THE RIGHT AND WRONG OF COMPULSION BY THE STATE, AND OTHER ESSAYS

Auberon Herbert

THE RIGHT AND WRONG OF COMPULSION BY THE STATE, AND OTHER ESSAYS

AUBERON HERBERT

*Edited and with an
Introduction by Eric Mack*

Liberty Fund
Indianapolis
1978

This book is published by Liberty Fund, Inc., a foundation established to encourage study of the ideal of a society of free and responsible individuals.

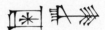

The cuneiform inscription that serves as our logo and as the design motif for our endpapers is the earliest-known written appearance of the word "freedom" *(ama-gi)*, or "liberty." It is taken from a clay document written about 2300 B.C. in the Sumerian city-state of Lagash.

© 1978 by Liberty Fund, Inc.
All rights reserved
Printed in the United States of America

Library of Congress Cataloging in Publication Data

Herbert, Auberon Edward William Molyneux, Hon., 1838–1906.
   The right and wrong of compulsion by the state, and other essays.
   Bibliography: pp. 27–29.
   Includes index.
   CONTENTS: The choices between personal freedom and state protection.—
State education: a help or hindrance?—A politician in sight of haven.—The right and wrong of compulsion by the state. (etc.)
    1. Individualism—Addresses, essays, lectures. 2. Liberty—Addresses, essays, lectures.
I. Mack, Eric II. Title.
JC571.H39 1978   323.4'01   78–4879
ISBN 0-913966-41-X (acid-free paper).—ISBN 0-913966-42-8 (pbk.: acid-free paper)

Liberty Fund, Inc.
8335 Allison Pointe Trail, Suite 300
Indianapolis, IN 46250–1687
(317) 842-0880

00 99 98 97 96 C 6 5 4 3 2
00 99 98 97 96 P 6 5 4 3 2

For my parents
—E.M.

CONTENTS

ESSAY SIX

ESSAY SEVEN

ESSAY EIGHT

ESSAY NINE

ESSAY TEN

INTRODUCTION
by Eric Mack

This collection of essays makes available the major and representative writings in political philosophy of one of the distinctive figures in the profound and wide-ranging intellectual debate which took place during the late Victorian age. It was during this period, in the intellectual and social ferment of the 1880s and 1890s, that Auberon Herbert (1838–1906) formulated and expounded voluntaryism, his system of "thorough" individualism. Carrying natural rights theory to its logical limits, Herbert demanded complete social and economic freedom for all noncoercive individuals and the radical restriction of the use of force to the role of protecting those freedoms— including the freedom of peaceful persons to withhold support from any or all state activities. All cooperative activity, he argued, must be founded upon the free agreement of all those parties whose rightful possessions are involved.

Auberon Herbert was by birth and marriage a well-placed member of the British aristocracy. He was educated at Eton and at St. John's College, Oxford. As a young man he held commissions in the army for several years and served briefly with the Seventh Hussars in India (1860). On his return to Oxford he formed several Conservative debating societies, was elected a Fellow of St. John's, and lectured occasionally in history and jurisprudence. In 1865, as a Conservative, he unsuccessfully sought a seat in the House of Commons. By 1868, however, he was seeking a parliamentary seat, again unsuccessfully, as a Liberal. Finally, in 1870, Herbert successfully contested a by-election and entered the Commons as a Liberal representing Nottingham. Most notably, during his time in the House of Commons, Herbert joined Sir Charles Dilke in declaring his republicanism and Herbert supported Joseph Arch's attempts to form an agricultural laborer's union. Although, through hindsight, many of Herbert's actions and words during the sixties and early seventies can be read as harbingers of his later consistent libertarianism, he actually lacked, throughout this period, any consistent set of political principles. During this period, for instance, he supported compulsory state education—albeit with strong insistence on its being religiously neutral.

In late 1873 Herbert met and was much impressed by Herbert Spencer. As he recounts in "Mr. Spencer and the Great Machine," a study of Spencer led to the insight that

> thinking and acting for others had always hindered, not helped, the real progress; that all forms of compulsion deadened the living forces in a nation; that every evil vio-

lently stamped out still persisted, almost always in a worse form, when driven out of sight, and festered under the surface. I no longer believed that the handful of us—however well-intentioned we might be—spending our nights in the House, could manufacture the life of a nation, could endow it out of hand with happiness, wisdom, and prosperity, and clothe it in all the virtues.[1]

However, it was even before this intellectual transformation that Herbert had decided, perhaps out of disgust with party politics or uncertainty about his own convictions, not to stand for reelection in 1874. Later, in 1879, he again sought Liberal support to regain a seat from Nottingham. But at that point his uncompromising individualist radicalism was not acceptable to the majority of the Central Council of the Liberal Union of Nottingham. In the interim, in 1877, he had organized the Personal Rights and Self-Help Association. And in 1878 he had been one of the chief organizers of the antijingoism rallies in Hyde Park against war with Russia. Along with other consistent classical liberals, Herbert repeatedly took anti-imperialist stands. He called for Irish self-determination. He opposed British intervention in Egypt and later opposed the Boer War.

In 1880, following his rejection by the Liberals of Nottingham, Herbert turned to the publication of addresses, essays, and books in defense of consistent individualism and against all forms of political regimentation.

---

[1] Auberon Herbert, "Mr. Spencer and the Great Machine," p. 260. For additional bibliographic information see the bibliography. Page citations for material reproduced here are to pages in this volume. All other page citations refer to items listed in the bibliography.

Even in 1877 he had been disturbed by "a constant undertone of cynicism" in the writings of his mentor, Herbert Spencer, and had resolved to do full justice to "the moral side" of the case for a society of fully free and voluntarily cooperative individuals.[2] And while Spencer grew more and more crusty, conservative, and pessimistic during the last decades of the nineteenth century, Herbert, who continued to think of himself as Spencer's disciple, remained idealistic, radical, and hopeful. And though he refused to join, he willingly addressed such organizations as the Liberty and Property Defense League which he felt to be "a little more warmly attached to the fair sister Property than . . . to the fair sister Liberty."[3] Similarly, Herbert held himself separate from the Personal Rights Association, whose chief mover, J. H. Levy, favored compulsory taxation for the funding of state protective activities. With the exception of the individualistic "reasonable anarchists," Herbert thought of himself as occupying the left wing of the individualist camp, that is, the wing most willing to carry liberty furthest.[4]

In 1885 Herbert sought to establish the Party of Individual Liberty and under this rubric gave addresses across England. The title essay for this collection, *The Right and Wrong of Compulsion by the State*, was written as a statement of the basis for, the character of, and the implications of, the principles of this party. Again with

---

[2] S. Hutchinson Harris, *Auberon Herbert: Crusader for Liberty*, p. 248.
[3] Auberon Herbert, "The Rights of Property," p. 7.
[4] Ibid., p. 39.

the aim of advancing libertarian opinion, Herbert published the weekly (later changed to monthly) paper *Free Life*, "The Organ of Voluntary Taxation and the Voluntary State," from 1890 to 1901. *Free Life* was devoted to "One Fight More—The Best and the Last," the fight against the aggressive use of force which is "a mere survival of barbarism, a mere perpetuation of slavery under new names, against which the reason and moral sense of the civilized world have to be called into rebellion."[5] Also during the 1890s, Herbert engaged in lengthy published exchanges with two prominent socialists of his day, E. Belfort Bax and J. A. Hobson. Herbert continued to write and speak into this century, and two of his best essays, "Mr. Spencer and the Great Machine" and "A Plea for Voluntaryism," were written in 1906, the last year of his life.

In all his mature writings Auberon Herbert defended a Lockean-Spencerian conception of natural rights according to which each person has a right to his own person, his mind and body, and hence to his own labor. Furthermore, each person has a right to the products of the productive employment of his labor and faculties. Since each person has these rights, each is under a moral obligation to respect these rights in all others. In virtue of each person's sovereignty over himself, each individual must consent to any activity which directly affects his person or property before any such activity can be morally legitimate. Specifically, each must forgo the use of

---

[5] S. Hutchinson Harris, "Auberon Herbert," pp. 700-701.

force and fraud. Each has a right to live and produce in peace and in voluntary consort with others, and all are obligated to respect this peace.

In *The Right and Wrong of Compulsion by the State*, Herbert is anxious to point out that there is a potentially dangerous confusion between "two meanings which belong to the word force."[6] Direct force is employed when person A, without his consent, is deprived, or threatened with the deprivation, of something to which he has a right—for example, some portion of his life, liberty, or property. Anyone subject to such a deprivation or threat is, in his own eyes, the worse for it. His interaction with the wielder of force (or fraud) is something to be regretted, something to which he does not consent. In contrast, if B induces A to act by threatening (so-called) merely to withhold something that B rightfully owns and A values, then, according to Herbert, we can say that B has used "indirect force" upon A. But such indirect force is radically different from direct force. In the case of indirect force, A does not act under a genuine threat. For he is not faced with being deprived of something rightfully his (his arm or his life). Instead he is bribed, coaxed, induced into acting by the *lure* of B's offer of something which is rightfully B's. No action endangering rights plays any role in motivating A. A may, of course, wish that B had offered even more. But in accepting B's offer, whatever it may be, A indicates that on the whole he consents to the exchange with B. He indicates that he values this interchange with B over the status quo. He

---

6 Herbert, *The Right and Wrong of Compulsion by the State.* p. 144.

indicates that he sees it as beneficial—unlike all inter-
actions involving direct force.

> The employer may be indirectly forced to accept the work-
> man's offer, or the workman may be indirectly forced to accept
> the employer's offer; but before either does so, it is necessary
> that they should consent, as far as their own selves are con-
> cerned, to the act that is in question. And this distinction is of
> the most vital kind, since the world can and will get rid of
> direct compulsion; but it can never of indirect compulsion. . . .[7]

Besides, Herbert argues, any attempt to rid the world of
indirect force must proceed by expanding the role of
direct force. And "when you do so, you at once destroy
the immense safeguard that exists so long as [each man]
. . . must give his consent to every action that he does."[8]
The believer in strong government cannot claim, says
Herbert, that in proposing to regulate the terms by which
individuals may associate, he is merely seeking to diminish the use of force in the world.

What, then, may be done when the violation of rights
threatens? So strong is Herbert's critique of force that,
especially in his early writings, he is uncomfortable about
affirming the propriety of even defensive force. Thus, in
"A Politician in Sight of Haven" the emphasis is on the
fact that the initiator of force places his victim "outside
the moral-relation" and into "the force-relation." Force,
even by a defender, is not "moral." The defender's only
justification is the necessity of dealing with the aggressor
as one would with "a wild beast." Indeed, so pressed is

---

[7] Ibid., pp. 144–45.
[8] Ibid., pp. 145–46.

Herbert in his search for some justification that he says, in justification of his defense *of himself*, "The act on my part was so far a moral one, inasmuch as I obeyed the derived moral command to help *my neighbor*."[9]

In *The Right and Wrong of Compulsion by the State*, Herbert starts by identifying the task of finding moral authority for any use of force and the task of finding moral authority for any government. He declares that no "perfect" foundation for such authority can be found, that all such authority is a usurpation—though "when *confined within certain exact limits* . . . a justifiable usurpation."[10]

In his later writings, Herbert seems to have fully overcome his hesitancy about defensive force. Possibly his most forceful statement appears in the essay "A Voluntaryist Appeal":

> If you ask us why force should be used to defend the rights of self-ownership, and not for any other purpose, we reply by reminding you that the rights of self-ownership are . . . supreme moral rights, of higher rank than all other human interests or institutions; and therefore force may be employed on behalf of these rights, but not in opposition to them. All social and political arrangements, all employments of force, are subordinate to these universal rights, and must receive just such character and form as are required in the interest of these rights.[11]

According to Herbert, each person's absolute right to what he has peacefully acquired through the exercise of

---

9 Herbert, "Politician," p. 101. Italics added.
10 Herbert, *Right and Wrong*, p. 141.
11 Herbert, "A Voluntaryist Appeal," p. 317.

his faculties requires the abolition of compulsory taxation. The demand for "voluntary taxation" only is a simple instance of the demand for freedom in all human interaction. An individual does not place himself outside the moral relation by merely retaining his property, by not donating it for some other person's conception of a worthy project. Such a peaceful individual is not a criminal and is not properly subject to the punishment of having a portion of his property confiscated. Herbert particularly urged those in the individualist camp to reject compulsory taxation.

> I deny that A and B can go to C and force him to form a state and extract from him certain payments and services in the name of such state; and I go on to maintain that if you act in this manner, you at once justify state socialism. The only difference between the tax-compelling individualist and the state socialist is that while they both have vested ownership of C in A and B, the tax-compelling individualist proposes to use the powers of ownership in a very limited fashion, the socialist in a very complete fashion. I object to the ownership in any fashion.[12]

It is compulsory taxation which generates and sustains the corrupt game of politics—the game in which all participants strive to further their aims with resources forcefully extracted from those who do not share their aims. Compulsory taxation breaks the link between the preferences of the producers and peaceful holders of resources with respect to how those resources (their property, their

---

[12] J. H. Levy, ed., *Taxation and Anarchism*, p. 3. For a discussion of the views of J. H. Levy, Herbert's antagonist in the exchange reprinted as *Taxation and Anarchism*, see *Liberty*, vol. 7, no. 14, p. 4.

faculties, their minds and bodies) should be used, and the actual use of those resources. For instance, compulsory taxation

> gives great and undue facility for engaging a whole nation in war. If it were necessary to raise the sum required from those who individually agreed in the necessity of war, we should have the strongest guarantee for the preservation of peace. . . . Compulsory taxation means everywhere the persistent probability of a war made by the ambitions or passions of politicians.[13]

Herbert's demand for a "voluntary state," that is, a state devoted solely to the protection of Lockean-Spencerian rights and funded voluntarily, combined with his continual condemnation of existing state activities led to Herbert's being commonly perceived as an anarchist. Often these perceptions were based on hostility and ignorance, but Herbert was also regarded as an anarchist by serious and reasonably well-informed prostate critics like J. A. Hobson and T. H. Huxley. Similarly, J. H. Levy thought that to reject the compulsory state was to reject the state as such. And while, for these men, Herbert's purported anarchism was a fault, the individualist anarchist Benjamin Tucker always insisted that, to his credit, Auberon Herbert was a true anarchist.[14]

---

[13] Herbert, "The Principles of Voluntaryism and Free Life," p. 398.
[14] See J. A. Hobson, "Rich Man's Anarchism"; T. H. Huxley, "Anarchy or Regimentation"; Levy, ed., *Taxation and Anarchism*, p. 7; and Tucker's announcement of Herbert's death in *Liberty* (vol. 15, no. 6, p. 16)— "Auberon Herbert is dead. He was a true anarchist in everything but name. How much better (and how much rarer) to be an anarchist in everything but name than to be an anarchist in name only!"

Of course, there can be no question of whether Auberon Herbert was an anarchist of the coercive collectivizing or terrorist sort. Nothing could be further from his own position. For as Herbert points out in his "The Ethics of Dynamite," coercion, systematic or random, is nothing but a celebration of the principles on which the coercive state rests. Whether Herbert was an anarchist of the individualist, private property, free market sort is another and far more complex question. Herbert himself continually rejected the label; and although he maintained cordial relationships with men like Benjamin Tucker and Wordsworth Donisthorpe, he insisted that his views were sufficiently different from theirs in important respects to place him outside the camp of "reasonable" anarchists.

In what ways did Herbert's views differ from those of the individualist anarchists as represented by Tucker? Tucker had tied himself to a labor theory of value. It followed for him that such activities as lending money and renting property were not genuinely productive and that those who gained by such activities advanced themselves improperly at the expense of less-propertied people. Thus, Tucker took the laboring class to be an exploited class, exploited by the holders of capital. And he duly sympathized with, and often shared the rhetoric of, others who were announced champions of the proletariat against the capitalist class. Herbert did not accept this sort of economic analysis. He saw interest as a natural market phenomenon, not, as Tucker did, as the product of state-enforced monopolization of credit. And Herbert saw rent as legitimate because he believed, contrary to Tucker, that one did not have to be continually using an object in order to retain just title to it and therefore morally charge others for their use of that object.[15]

I suspect it was these differences—differences not actually relevant to the issue of Herbert's anarchism—along with Herbert's desire not to grant the political idiots of his day the verbal advantage of tagging him an anarchist, that sustained Herbert's insistence that what he favored was, in fact, a type of state. But other factors and nuances entered in. Herbert argued that a voluntarily supported state would do a better job at defining and enforcing property rights than would the cooperative associations which anarchists saw as taking the place of the state and protecting individual liberty and property. Unfortunately, in his exchanges with Tucker on this matter, the question of what sort of institution or legal structure was needed for, or consistent with, the protection of individual life, liberty, and property tended to be conflated with the question of the genuine basis for particular claims to property.[16] Finally, Herbert's considered judgment was that individualistic supporters of liberty and property who, like Tucker, favored the free establishment of defensive associations and juridical institutions were simply making a verbal error in calling themselves anarchists. They were not for no government, Herbert thought, but for decentralized, scattered, fragmented government. Her-

---

[15] Whereas Herbert grounded his views in a belief in moral rights and obligations, Tucker came to espouse a purportedly postmoralistic egoism, and whereas Herbert was at least sympathetic to theism, Tucker was aggressively antireligious. But these differences seem never to have been factors in their disputes.

[16] *Liberty*, vol. 7, no. 6, p. 5.

bert's position was that, although it would be better to have many governments within a given territory (a republican one for republicans, a monarchical one for monarchists, etc.) than to compel everyone to support a single state,[17] individuals, if given the choice, would converge on a single government as their common judge and defender within a given territory.[18] How we ultimately classify Herbert depends upon our answers to these two questions: (1) Does the fact that Herbert would allow individuals to withhold support from "the state" and to form their own alternative rights-respecting associations, show him to be an anarchist? (2) Does the fact that Herbert thought that it would be unwise for individuals to form such splinter associations, and unlikely that they would form them, show that the central institution which he favored was a state?[19]

No sketch of Herbert's views could be complete, even as a sketch, without some mention of Herbert's multi-dimensional analysis of power—"the sorrow and the curse of the world."[20] Following Spencer's distinction between industrial and militant societies, Herbert continually emphasized the differences between two basic modes of interpersonal coordination. There is the "way

---

[17] See Levy, ed., *Taxation and Anarchism*, pp. 3–4.

[18] Herbert, "A Voluntaryist Appeal," p. 329, and "Principles," p. 383.

[19] See *Liberty*, vol. 10, no. 12, p. 3. For a portion of the contemporary version of this dispute, see Robert Nozick, *Anarchy, State, and Utopia* (New York: Basic Books, 1974), Tibor Machan, *Human Rights and Human Liberties* (Chicago: Nelson-Hall, 1975), and the essays by Eric Mack and Murray Rothbard in *Anarchism*, ed. J. W. Chapman and J. R. Pennock (New York: New York University Press, 1978).

[20] Herbert, "A Plea for Voluntaryism," p. 316.

of peace and cooperation" founded upon respect for self-
ownership and the demand for only voluntary association. And there is the "way of force and strife" founded
upon either the belief in the ownership of some by others
or the simple reverence of brute force.[21]

It is difficult, however, to summarize Herbert's analysis of these modes since it involves a great number of
interwoven moral, psychological, and sociological in-
sights. One of course must look to his writings, but
chiefly his two last essays, "Mr. Spencer and the Great
Machine," and "A Plea for Voluntaryism." Insofar as
there is a division of labor between these two essays, the
former focuses on the inherent dynamic of political
power—the ways in which the great game of politics
captures its participants no matter what their own initial
intentions—while the latter essay focuses on the corrupting results of this captivity within those participants.
According to Herbert, no man's integrity or moral or intellectual selfhood can withstand participation in the battle of power politics.

> The soul of the high-minded man is one thing; and the great
> game of politics is another thing. You are now part of a ma-
> chine with a purpose of its own—not the purpose of serving
> the fixed and supreme principles—the great game laughs at all
> things that stand before and above itself, and brushes them
> scornfully aside, but the purpose of securing victory. . . . When
> once we have taken our place in the great game, all choice as
> regards ourselves is at an end. We must win; and we must do
> the things which mean winning, even if those things are not
> very beautiful in themselves.[22]

---

[21] Ibid., p. 358.
[22] Herbert, "Mr. Spencer," p. 267.

Progress is a matter of the development of human individuality, not the growth of uniformity and regimentation. Hence,

> Progress depends upon a great number of small changes and adaptations and experiments constantly taking place, each carried out by those who have strong beliefs and clear perceptions of their own in the matter. . . . But . . . true experimentation is impossible under universal systems. . . . Progress and improvement are not amongst the things that great machines are able to supply at demand.[23]

Progress, then, is part of the price we all pay for power. But the possessors of power pay a further price. For, according to Herbert, power is a "fatal gift."

> If you mean to have and to hold power, you must do whatever is necessary for the having and holding of it. You may have doubts and hesitations and scruples, but power is the hardest of all taskmasters, and you must either lay these aside, when you once stand on that dangerous, dizzy height, or yield your place to others, and renounce your part in the great conflict. And when power is won, don't suppose that you are a free man, able to choose your path and do as you like. From the moment you possess power, you are but its slave, fast bound by its many tyrant necessities.[24]

Ultimately, therefore, it is in no one's interest to seek power over others. Such an endeavor simply generates a dreadful war of all upon all which, even when momentarily won, makes the victor the slave of the vanquished

---

[23] Ibid., pp. 300–01.
[24] Herbert, "A Plea for Voluntaryism," p. 321.

and which robs all contestants of their dignity as self-owning and self-respecting beings. It is necessary to emphasize that, according to Herbert, liberty and respect for all rights are, ultimately, in each individual's interest. For Herbert often couched his appeals in terms of self-denial and self-sacrifice. This was especially true of his appeals to the working class, which he envisioned as forming electoral majorities for the purpose of legislating downward redistributions of property. In fact, it seems that Herbert's calls for self-denial were calls for the discipline to withstand the temptations of (merely) short-term political windfalls and to appreciate the long-term moral, psychological, and economic importance, for each person, of respect for all individual rights. Thus, on the moral and psychological level, Herbert rhetorically asks,

> If you lose all respect for the rights of others, and with it your own self-respect; if you lose your own sense of right and fairness; if you lose your belief in liberty, and with it the sense of your own worth and true rank; if you lose your own will and self-guidance and control over your own lives and actions, . . . what can all the gifts of politicians give you in return?[25]

And on the tactical level he adds, "In the end you will gain far more by clinging faithfully to the methods of peace and respect for the rights of others than by allowing yourselves to use the force that always calls out force in reply. . . ."[26] The skepticism of Herbert's contempo-

---

[25] Ibid., p. 341.
[26] Ibid., p. 358.

raries about whether they would have to live with such long-term consequences was, for them, no virtue, and, for us, no favor.

Tulane University
New Orleans, La.
February 1978

SELECTIVE BIBLIOGRAPHY

Auberon Herbert's Political Writings

"The Canadian Confederation." *Fortnightly Review*, 1867.
"Address on the Choices between Personal Freedom and State Protection." Delivered at the annual meeting of the Vigilance Association for the Defense of Personal Rights, March 9, 1880. London: Vigilance Association, 1880.
"State Education: A Help or Hindrance?" *Fortnightly Review*, 1880.
"A Politician in Trouble About His Soul." *Fortnightly Review* (in five parts) 1883, 1884. The last sequel bore the separate title, "A Politician in Sight of Haven." The whole work was reprinted as *A Politician in Trouble About His Soul* (London: Chapman & Hill, 1884). "A Politician in Sight of Haven" was serialized in Benjamin Tucker's *Liberty* in 1884, and published by Tucker in Boston in 1884 and 1890.
The Right and Wrong of Compulsion by the State. London: Williams & Norgate, 1885—based on a series of articles in and on letters to the *Newcastle Weekly Chronicle*.
"The Rights of Property." The proceedings of and Herbert's address at the seventh annual meeting of the Liberty and Property

Defense League, December 10, 1889. London: Liberty & Property Defense League, 1890.

Free Life. Edited by Herbert (weekly, later monthly). London, 1890–1901.

" 'The Rake's Progress' in Irish Politics." *Fortnightly Review,* 1891.

"The True Line of Deliverance." In *A Plea of Liberty.* Edited by T. Mackay. London: John Murray, 1891.

"Under the Yoke of the Butterflies." *Fortnightly Review* (in two parts), 1891, 1892.

"A Cabinet Minister's Vade-mecum; a Satire." *Nineteenth Century,* 1893.

"Is the Hope of Our Country an Illusion?" *New Review,* 1894.

"The Ethics of Dynamite," *Contemporary Review,* 1894.

"Wares for Sale in the Political Market." *The Humanitarian: A Monthly Review of Sociological Science* (in two parts), 1895.

"State Socialism in the Court of Reason." *The Humanitarian: A Monthly Review of Sociological Science* (in two parts), 1895.

"The Principles of Voluntaryism and Free Life." Edited by E. E. Krott. Burlington, Vt.: Free Press Assoc., 1897. Second edition, 1899.

"A Voluntaryist Appeal." *The Humanitarian: A Monthly Review of Sociological Science,* 1898.

"Salvation by Force." *The Humanitarian: A Monthly Review of Sociological Science,* 1898.

"Lost in the Region of Phrases." *The Humanitarian: A Monthly Review of Sociological Science,* 1899.

"The Tragedy of Errors in the War in Transvaal." *Contemporary Review,* 1900.

"How the Pot Called the Kettle Black." *Contemporary Review,* 1902.

The Voluntaryist Creed (consisting of "Mr. Spencer and the Great Machine" and "A Plea of Voluntaryism"). London: W. J. Simpson, 1908.

Taxation and Anarchism. With and edited by J. H. Levy. London: Personal Rights Assoc., 1912.

Secondary Material

E. Belfort Bax. "Voluntaryism Versus Socialism." *The Humanitarian: A Monthly Review of Sociological Science,* 1895.

Dictionary of National Biography. Second Supplement. London: Smith, Elder & Co., 1912.

S. Hutchinson Harris. *Auberon Herbert: Crusader for Liberty.* London: Williams & Norgate, 1943.

————. "Auberon Herbert." *Nineteenth Century and After,* 1938.

J. A. Hobson. "Rich Man's Anarchism." *The Humanitarian: A Monthly Review of Sociological Science,* 1898.

T. H. Huxley. "Government: Anarchy or Regimentation." *Nineteenth Century,* 1890.

Liberty. Edited by Benjamin Tucker. Boston and New York, 1881–1908. Reprinted by Greenwood Press (Westport, Conn., 1970). Some of the relevant material appears in Tucker's *Instead of a Book* (New York: Tucker, 1893), reprinted by Arno Press (New York, 1972).

THE RIGHT AND WRONG OF COMPULSION BY THE STATE, AND OTHER ESSAYS

ESSAY ONE

THE CHOICES
BETWEEN PERSONAL FREEDOM
AND STATE PROTECTION

*This address was given by Auberon Herbert before a meeting
of the Vigilance Association for the Defense of Personal
Rights in London on March 9, 1880. It was published shortly
thereafter by the Vigilance Association.*

In the midst of much that is written and said about progress and improvement, it is seldom perceived how disorderly are our usual habits of political thinking. Those who are engaged in political work usually reject any kind of systematic thought, and disdain the authority of general principles. Whether they are writers or speakers they dislike to look forward and to consider questions that are not already well above their horizon; they have a generous confidence in the guidance of the future and their own unprepared instincts. They could with difficulty, and perhaps not altogether with satisfaction to themselves, reconcile their votes or opinions on different subjects, and the history of their conduct would contain nearly as many anomalies as does the British constitution. Except in the most general terms they could not describe the goal toward which their efforts are directed, nor have they ever placed before their own minds a distinct and coherent picture of what they seek to make of this England which is subjected to their treatment. They cannot see the forest on account of the trees, and their horizon is inexorably bounded by the immediate struggles in which their party is engaged. Like the rest of the world, they are not unwilling to dislike and condemn what they do not practice. They look on every system of thought as a newfangled invention of the doctrinaires, a sign both of want of practicality and of intellectual conceit, and they resent it vigorously as an attempt to restrain their intelligence from flowing, like Wordsworth's river, "at its own sweet will." Expressions of pious thankfulness for the prosperous flowings of this mental river meet us on every side. "Thank Heaven!" we hear men say, "we are not as our neighbors! We are not enslaved by formulas! We are not afraid of doing any wise or useful thing, because it is inconsistent with our general views! We have the gift of always stopping in time, and we can therefore safely move to any point, north, south, east, or west, of our political compass. We can never go far wrong, for we always have our good sense ready to protect us!"

In listening to such language we are tempted to ask, does anyone in reality escape the thraldom—if thraldom it be—of general principles? We may not recognize in our own minds the general principles which direct our conduct; we may be profoundly ignorant of their existence; but I think in every case, putting out of consideration actions which are instinctive, it may be shown that whether these general principles are, or are not known to us, nevertheless we are all acting under their guidance. One man may be quite conscious of the principles he is following; he has deliberately examined, tested, and chosen them as his guides; another man is equally under the authority of some other set of principles, though he has never consciously placed himself in that position, and does not even know the name or nature of what he obeys; in one case they may be narrower; in another case, wider; more consistently or more uncertainly applied; but in every case, however carelessly adopted or inconsistently followed, or however little recognized they may be, general principles of some kind or another will be found as the guides of conduct. This will become plainer when we remember that a general principle implies the classing together of certain facts—with or without an injunction added to it—and that daily life is only carried on from hour to hour by means of the knowledge which results from such classifications. We perceive that a certain thing acting under similar conditions produces a certain effect, and having repeatedly observed this same cause and this same effect accompanying each other, we enact for ourselves a command to do or to forbear, and we act so as to produce or avoid a foreseen effect. It will be plain to everyone who considers the matter, that there could be no advance in knowledge of any kind, unless facts were always being classified, and unless, with the enormous increase of facts so classified, the further work were to go on of arranging them in groups according to their relations amongst themselves. This is the work on which the race has been engaged ever since the dim early days when it first classified the effect of fire and water, by saying fire burns and water quenches. Advance of knowledge means that we are learning as regards some substance whatever it may be, metal, plant, animal, that the same cause is accompanied by the same effect—by placing this effect in

connection with other effects, and gathering from the
members of the group the law which is common to them
all. It means not only learning new facts, but introducing
order amongst facts already learned. All available knowledge consists of classification, since facts unarranged and
unclassified are of no more present use to us, than bricks
are until they are built into some kind of a building.
What is true as regards material substances of the world
is true as regards human nature. Now politics are essentially one part of the science of human nature, and it is
the same human nature, neither more nor less, as that
with which we come in contact every hour of our lives.
This simple truth is often forgotten in presence of the
machinery of Parliaments, public offices, parties, organizations, caucuses, and all the other instruments of political
life, but we cannot go back in mind too often to the fundamental facts, first, that we are dealing with the simple
human nature of every day, and, second, that human nature must be studied and understood—its facts must be
classified—like causes connected with like effects, furnishing us with their own special generalizations—then
these effects connected with other effects furnishing us
with their own special generalizations—then these effects
connected with other effects furnishing us with wider
generalizations—if we are to act as successfully upon it
as we do upon any of the materials that we use in our
manufactures. It seems almost like urging the importance
of study of the alphabet to urge that all successful political
conduct must be founded upon the classification of those
facts that affect human nature, of those conditions which
as we learn from the common everyday experience of

life, either aid or impede its development. Is proof required that in our views of human nature we recognize general principles? *Si quaeris signa, circumspice!* A speech that wins the applause of its hearers, a character skillfully drawn in a novel, a successful play bear witness to the self-evident proposition that men have classified certain facts regarding their own selves, and recognized what are called laws of human nature. Otherwise we could not by a sort of common agreement praise the skill and truth of the artist; the effect upon each of us would be purely personal, subjective and accidental. We should be without that common standard of reference which we now possess and of which our common judgments of praise and blame are the evidence. And yet the very words "general principles" cause a sort of horror to those who are engaged in politics. There is a vague superstitious dread about the use of them; and men feel, when an appeal is made in their name, almost as if they were asked to give up the study of facts and to return to those verbal explanations of earlier days, which merely supplied a new clothing of words and left the matter itself standing where it did before.

But amongst the objectors to general principles in politics will be found some men of cautious and exact thought whose mental inclination will be to hand over each question as it arises to the decision of those who have given special attention to it, and may be looked on as authorities in the matter. These men will deny that there is at present sufficient material to justify the laying down of wide general principles; they will be on the side of experiment; they will wish each question to be separately treated, and treated according to the recommendations of those most familiar with it; they will attach immense importance to special knowledge and special experience, and exceedingly little importance to knowledge and experience of a wider kind. I cannot attempt to reply at length here to such objections, which must however be treated with respect. It is sufficient to point out that those great advances in knowledge, which cause mental and moral revolutions, are more often made by those men who fit themselves to connect existing groups of facts, than by those who add one more group to the many thousand groups now in existence. Without undervaluing the gain of a new fact in any department of life, I think one is justified in saying that at present the accumulation of facts is in advance of the power of using and connecting facts, and that the balance seems likely to be still further inclined in this direction; especially as regards the science of human nature the mass of unused facts is enormous. Every history, every novel, every newspaper, every household is full of them; but they are lost to the world for want of careful attempts to follow their connections and to introduce order amongst them. I must also urge as against following the advice of political specialists, that they are seldom if ever men who have studied the body politic as a whole, or who have given much thought to the effect on the general system of the local remedy they would apply. A specialist in medicine is only really deserving of confidence if, in addition to his knowledge of the part, he has thorough knowledge of the whole system, but our local advisers in politics, who are often men of great thoroughness and worthy of all respect for their own special knowledge, would generally disclaim such wider knowledge. In politics quite as much as in medicine the local evil is often but a symptom of the systematic evil, and only to be removed when some condition of life, at first sight unconnected with it, is altered.

But it may be urged that the acceptance of general principles in politics would lead to an idle way of thinking. All questions would be dismissed from political consideration at the dictation of an assumed formula which, as it is remarked, might not be true after all. No doubt there is a saving of intellectual labor. So there is when an astronomer takes the law of gravitation for granted; or a mechanician the properties of the lever; or a chemist the laws of the combining weights of the elements; or a physiologist the law that work implies waste. No worker in any of these departments would be grateful for the obligation to do such work over again on each occasion for himself. He would complain that a science that was not in possession of certain accepted generalizations, could not be treated as a science at all, but as a mere aggregate of floating facts. As regards the objection that incalculable harm might follow from the acceptance of a false general principle, we must bear in mind that every wide generalization that continues to live and gather strength in the world, bears in itself a certain evidence of its truth. It is so far true, that presumably the existing generation of men have not the requisite knowledge to disprove it. The wider it is, the more exposed to attack it is in many places and at many times. It stands in the presence of all men, always inviting attack. The wider it is spread amongst an intelligent people, the more probable it becomes that if not true in itself, the experience of some person or other will provide the weapon for its destruction. Unless, as some persons believe, the human race is born to err, it is as nearly certain as can be that the doom of refutation sooner or later will descend upon any false first principle that has been exalted into a law of conduct.

We must also remember that in seeking for a guide for conduct, we have not really the choice of either consistently following general principles, or being guided in each case by special knowledge. Few men can have special knowledge on many subjects, and what are those to do who are not amongst the happy few? Follow the specialists? but generally the specialists are divided. The more carefully we examine the springs which move those who reject the guidance of general principles, the more clearly we shall see that either they are swayed by general principles, which they have never examined, and are scarcely conscious of, and which in such a case are degenerated into mere prejudices (prejudice being I think a general principle that has never been submitted to the examination of reason), and therefore that they are likely to select that specialist as their guide who most agrees with their ordinary way of thinking; or else that they leave themselves at the mercy of that chapter of accidents, popular excitement, private interest, advantage of party, contagion of emotion, or whatever it may be which is responsible for so many of our actions, and which explains why our actions so often present startling contrasts between themselves.

Last, it must be said, that those who object to general

principles in politics and disclaim their supremacy, are themselves betrayed by their incautious caution—*nimium premendo littus iniquum*—into making a generalization of a very wide and rash character. Those like effects which follow from like causes—that unbroken interdependence of every group of facts with every other group of facts— that order and that arrangement which prevail every- where else in the world—these things are suddenly and miraculously to be suspended in the political world, here alone in the whole realm of nature, for the benefit of the politician who wishes to have no further embarrassment than those of the present time, and to fulfill from hour to hour of his shifting course, the maxim "sufficient for the day is the evil thereof." This is the startling general principle to which we find ourselves committed in our vain attempt to discover a region behind the north wind. I have spent much of your time today in trying to show that our great work in politics, as in every other science, is to bring facts into groups, or to use the more common expression, under law, to connect these groups with each other, until from them we establish the great principles which are to be the guides of our action. I believe until this is done, whatever work of reform we undertake for special objects is in a great measure wasted. You break off today with infinite labor the chains that fasten one limb, to find tomorrow that chains of the same kind have been placed on another limb. At present in England no reform can be attempted until the part affected is in an acute state of suffering and the effects are visible to all men. No reform has the least chance of success which appeals to abstract justice, and which simply says, "Evil must follow, because the primary laws are broken." I do not wish to undervalue the fair-mindedness of Englishmen; we have some small measure of that quality which is scarcely as yet at all developed amongst civilized men, the power of being convinced; but I wish to attack the self-complacency with which Englishmen regard their present state of mental disorder, and their satisfaction at placing their convictions at the mercy of the chapter of accidents. Half the evils in politics arise from our being obliged, whenever and wherever a reform is needed, to show that the immediate (and I may say the lower) interests of some class are involved in the matter; until at last, thanks to such constant appeals, the feeling arises in those classes that their immediate interest is the right standpoint from which to view every political question. If, instead of such appeals, we stood on those great and primary principles which underlie every group of political facts, then there would be an ennobling and transforming influence in politics, because the sense of direct personal interest would be put on one side, and men would seek to interpret rightly in each case the universal law. The universal law cannot be disregarded without injury to every part of society, and it is a truer method to regard political questions from this point of view, than to attempt to balance the loss or profit which will accrue to some special class.

And now, if there be great primary laws controlling the intercourse of men and regulating their relations with each other; if order prevails in human science as it does in every other science, can we yet speak confidently as to what these laws are? Mr. Herbert Spencer, to whom in all this matter we owe largely, to whom I am convinced the world owes a debt which it will some day much more fully recognize than it has yet done, to whom personally I owe directly or indirectly every belief for which this paper contends, has expressed the law which binds men in their relations to each other. We can suppose no other object to be placed before ourselves but happiness, though we may differently interpret the word, in a higher or in a lower sense. We are then entitled to pursue happiness in that way in which it can be shown we are most likely to find it, and as each man can be the only judge of his own happiness, it follows that each man must be left free so to exercise his faculties and so to direct his energies as he may think fittest to produce happiness;—with one most important limitation, which must always be understood as accompanying the liberty of which I speak. His freedom in this pursuit of happiness must not interfere with the exactly corresponding freedom of others. Neither by force nor by fraud may he restrain the same free use of faculties enjoyed by every other man. This then, the widest possible liberty, is the great primary law on which all human intercourse must be founded if it is to be happy, peaceful, and progressive. Perfect obedience to it will produce constant advance in our capabilities for happiness, in our feelings of kindliness and good will toward each other, in our intellectual acquisitions. Just as I believe this to be the master-principle of good in human affairs, so do I believe that old desire which is so firmly planted in the breasts of men—the desire to exercise force over each other—to be the master-principle of evil. Where liberty is to be bounded by liberty, it is necessary for us to define liberty and to restrain all aggressions upon it. In this one case force acquires its true sanction, that of being employed in the immediate defense of liberty, but except in this case physical force has no place or part in civilized life, and represents the antiprogressive power that still exists amongst us. If this principle be true—and I believe that the more it is examined and subjected to attacks, the more clearly will it be seen to be true—then how sure and how simple is the guide which we possess in political life, and how mischievous though well intentioned are all those efforts of the reformer or the philanthropist who believes in his own special method of coercion and restraint, and has never learned to believe in the all-healing method of liberty. I do not ask that the principle of liberty should be accepted by any man until he has most carefully and most anxiously viewed it in its every bearing, and has examined every group of political facts with the purpose of ascertaining whether mischievous results, like in kind, do not, sooner or later, follow wherever there is a neglect or contempt of liberty. If the principle be true we shall be able, with increasing knowledge and better methods of examination, to vindicate it at every point. Of all the serious steps in life, that is the most serious when a man chooses the guiding principle of his actions. I think, therefore, we ought to search out for ourselves and to listen to all that can be said against the principle of liberty. Let us hear all the counter evidence possible before we finally exalt it as our rule and guide, though, perhaps, when we have once done so, we shall be as much inclined to smile when it is impatiently proposed to disregard it for the sake of some passing evil, as the Astronomer Royal would be if some new group of facts were to be hastily explained in disregard of the influence of gravitation. Nor must we assign to liberty qualities which it does not possess, and which, if we were in a mood of unreasoning enthusiasm to attribute to it, would only lead to our disappointment. Like other great beneficent forces in nature, such as natural selection, there is a sternness in it, and its direct effects are often accompanied with pain. It is, as I believe, the great all-healer, but healing must sometimes be a painful process.

Now let me point out to you that we have not arrived simply at an abstract result, but that this question of liberty as against force will be found to enter into all the great questions of the day. It is the only one real and permanent dividing line between opinions. Whatever party names we may give ourselves, this is the question always waiting for an answer, Do you believe in force and authority, or do you believe in liberty? Hesitations, inconsistencies there may be—men shading off from each side into that third party which in critical and decisive times has become a proverb of weakness—but the two great masses of the thinking world are ever ranged on the one side or the other, supporters of authority, believers in liberty.

What, then, is the creed of liberty, and to what, in accepting it, are we committed? We have seen that there exists a great primary right that as men are placed here for happiness (we need not dispute as to the meaning of the term), so each man must be held to be the judge of his own happiness. No man, or body of men, has the right to wrest this judgment away from their fellow man. It is impossible to deny this, for no man can have rights over another man unless he first have rights over himself. He cannot possess the right to direct the happiness of another man, unless he possess rights to direct his own happiness: and if we grant him the latter right, this is at once fatal to the former right. Indeed to deny this right, or to abridge anything from it, is to reduce the moral world to complete disorder. Deny this right and you have no foundation left for rights of any kind—for justice, political freedom, or political equality—you have established the reign of force, and whatever gloss of civilization you may place over it, you have brought men once more to the "good old plan" on which our fathers stood.

This I believe to be the plain truth. There is this one strong simple foundation, or there is nothing. We may accustom our minds to Houses of Parliament, to majorities in the House, or majorities in the nation; we may talk our political jargon and push forward our party schemes, but this great truth remains unaltered through all our sayings and doings. It is true that here, as elsewhere in nature, we may live in disregard of the law, but here, as elsewhere, there is no escape from the consequences. All the partialities and privileges—all the bitter envyings and hostilities which exist amongst us—all the craving for power—all the painful unrest and blind efforts—all the wild and dangerous remedies—all the clinging to old forms, and the want of faith and courage to choose the new—all these will be found in an ultimate analysis to be amongst the consequences—and serious enough they are—of not recognizing and obeying the law on which our intercourse with each other is founded.

In very few words I will point out what are the derivatives from this law of liberty. Granted that a man is to be judge of his own happiness, and to direct his exertions in whatever manner he will, he is entitled to receive the full reward of those exertions. *Except for the defense of liberty itself,** which defense is necessary to ensure the

---

* This "defense of liberty" involves the administration of civil and criminal law. If liberty is a human right, its applications to human matters must be defined, and it must be protected by such arrangements as are necessary, otherwise it is a right which cannot be enjoyed. The state, therefore, is armed with certain powers, but it simply derives these powers from this principle of liberty; it is completely subordinate to the latter, and its powers over those who are its members end as soon as these arrangements in defense of liberty are made.

In other words, the state exists as the instrument of liberty. Liberty is not one of the creations of the state.

The importance of clearly keeping the view of the state before our minds will be seen, when we remember that under any other view we cannot refuse it the power of dealing with the minds and bodies of its members, as seems most convenient to the ruling majority at any particular moment. There is no other alternative. Either men acting in combination, or in other words, forming a state, become possessed, as a consequence, of unlimited powers over each other, or they do not. If they do, then we must sanctify the will of the majority, and make it our conscience and our law; if they do not, then we must be able to represent clearly to ourselves, what is the principle which is morally supreme over the actions of men thus acting in combination; and if we are once agreed that there be such a principle, we shall necessarily admit that it is itself the measure and the limit of those powers which it has for its own ends called into existence.

It is not difficult to discover the insufficient foundations on which the first view rests. How should it happen that the individual should be without rights, but that the combination of individuals should possess unlimited rights? Except by some process of magic, a whole made up of similar parts cannot become possessed of a quality which does not exist in the parts.

receiving of this full reward, no man or body of men may rightfully step in and intercept any part of that reward. We know as a fact that governments—who are the last to recognize rights—are not encumbered with scruples in this matter, and that they do not hesitate to help themselves out of the resources of their subjects, as largely as they consider necessary for the furtherance of any and every kind of object, which they either consider is desired by some influential part of the nation, or which they have personal motives for desiring themselves. But few men will contend that the actions of governments are founded on right; and few men amongst those who look for the foundations of right below existing customs and current expressions, will accept the will of a majority as a sanction for taking from a man what he has won by his own exertions. It may be inconvenient, and it is often highly so in politics, to recognize the truth; but there the truth is, that if a man possesses rights—I mean primary rights, rights belonging to human existence, not created by any majority of his fellow men—neither that majority nor any other majority outside that man can dispossess him of those rights. To do so is to abolish the very word "rights" from any place in civilized language.

To resume the argument, once let this right be granted —this right of free action and full enjoyment—and what follows? By it all those attempts of government to restrain people for their own good, are condemned. The man is to be his own judge, and you are not to tell him in what fashion he is to follow his religion, pursue his trade, enjoy his amusements, or in a word, live any part of his life. Neither are you to protect him in either body or mind.

To protect one man you must take from the resources of another man—you must abridge the amount which the latter by his exertions has earned for himself. It is impossible to protect any one man save by diminishing the result of what the perfect enjoyment of liberty—that is the free use of his own faculties—has brought to another man, and therefore without taking into consideration here the weakening and destroying effects of protection upon the person protected, all protection equally with all restraint by force of government, must be held as a diminution from perfect liberty. It comes then to this, that except to protect the liberty of one man from the aggression of another man, that is, to repel force and fraud, which latter is force in disguise, you cannot justify the interferences of government in the affairs of the people, however benevolent or philanthropic may be the cloak you throw over them. That there may be certain cases which, from their very nature, are not cases to which the law applies, and which require special consideration, such, for example, as the management of property, wisely or unwisely placed in the hands of a government, I at once admit; into these I need not here enter. But bearing in mind that which Mr. Spencer has pointed out, the imperfection of all human definitions, and that at the boundary of every division into which we place existences of any kind, whether physical or mental, there is a point where it is impossible to say on which side of the line the thing in question lies; remembering that nature has not divided plant or animal, qualities of the mind, or even those ancient opposites, good and bad, into black and white squares, like those of a chessboard; but that, however complete and manifest may be their differences today, in virtue of that common root which existed in the ages of long ago, they still melt into each other by gradations too delicate for any point of separation to be fixed; remembering this, and making such allowance for it as is necessary, we may still say, and say truly, that the law knows no exception. You must accept human liberty whole or entire, or you must give up all cogency of reasoning by which to defend any part of it. Either it is a right, as sacred in one part as in another, an intelligible and demonstrable right, from which political justice and political equality intelligibly and demonstrably descend, or else it only exists in the world as a political luxury, a passing fashion, a convenience for obtaining certain economical advantages, which today is and tomorrow is not. Either you must treat men as self-responsible, as bearing their own burdens, and making their own lives, as free in thought, word and action, or you must treat them as so much political matter, which any government that can get into power may protect, restrain and fashion as it likes. In this case it all becomes subject matter for experiment, and Tory or Communist are alike free to work out their theories upon it, if they can only once count hands enough to transfer the magic possession of power to themselves. It is easy to perceive how long the reign of force has lasted in the world, how withering to conscience and to intellect has been its influence, when we find the great mass of men practically supporting such a creed. Out belief in force, our readiness to use it, and our obedience yielded to it, are but forms of fetish worship still left amongst us. Written in almost every heart, though unknown to the owner of it, are the words "force makes right." Those who wish to escape from this baneful superstition, who wish to destroy its altar and cut down its groves, can only do so by taking their stand on plain, intelligible principle; can only do so by recognizing that there are moral laws standing above our human dealings with each other, laws which we cannot depart from, which we cannot recognize at one moment and ignore at the next to suit our party conveniences. No detached effort, no rising of a few people against some special wrong which personally affects them, will ever alter the world's present way of thinking. It must be the battle of principles—the principle of liberty against the principle of force. With slight alterations we may take the words of Lowell, and read our own meaning in them:

> Not this man up and that man down,
>   But rights for all, say we;
> For rich and poor, for great and small—
>   Now what is your idee?
> God means to make this land, John,
>   Clear through from sea to sea,
> Believe and understand, John,
>   The worth of being free.
> Old Uncle S., sez he, I guess
>   God's price is high, sez he,
> But nothing else than what He sells
>   Wears long; and that J. B.
> May learn, like you and me.

ESSAY TWO

STATE EDUCATION:
A HELP OR HINDRANCE?

This article appeared in the Fortnightly Review *for July 1880.*

For ten years we have been busy organizing national education. A vigorous use of bricks and mortar is not generally accompanied by a careful examination of first principles,[1] but now that we have built our buildings and spent our millions of public money, and civilized our children in as speedy a fashion as that in which the great Frank christianized his soldiers, we may perhaps find time to ask a question which is waiting to be discussed by every nation that is free enough to think, whether a state education is or is not favorable to progress?[2]

It may seem rash at first sight to attack an institution so newly created and so strong in the support which it receives. But there are some persons at all events whom one need not remind, that no external grandeur and in-

---

[1] Has Mr. Leslie Stephen said somewhere, that it is easier to build churches than to think about what is to be taught inside of them?

[2] I ought to say that I have changed my opinions as regards the action of the state since 1870. I could not have made this change without the assistance of Mr. Herbert Spencer's writings.

fluence, no hosts of worshipers can turn wrong principles into right principles, or prevent the discovery by those who are determined to see the truth at any cost that the principles are wrong. Sooner or later every institution has to answer the challenge, "Are you founded on justice? Are you for or against the liberty of men?" And to this challenge the answer must be simple and straightforward; it must not be in the nature of an outburst of indignation that such a question should be asked; or a mere plea of sentiment; or the putting forward of usefulness of another kind. These questions of justice and liberty stand first; they cannot take second rank behind any other considerations, and if in our hurry we throw them on one side, unconsidered and unanswered, in time they will find their revenge in the imperfections and failure of our work.

National education is a measure carried out in the supposed interest of the workmen and the lower middle class, and it is they especially—the men in whose behalf the institution exists—whom I wish to persuade that the inherent evils of the system more than counterbalance the conveniences belonging to it.

I would first of all remind them of that principle which many of us have learned to accept, that no man or class accepts the position of receiving favors without learning, in the end, that these favors become disadvantages. The small wealthy class which once ruled this country helped themselves to favors of many kinds. It would be easy to show that all these favors, whether they were laws in protection of corn, or laws favoring the entail of estates, creating sinecures, or limiting political power to themselves, have become in the due course of time unpleasant and dangerous burdens tied round their own necks. Now, is state education of the nature of a political favor?

It is necessary, if discussion is in any way to help us, to speak the truth in the plainest fashion, and therefore I have no hesitation in affirming that it is so. Whenever one set of people pay for what they do not use themselves, but what is used by another set of people, their payment is and must be of the nature of a favor, and does and must create a sort of dependence. All those of us who like living surrounded with a slight mental fog, and are not overanxious to see too clearly, may indignantly deny this; but if we honestly care to follow Dr. Johnson's advice, and clear our minds of cant, we shall perceive that the statement is true, and if true, ought to be frankly acknowledged. The one thing to be got rid of at any cost is cant, whether it be employed on behalf of the many or the few.

Now, what are the results of this particular favor? The most striking result is that the wealthier class think that it is their right and their duty to direct the education of the people. They deserve no blame. As long as they pay by rate and tax for a part of this education, they undoubtedly possess a corresponding right of direction. But having the right they use it; and in consequence the workman of today finds that he does not count for much in the education of his children. The richer classes, the disputing churches, the political organizers are too powerful for him. If he wishes to realize the fact for himself let him read over the names of those who make up the school boards of this country. Let him first count the ministers of all denominations, then of the merchants, manufacturers, and squires. There is something abnormal here. These ministers and gentlemen do not place the workmen on committees to manage the education of their children. How, then, comes it about that they are directing the education of the workmen's children? The answer is plain. The workman is selling his birthright for the mess of pottage. Because he accepts the rate and tax paid by others, he must accept the intrusion of these others into his own home affairs—the management and education of his children. Remember, I am not urging, as some do, the workmen to organize themselves into a separate class, and return only their own representatives as members of school boards; such action would not mend the unprofitable bargain. To take away money from other classes, and not to concede to them any direction in the spending of it, would be simply unjust—would be an unscrupulous use of voting power. No, the remedy must be looked for in another direction. It lies in the one real form of independence—the renunciation of all obligations. The course that will restore to the workmen a father's duties and responsibilities, between which and themselves the state has now stepped, is for them to reject all forced contributions from others, and to do their own work through their own voluntary combinations. Until that is done no workman has more, or has a claim to have more, than half rights over his own children. He is stripped of one-half of the thought, care, anxiety, affection, responsibility, and need of judgment which belong to other parents.

I used the expression, the forced contributions of the rich. There are some persons who hold that the more money you can extract by legislation from the richer classes for the benefit of the poorer classes the better are your arrangements. I entirely dissent from such a view. It is fatal to any clear perception of justice. Justice requires that you should not place the burdens of one man on the shoulders of another man, even though he is better able to bear them. In plainer words, that you should not make one set of men pay for what is used by another set of men. If this law be once disregarded it simply reduces politics to a universal scramble, in which the most selfish will have the most success. It turns might into right, and proclaims that each man may rightfully possess whatever he can vote into his pocket. Whoever is intent on justice must be as just to the rich man as to the poor man; and because so-called national education is not for the children of the rich man, it is simply not just to take by compulsion one penny from him. No columns of sophistry can alter this fact. And yet, when once the obligation disappears, and the grace of free-giving is restored, it is a channel in which the money of the richer classes may most worthily flow. Whatever the faults are of our richer classes, there is no lack amongst them of generous giving. Take any newspaper and you will find that although by unwise legislation we are closing many of the great channels existing for their gifts, yet the quality persists. The endowment of colleges at one period, the endowment of grammar schools at another period, gifts to religious institutions, and the support given to that narrow, partial, vexatious, and official-minded system of education which prevailed up to 1870, are all evidence of what the richer people are ready to do as long as you do not withhold the opportunities. It may, however, be said, "Do not rich gifts bring obligations, and with them their mischievous consequences?" It is plain that the most healthy state of education will exist when the workmen, dividing themselves into natural groups according to their own tastes and feelings, organize the education of their children without help, or need of help, from outside. But between obligatory and voluntary contributions there is the widest distinction. There is but slight moral hurt to the giver or receiver in the voluntary gift, provided only that the spirit on both sides be one of friendly equality. It is the forced contribution, bringing neither grace to the giver nor to the receiver, which has the evil savor about it, and brings the evil consequence. The contribution taken forcibly from the rich is justified on the ground that the thing to be provided is a necessity for which the poorer man cannot pay. Thus the workman is placed in the odious position of putting forward the pauper's plea, and two statments equally deficient in truth are made for him: one, that book education is a necessity of life—a statement which for those who look for an exact meaning in words that are used is simply not true—and the other, that our people cannot provide it for themselves if left to do so in their own fashion.[3]

I wish to push still further the question of how much real power the workman possesses over the education of his children. I maintain that, setting aside the interference

---

[3] At the same time a thorough and radical readjustment of our educational endowments is required in the interest of the workmen, who, though in most cases having the first claim, derive little or no advantage from them.

of ministers, merchants, manufacturers, doctors, lawyers, and squires in his affairs, he has only the shadow and semblance of power, and that he never will possess anything more substantial under a political system. Let us see for what purposes political organization can be usefully applied. It is well adapted to those occasions when some definite reply has to be made to a simple question. Shall there be peace or war? Shall political power be extended to a certain class? Shall certain punishments follow certain crimes? Shall the form of government be republican or monarchical? Shall taxes be levied by direct or indirect taxation? These are all questions which can be fairly answered by yes or no, and on which every man enrolled in a party can fairly express his opinion if he has once decided to affirm or deny. But whenever you call upon part of the nation to administer some great institution the case becomes wholly different. Here all the various and personal views of men cannot be represented by a simple yes or no. A mixed mass of men, like a nation, can only administer by suppressing differences and disregarding convictions. Take some simple instance. Suppose a town of 50,000 electors should elect a representative to assist in administering some large and complicated institution. Let us observe what happens. It is only possible to represent these 50,000 people, who will be of many different mental kinds and conditions, by some principle which readily commands their assent. It will probably be some principle which, from its connection with other matters, is already familiar to their mind—made familiar by preceding controversies. For example, the electors may be well represented on such questions as "Shall the institution be open or closed on Sundays? Shall it be open to women? Shall the people be obliged to support it by rate? and, When rate-supported, to make use of it?" But it will at once be seen that these are principles which do not specially apply to any one institution but to many institutions. They are principles of common political application —they are, in fact, external to the institution itself, and distinct from its own special principles and methods. The effect then will be that the representative will be chosen on principles that are already familiar to the minds of the electors, and not on principles that peculiarly and specially affect the institution in question. Existing controversies will influence the minds of the electors, and the constituency will be divided according to the lines of existing party divisions. Both school boards and municipal government yield an example that popular elections must be fought out on simple and familiar questions. The existing political grooves are cut too deeply to allow of any escape from them.

"But," it may be replied, "as intelligence increases, and certain great political questions which are always protruding themselves are definitely settled, the electorate may become capable of conducting their contests simply with regard to the principles which really belong to the matter itself." Another difficulty arises here. Without discussing the possible settlement of these ever-recurring political questions, it ought to be remembered that, in the case of increased intelligence, we should have an increase in the number of different views affecting the principles and methods of the institution in question; and, as we should still have only one representative to represent us, it would be less possible for him than before to represent our individual convictions. If he represent A he cannot represent B, or C, or any of those that come after C; that is to say, if A, B, C, and the others are all thinking units, and therefore, do not accept submissively whatever is offered to them. He can only represent one section, and must leave other sections unrepresented. But as these individual differences are both the accompaniment and sign of increasing intelligence, this unhappy result follows, that the more intelligent a nation becomes, the greater pain it must suffer from a system which forces its various parts to think and act alike when they would naturally be thinking and acting differently.

"But if this is so, then there is no such thing possible as representation. If one person cannot represent many persons, then administration of all kinds fails equally in fulfilling a common purpose. All united effort therefore becomes impossible."

No doubt effective personal representation is under any circumstances a matter of difficulty; but political organization admits only of the most imperfect form of it, voluntary organization of the most perfect. Under political organization you mix everybody together, like and unlike, and compel them to speak and act through the same representative; under voluntary organization like attracts like, and those who share the same views form groups and act together, leaving any dissident free to transfer his action and energy elsewhere. The consequence is that under voluntary systems there is continual progress, the constant development of new views, and the action necessary for their practical application; under political systems, immobility on the part of the administrators, discontented helplessness on the part of those for whom they administer.

"But still there remain certain things which, however much you may desire to respect personal differences, the state must administer; such, for example, as civil and criminal law, or the defense of the country."

The reason why the nation should administer a system of law, or should provide for external defense, and yet abstain from interference in religion and education, will not be recognized until men study with more care the foundations on which the principle of liberty rests. Many persons talk as if the mere fact of men acting together as a nation gave them unlimited rights over each other; and that they might concede as much or as little liberty as they liked one to the other. The instinct of worship is still so strong upon us that, having nearly worn out our capacity for treating kings and such kind of persons as sacred, we are ready to invest a majority of our own selves with the same kind of reverence. Without perceiving how absurd is the contradiction in which we are involved, we are ready to assign to a mass of human being unlimited rights, while we acknowledge none for the individuals of whom the mass is made up. We owe to Mr. Herbert Spencer— the truth of those writings the world will one day be more prepared to acknowledge, after it has traveled a certain number of times from Bismarckism to communism, and back from communism to Bismarckism—the one complete and defensible view as to the relations of the state and the individual. He holds that the great condition regulating human intercourse is the widest possible liberty for all. Happiness is the aim that we must suppose attached to human existence; and therefore each man must be free—within those limits which the like freedom of others imposes on him—to judge for himself in what consists his happiness. As soon as this view is once clearly seen, we then see what the state has to do and from what it has to abstain. It has to make such arrangements as are necessary to ensure the enjoyment of this liberty by all, and to restrain aggressions upon it. Wherever it undertakes duties outside this special trust belonging to it, it is simply exaggerating the rights of some who make up the nation and diminishing the rights of others. Being itself the creature of liberty, that is to say, called into existence for the purposes of liberty, it becomes organized against its own end whenever it deprives men of the rights of free judgment and free action for the sake of other objects, however useful or desirable they may be.

It is on account of our continued failure to recognize this law of liberty that we still live, like the old border chieftains, in a state of mutual suspicion and terror. Far the larger amount of intolerance that exists in the world is the result of our own political arrangements, by which we compel ourselves to struggle, man against man, like beasts of different kinds bound together by a cord, each trying to destroy the other out of a sense of self-preservation. It is evident that the most fair-minded man must become intolerant if you place him in a position where he has only the unpleasant choice either to eat or be eaten, either to submit to his neighbor's views or force his own views upon his neighbor. Cut the cord, give us full freedom for differing amongst ourselves, and it at once becomes possible for a man to hold by his own convictions and yet be completely tolerant of what his neighbor says and does.

I come now to another great evil belonging to our system. The effort to provide for the education of children is a great moral and mental stimulus. It is the great natural opportunity of forethought and self-denial; it is the one daily lesson of unselfishness which men will learn when they will pay heed to none other. There is no factor that has played so large a part in the civilization of men as the slow formation in parents of those qualities which lead them to provide for their children. In this early care and forethought are probably to be found the roots of those things which we value so highly—affection, sympathy, and restraint of the graspings of self for the good of others. We may be uncertain about many of the agents that have helped to civilize men, but here we can hardly doubt. What, then, is likely to be the effect when, heedless of the slow and painful influences under which character is formed, you intrude a huge all-powerful something, you call the state, between parents and children, and allow it to say to the former, "You need trouble yourself no more about the education of your children. There is no longer any occasion for that patience and unselfishness which you were beginning to acquire, and under the influence of which you were learning to forego the advantage of their labor, that they might get the advantage of education. We will give you henceforth free dispensation from all such painful efforts. You shall at once be made virtuous and unselfish by a special clause in our act. You shall be placed under legal obligations, under penalty and fine, to have all the proper feelings of a parent. Why toil by the slow irksome process of voluntary efforts and your own growing sense of right to do your duty, when we can do it so easily for you in five minutes? We will provide all for you—masters, standards, examinations, subjects, and hours. You need have no strong convictions, and need make no efforts of your own, as you did when you organized your chapels, your benefit societies, your trade societies, or your cooperative institutions. We are the brain that thinks; you are but the bone and muscles that are moved. Should you desire some occupation, we will throw you an old bare bone or two of theological dispute. You may settle for yourselves which dogmas of the religious bodies you prefer; and while you are fighting over these things our department shall see to the rest of you. Lastly, we will make no distinctions between you all. The good and the bad parent shall stand on the same footing, and our statutes shall assume with perfect impartiality that every parent intends to defraud his child, and can only be supplied with a conscience at the police court." This cynical assumption of the weakness and selfishness of parents, this disbelief in the power of better motives, this faith in the inspector and the policeman, can have but one result. Treat the people as unworthy of trust, and they will justify your expectation. Tell them that you do not expect them to possess a sense of responsibility, to think or act for themselves, withhold from them the most natural and the most important opportunities for such things, and in due time they will passively accept the mental and moral condition you have made for them. I repeat that the great natural duties are the great natural opportunities of improvement for all of us. We can see every day how the wealthy man, who strips himself entirely of the care of his children, and leaves them wholly in the hands of tutors, governesses, and schoolmasters, how little his life is influenced by them, how little he ends by learning from them. Whereas to the man whose are much occupied with what is best for them, who is busied with the delicate problems which they are ever suggesting to him, they are a constant means of both moral and mental change. I repeat that no man's character, be he rich or poor, can afford the intrusion of a great power like the state between himself and his thoughts for his children. Observe the corresponding effect in another of our great state institutions. The effect of the Poor Law —which undertakes the care in the last resort of the old and helpless—has been to break down to a great extent the family feelings and affections of our people. It is simply and solely on account of this great machine that our people, naturally so generous, recognize much less the duty of providing for an old parent than is the case either in France or in Germany. With us, each man unconsciously reasons, "Why should I do that which the state will do for me?" All such institutions possess a philanthropical outside, but inwardly they are full of moral helplessness and selfishness.

These, then, are the first charges that I bring against state education; that the forced payments taken from other classes place the workman under an obligation; that, in consequence, the upper and middle classes interfere in the education of his children; that under a political system there is no place for his personal views, but that practically the only course of action left open to him is to join one of the two parties who are already organized in opposition to each other, and record a vote in favor of one of them once in three years. I do not mean to make the extreme statement that it is impossible to persuade either one party or both parties to adopt some educational reform, but I mean to say that one body acting for a whole country or a whole town can only pursue one method, and, therefore, must act to the exclusion of all views which are not in accordance with that one method; and that bodies which are organized for fighting purposes, and whose first great object is to defeat other great bodies nearly as powerful as themselves, are bound by the law of their own condition not to be easily moved by considerations which do not increase their fighting efficiency.

I have just touched upon the evils of uniformity in education; but there is more to say on the matter. At present we have one system of education applied to the whole of England. The local character of school boards deceives us, and makes us believe that some variety and freedom of action exist. In reality they have only the power to apply an established system. They must use the same class of teachers; they must submit to the same inspectors; the children must be prepared for the same examination, and pass in the same standards. There are some slight differences, but they are few and of little value. Now, if any one wishes to realize the full mischief which this uniformity works, let him think of what would be the result of a uniform method being established everywhere—in religion, art, science, or any trade or profession. Let him remember that canon of Mr. Herbert

Spencer, so pregnant with meaning, that progress is difference. Therefore, if you desire progress, you must not make it difficult for men to think and act differently; you must not dull their senses with routine or stamp their imagination with the official pattern of some great department. If you desire progress, you must remove all obstacles that impede for each man the exercise of his reasoning and imaginative faculties in his own way; and you must do nothing to lessen the rewards which he expects in return for his exertions. And in what does this reward consist? Often in the simple triumph of the truth of some opinion. It is marvelous how much toil men will undergo for the sake of their ideas; how cheerfully they will devote life, strength, and enjoyment to the work of convincing others of the existence of some fact or the truth of some view. But if such forces are to be placed at the service of society, it must be on the condition that society should not throw artificial and almost insuperable obstacles in the way of those reformers who search for better methods. If, for example, a man holding new views about education can at once address himself to those in sympathy with him, can at once collect funds and proceed to try his experiment, he sees his goal in front of him, and labors in the expectation of obtaining some practical result to his labor. But if some great official system blocks the way, if he has to overcome the stolid resistance of a department, to persuade a political party, which has no sympathy with views holding out no promise of political advantage, to satisfy inspectors, whose eyes are trained to see perfection of only one kind, and who may summarily condemn his school as "inefficient," and therefore disallowed by law, if in the meantime he is obliged by rates and taxes to support a system to which he is opposed, it becomes unlikely that his energy and confidence in his own views will be sufficient to inspire a successful resistance to such obstacles. It may be said that a great official department, if quickened by an active public opinion, will be ready to take up the ideas urged on it from outside. But there are reasons why this should not be so. When a state department becomes charged with some great undertaking, there accumulates so much technical knowledge round its proceedings, that without much labor and favorable opportunities it becomes exceedingly difficult to criticize successfully its action. It is a serious study in itself to follow the minutes and the history of a great department, either like the Local Board or the Education Department. And if a discussion should arise, the same reason makes it difficult for the public to form a judgment in the matter. A great office which is attacked envelopes itself, like a cuttlefish, in a cloud of technical statements which successfully confuses the public, until its attention is drawn off in some other direction. It is for this reason, I think, that state departments escape so easily from all control, and that such astounding cases of recklessness and mismanagement come periodically to light, making a crash which startles everybody for the moment. The history of our state departments is like that of some continental governments, unintelligent endurance through long periods on the part of the people, tempered by spasmodic outbursts of indignation and ineffectual reorganization of the institutions themselves. It must also be remembered that the manner in which new ideas produce the most favorable results is not by a system under which many persons are engaged in suggesting and inventing, and one person only in the work of practical application. Clearly the most progressive method is that whoever perceives new facts should possess free opportunities to apply and experiment upon them.

Add one more consideration. A great department must be by the law of its own condition unfavorable to new ideas. To make a change it must make a revolution. Our Education Department, for example, cannot issue an edict which applies to certain school boards and not to others. It knows and can know of no exceptions. Our bastard system of half-central half-local government is contrived with great ingenuity to render all such experiments impossible. If the center were completely autocratic (which Heaven forbid) it could try experiments as it chose; if the localities were independent, each could act for itself. At present our arrangements permit of only intolerable uniformity. Follow still further the awkward attempts of a department at improvement. Influenced by a long-continued public pressure, or moved by some new mind that has taken direction of it, it determines to introduce a change, and it issues in consequence a wholesale edict to its thousands of subordinates. But the conditions required for the successful application of a new idea are, that it should be only tentatively applied; that it should be applied by those persons who have some mental or moral affinity with it, who in applying it, work intelligently and with the grain, not mechanically and against the grain. No wonder, therefore, that departments are so shy of new ideas, and by a sort of instinct become aware of their own unfitness to deal with them. If only one wishes to realize why officialism is what it is, let him imagine himself at the center of some great department which directs an operation in every part of the country. Whoever he was he must become possessed with the idea of perfect regularity and uniformity. His waking and sleeping thought would be the desire that each wheel should perform in its own place exactly the same rotation in the same time. His life would simply become intolerable to him if any of his thousands of wheels began to show signs of consciousness, and to make independent movements of their own.

But suppose that a man of fresh mind and personal energy were to be placed at the head of our Education Department who perceived the mischievous effect of uniformity, could not this official tendency be counteracted? It might for a short space of time, just as the muscles of a strong man can for some hours defeat the pull of gravitation, but gravitation wins in the end. Such changes would be only spasmodic; they would not be the natural outcome of the system, and therefore could not last. Moreover, for those who understand the value of liberty and of responsibility, it is needless to point out how utterly false the system must be which makes the nation depend upon the intelligence of a minister, and not upon the free movement of the different minds within itself.

I come now to another great evil which accompanies an official system. In granting public money for education you must either give it on the judgment of certain public officers, which exposes you to different standards of distribution and to personal caprice, or you must give it according to some such system of results as exists at present with us. Payment by results has the merit, as a system, of being simple, easy to administer, and fairly equal; but it necessarily restricts and vulgarizes our conceptions of education. It reduces everybody concerned, managers, teachers, pupils, to the one aim and object of satisfying certain regulations made for them, of considering success in passing standards and success in education as the same thing. It is one long unbroken grind.[4] From boyhood to manhood the teacher himself is undergoing examinations; for the rest of his life he is reproducing on others what he himself has gone through. It is needless to say that the higher aims of the teacher, methods of arousing the imagination and developing the reasoning powers, which only bear fruit slowly and cannot be tested by a yearly examination of an inspector—whose fly will be waiting at the school door during the few hours at the disposal of himself or his subordinate—new attempts to connect the meaning of what is being learned with life itself, and to create an interest in work for work's own sake instead of for the inspector's sake, above all, the personal influences of men who have chosen teaching as their vocation, because the real outcome of their nature is sympathy with the young, and have not been drilled into it through a series of examinations owing to some accident of early days, all these things must be laid aside as subordinate to the one great aim of driving large batches successfully through the standards and making large hauls of public money. In our ignorant and unreasoning

---

[4] See an article bearing on this point by Mr. Fitch. I have not the reference by me at this moment.

belief in examinations we have not perceived how fatal
the system is to all original talent and strong personality
in the teacher. Whether it be a professor at a university
or a master in a board school, this modern exaggeration of
the use of examinations makes it impossible for him to
treat his subjects of teaching from that point of view
which is real and living to himself, or to follow his own
methods of influencing his pupils. In all cases he must
subdue his strongest tastes and feelings, and recast and
remodel himself until he is a sufficiently humble copy of
the inspector or examiner, upon whose verdict his success
depends. Any plan better fitted to reduce managers, teachers, and pupils to one level of commonplace and stupidity
could scarcely be found. The state rules a great copybook,
and the nation simply copies what it finds between the
lines.

I cannot escape a few words on the much-vexed religious question. Under our present system the Nonconformists are putting a grievous strain upon their own
principles. Whoever fairly faces the question must admit
that the same set of arguments which condemns a national religion also condemns a national system of education.
It is hard to pronounce sentence on the one and absolve
the other. Does a national church compel some to support
a system to which they are opposed? So does a national
system of education. Does the one exalt the principle of
majorities over the individual conscience? So does the
other. Does a national church imply a distrust of the
people, of their willingness to make sacrifices, of their
capacity to manage their own affairs? So does a national
system of education. Does the one chill and repress the

higher meanings and produce formalism? So does the other. But everywhere Nonconformists are being drawn into supporting the present school system, into obtaining popular influence by means of it, and, what is most inconsistent and undesirable, into using it as an instrument for spreading their own religious teaching. It is rapidly becoming their established church, and it will have, we may safely predict, the same narrowing effect upon their mind, it will beget the same inability to perceive the injustice of a political advantage, which the national church has had upon its supporters. Such a result is matter for much regret. First, because there is already but little steady adherence to principle in politics; and where a large body of influential men put themselves in a position which is inconsistent with the application of their own principles there is a sensible national deterioration. Second, if school boards are to be instruments of authoritatively teaching subjects of common dispute amongst us, such as the inspiration of the Bible and the performance of miracles, the struggle between the supporters of revealed religion and the different schools of free thought must be embittered. It is the question of political advantage and disadvantage which fans these disputes into red heat. Should this be the case, much of the better side of the present religious teaching will be lost sight of by a large part of the nation under the irritation of the political injustice, and its influence lost at a moment when its influence is specially wanted in shaping the new beliefs.

It may be said that secular education will prevent such antagonism, and that every year brings us nearer to the establishment of it. But secular education, even if it be the most just arrangement of trying to meet the injustice which a state system necessarily brings with it, is at best a miserable expedient. It is as if everybody agreed by common contract to tie up their right hand in doing a special piece of work in which they were most interested. Far healthier would it be for each section in the nation, from the Catholic to the materialist, to regain perfect freedom, and to do his best to place before children the scheme of life as he himself sees and feels it. If the common argument that such separate teaching will produce narrowness of mind and sectarian jealousy, is to be regarded, it thould be carried a step further, and the children on Sundays should not be permitted to go to their own churches and chapels, but the state should provide a universal temple with ceremonies adapted for all. I confess, for my own part, that I prefer to see intensity of conviction, even if joined with some narrowness, to a state of moral and intellectual sleepiness, and children waiting to be fed with such scanty crumbs as fall from official tables.

It only wants an effort to shake off the thraldom of familiar ideas and to see with fresh eyes, and then the monstrous fact that all England is placing itself under official restraints as regards that which it cares most about, would be enough to show us that there must be something radically wrong in a system which necessarily carries with it such a disqualification.

"But what are we to do?" is the impatient exclamation of many persons who feel both the pretentions and the poverty-stricken character of our present system? "Could education be supplied without official assistance?" My answer is that it could; that the combining and cooperative power of our people would provide for this great want, as it is providing for their religious and social wants; that money is waiting to flow from some of the richer people, if so plain and good an outlet were left open —money which is at present doing harm by creating scholarships and increasing the power of examinations; that good citizenship essentially consists in those who have learned to value some gift of civilization, awakening the same sense in those who remain indifferent. "But why did not education spread more quickly in the earlier part of the century?" No truly great thing grows like a mushroom. An intelligent value for education can only spread slowly like civilization itself. In our hurry to act we have not seen how much life and movement is sacrificed to make place for an official system. Those who administer such systems wish to get the flower ready-made without any process of growth. They do not recognize in the early and imperfect efforts the first stage of growth from which the better form will spring, but they wish to start at once with that which will satisfy their own rather prudish eyes. A certain uniform standard is fixed, and all that falls short of it is declared infamous. Of course it is always possible to smear education, religion, or anything else over a country, as you might smear paint, by departments or boards, and in five years be able to glorify your great work and to cram your speeches with statistics of what you have done. Every autocrat with ideas in his head has done the same thing, but he has also left it to his successors to moralize over the results of his work. Education when still left to itself did spread, perhaps too rapidly, in the beginning of the century. Presented to the English people by Lancaster, it was received like a gospel of good news; and although many of the early schools were of exceedingly humble and imperfect form, yet the want was beginning to be felt, and the supply was following. Then came the unwise, if well-intentioned, assistance of government. As usual, the political philanthropists could not endure to see a movement taking its own direction and shaping itself. As soon as the idea of government responsibility had taken root the evil was done. It is a mistake to suppose that government effort and individual effort can live side by side. The habits of mind which belong to each are so different that one must destroy the other. In the course of time there fell alike over everybody concerned the shadow of coming changes, and work which would have been done resolutely and manfully, if no idea of government interference had existed, remained undone, because the constant tendency of government to enlarge its operations was felt everywhere. The history of our race shows us that men will not do things for themselves or for others if they once believe that such things can come without exertion on their own part. There is not sufficient motive. As long as the hope endures that the shoulders of some second person are available, who will offer his own shoulders for the burden? It must also be remembered that unless men are left to their own resources they do not know what is or what is not possible for them. If government half a century ago had provided us all with dinners and breakfasts, it would be the practice of our orators today to assume the impossibility of our providing for ourselves.

And now, leaving much unsaid, I must ask what practical steps should be taken by those workmen who suspect that state education is but a part of that coercive drill which one half the human race delights to inflict upon the other half. First of all get rid of compulsion. It has been made the instrument of endless petty persecutions. It is fatal to the free growth of an intelligent love of education; to that moral influence which those of us who have learned the value of education ought to be exerting over others; to a true respect of man for man; for each man's right to judge what is morally best for himself and for those entrusted to him. It is an attempt to make one of those shortcuts to progress which end by making the goal recede from us. It is an exaggerated idea—as exaggerated, ill considered, and probably as short-lived as some other ideas of the present moment—of the value of book education, founded on a rigid and official idea that home duties and labors must in all cases be put aside before the official requirements. It is a copy of a continental institution, taken from a nation that, living under a paternal government, has not yet learned to spell the letters of the word *liberty*. The example of Germany and its highly organized state education is not alluring. In no country perhaps is there less respect of one class for the other class, or greater extremes of violent feeling. Where you subject people to strong official restraint, you seem fated to produce on the one side rigidity of thought and pedantry of feeling, on the other side those violent schemes against the possessions and the personal rights of the rich which we call socialism. Careful respect for the rights of others, vigorous and consistent defense of one's own rights, a deeply rooted love of freedom in thought, word, and action—these things are simply impossible wherever you entrust great powers to a government, and allow it to use them not simply within a sphere of strictly defined rights, but as supreme judge of what the momentary convenience requires.

Second, get rid of all dependence upon the central department. If you do not as yet perceive that public money cannot wisely, in any shape, be taken for education, still refuse the grant that the central department offers as a bribe for the acceptance of its mischievous interference. Until individual self-reliance has grown amongst us, let each town administer education in its own way. So, at least, we shall get local life and energy and variety thrown into the work, not the mere mechanical carrying out of regulations of two or three gentlemen sitting at their desks at Whitehall. But do not believe that you will get the highest results in this way. More freedom for action and experiment is wanted than you can get under any local board. Accustom yourself to the idea that men will act better in voluntary groups than if forced into union by external power. Many boards acting freely in a town, and learning gradually to cooperate together to some extent and for some purposes, is what we should look forward to. Perhaps the best step in advance, and in preparation for a purely free system, is to obtain powers from Parliament under which any considerable number of electors, say from one-sixth to one-tenth, according to the size of the town, might elect, and pay their rate to, their own board. Under such a plan there would be imperfections and possible evasions; but it would cast off the swaddling clothes imposed by the Privy Council, and would give a life to the work which would far more than compensate for the loss of mechanical regularity. It is always difficult to introduce freedom into a system that is founded on authority and officialism. You can only escape from anomalies and contradictions by being either rigidly despotic or completely free. But a little life and light are worth getting at almost any price, and will make us wish for more. The final step will be to render the rate purely voluntary, and to give full freedom and responsibility of action, for which the people will never be fit as long as they are persuaded to subject each other to official regulations under the much-abused name of self-government.

ESSAY THREE

A POLITICIAN
IN SIGHT OF HAVEN

This dialogue appeared in the Fortnightly Review *for March
1884 as the final sequel in the series of dialogues collectively
titled "A Politician in Trouble about his Soul."*

In a small but cheerful lodging overlooking the Thames,
Angus found Markham. After a few words he began
to pour out his old troubles. Was it possible to act honestly with party? Did it not lead to a constant sacrifice
of convictions, or, indeed, learning to live without them?
And then was party itself, morally speaking, better off;
would not convictions, if simply and straightforwardly
followed, place the party that so acted at a fatal disadvantage in its struggles with its rival? Were not politics
an art in which a clever manipulation of the electors, and
a nice opportunism in selecting measures that satisfied
one portion of the people without too much offending
another portion, possessed the first importance, while the
high motives and great causes to which all politicians
loved to appeal were as bits of broken mosaic that the
Jew dealer throws in as a make-weight to complete the
bargain?

"What course is open to a man," he asked, "who
wishes, above all, to be honest and to speak the truth;

who wishes neither himself to be corrupted nor to corrupt the people; who has no desire to preserve any privileges for the richer classes, but yet will not go one step beyond what he believes to be just in gaining favor of the masses? The common theory of modern government seems to be that we have given power to the people, and therefore, whatever may be our own opinions, we must acquiesce in their wishes. We may dexterously pare a little off here and there, at this or at that point, but, having placed power in their hands, we must accept and act upon their views. Should it happen that we can add a little semispontaneous enthusiasm on our own account, why, so much the better. Now, with this theory I cannot come to terms. I stick at the old difficulty. Shall a man look first and foremost to his own sense of what is right, or shall he follow his party?"

"Does not the question answer itself when stated in words?" replied Markham. "If the world is to make any real improvement, does it not depend more upon the individual resolution to see what is true, and to do it, than upon any possible combination into which men may enter? Is not the great thing that we have to hope for that a man should cherish and respect his own opinions beyond every other thing in life, so that it should be impossible for him to act in disregard of them? What form of slavery can be more debasing than that which a man undergoes when he allows either a party or a church to lead him to and fro when he is in no real agreement with it? Truth to your own self or faithful service to your party? Can you hesitate about the choice?"

"But might he not say," urged Angus, " 'the highest

truth to me personally is to follow faithfully my own party? I feel that I am doing the best of which I am capable when I act under and obey a man in whose capacity and devotion to great ends I believe. I prefer his judgment to my own. I do not trust my own views as regards all these complicated questions of the day; but I have faith in those who lead us, and wish to strengthen their hands in all ways possible.' "

"Yes, a man might speak in that sense who accepts the Catholic theory; who is ready to hand himself over to authority, and believes that he need not solve great questions himself, but may leave others to do it for him. If he slavishly give up the attempt to bring this world and that higher part of himself, his own intelligence, into harmony with each other; if he be content to act without seeing the just and the true and the reasonable in all that he does, then he may use this language, and plead an easy faith and easy devotion in excuse for effacing his own reason and making default, as far as he is concerned, in the great plan of the world. Your words are well chosen to snare a man's soul, but they cannot alter the fact that you are born a reasonable being, and that there is no rightful deliverance from the use of your own reason."

"But is not party a necessity?" replied Angus. "Here are two great parties in existence, and is it not a 'counsel of perfection' to say that a man must follow his sense of right, and act in complete independence of party? Suppose all the clearer-sighted and nobler-minded men did this, and retired from party, would it improve matters?"

"Have a little faith, Mr. Bramston, in right for right's sake. More good will come from the best men being true to themselves than from any cooperation of theirs with others. Unless the good man keeps true to himself you will get but little profit from his goodness which is sacrificed in order that he may work with others."

"But is not party," again urged Angus, "a reasonable thing in itself? Is not cooperation a natural and right means by which men unite their strength to obtain certain results?"

"Yes," replied Markham, "as an instrument, as a means toward a distinct end. A party organized for some common purpose in which men distinctly and definitely agree, in which each unit preserves his own consciousness and volition, is a natural and right instrument for men to use. But you politicians, Mr. Bramston, make party an end and not a means. You do not strive to live in real harmony with your own opinions; you care far more to be one of a party—to shout with it, fight with it, win with it."

"But suppose for a moment," said Angus, "that my sense of right went entirely with the most popular measures of the party; supposing that I sincerely approved of every gift which it was possible to take from the richer and give to the poorer. Suppose that I were Bastian—you probably know Bastian—with only this difference, that I believed heart and soul in which I promised, and so long as these services were done for the people I cared but little what was the exact form that they took?"

"And suppose the party were divided by two rival schemes for endowing the people?"

"I probably should be guided by the wishes of the people," said Angus hesitatingly.

"Yes; that is pretty nearly the only answer which is left you. As you have dismissed your own intelligence as your guide, what else can you do but follow the wishes of the people? And now please to say, Mr. Bramston, however good may be your intentions, is this a true position for any man to hold? Has he the right as regards himself to give others the keeping of his intelligence, to become in consciousness as a polype that leads but a semidetached life in the polype group? Can he really help his fellow-men by such mental subservience and denial of his own reason? Do you think that progress lies before us if we simply exchange holy mother church for holy mother party?

"And yet," said Angus hesitating, "granted that men ought not to accept a party program any more than they accept a Thirty-nine Articles, granted that no man who has freed his mind can take either his theology or his politics in a lump from others, still practically if any government is to do great services for the people, if it is to educate them, if it is to give them decent dwellings, to improve their sanitary condition, and on all sides to soften and improve the circumstances of life, I cannot disguise from myself that I can do more toward this end by simply supporting the government than by insisting on my own opinions."

"Ah, Mr. Bramston, you are introducing a large 'if.' You ask me, *if* a body we call government, enjoying certain honors and rewards at the expense of its rival, has for its object, in all the greatest matters that affect human life, to proclaim a certain number of universal schemes, be it for education, for regulating labor, for providing against distress, or for adding to the comforts of existence, whether in such a case we must not dismiss our separate intelligences to the second place, and simply support the government against the rival that waits to dislodge it. To which question I at once answer yes; as I should if you asked me whether the men who make up an army sent to conquer a neighboring country had better give up their own judgment in all things and be moved at will by the hands of their general. Defeating an enemy and defeating a political rival have only too many points in common; and in either case separate intelligences would be a great hindrance to success. It would be best in both cases—to use the mildest phrase—that they should be disciplined."

"Is it a fair comparison, Mr. Markham, between what men do in war and what they do in politics?" asked Angus, forgetting that he himself had often compared the two parties to two armies. "We almost all condemn war and its violence; you cannot compare these with the peaceful methods of discussing and voting."

"Are you sure," replied Markham, "that the two sys tems are so far apart? In war you use force, in politics you only imply force, but it is still there. What reason can you find why twelve million men should accept the views of sixteen million after they have voted, except that it is taken for granted that the sixteen million could smash up the twelve million, or as many of them as was necessary, were it a trial of strength between them? You take numbers, because they represent force, as conclusive of the verdict in what we call a constitutional country; but can you give me any moral reason that will bear five minutes' examination why you should do so, or why three men should compel two men to accept their views of life? Of course you cannot. Any moral scheme built upon numbers must break to pieces under its own inconsistencies and absurdities. There is only the one reason that superior numbers imply superior force. The sixteen million are presumably stronger than the twelve, and therefore the twelve submit without having recourse to practical tests."

"But is it impossible," said Angus, "to defend the authority of numbers? May it not be right that if five men differ, the two should give way to the three? It would be absurd to ask the three to submit to the two."

"Why should either two men live at the discretion of three, or three at the discretion of two? Both propositions are absurd from a reasonable point of view. If being a slave and owning a slave are both wrong relations, what difference does it make whether there are a million slave owners and one slave, or one slave owner and a million slaves? Do robbery and murder cease to be what they are if done by ninety-nine percent of the population? Clear your ideas on the subject, Mr. Bramston, and see that numbers cannot affect the question of what is right and wrong. Suppose some man with the cunning brain of a Napoleon were to train and organize the Chinamen, and should then lead them to annex such parts of the West as they desired; on your theory of numbers, if they exceeded the population of the country they appropriated it would be all right."

"I do not say that it is a satisfactory answer; but might not a majority inside a country afford a right method of decision, without extending the rule to the case of one country against another?"

"On what ground?" said Markham. "From where are
the rights to come which you have so suddenly discovered? Do you think that the moral laws that govern men
are made to appear and disappear at our convenience?
Forget that you are a politician, Mr. Bramston, and admit
that if you can plead any moral law as against the numbers of a stronger race, you must be able to plead it
equally against the stronger part of a nation; you must
be able to plead it whether on behalf of two men against
three, or of one man against a million. Either there are
or there are not moral conditions limiting force, but if
they exist they cannot depend upon numbers."

"Then you would condemn the Birmingham doctrine
of the sovereign rights of a majority, and refuse to treat
it as the foundation stone of democratic government,"
said Angus. "Bright preaches the doctrine eloquently, but
I am continually doubting the easygoing philosophy
which assumes that the majority will always be on the
right side and will only ask for what is just."

"I share the common respect which England has for
Mr. Bright," said Markham. "We all instinctively feel
that he is more of a man with living beliefs, and less of a
politician, than the rest. But can anything be less defensible than his position? He declares force to be no
remedy; he declares war, which is force nakedly asserted,
to be wrong; but he looks on the outcome of the ballot
box, which is as much force as the orders issued by a
Prussian field marshal, and is only obeyed because it involves the breaking of heads when necessary, almost as
a divine and inspired thing. What is the difference be-

tween force calling itself force or wrapped up in platform phrases, so long as it has the same self."

"Then you reject the rights of the majority, and with them the theory of democratic government?"

"I believe myself more democratic than your politicians," said Markham, "but I reject utterly their view of what democracy is. They have not the courage to bid the people to accept universal conditions, but wish, in imitation of departed kings and emperors, to build anew every sort of artificial privilege, as if such privileges, for whomsoever they are created, ever had lasted or could last in defiance of moral law. Well, Mr. Bramston, the world has lived through many lies; it has lived through the priestly lie, the kingly lie, the oligarchical lie, the ten-pound-householder lie, and it has now to live through the majority lie. These other lies are gone to their own place, and this last lie will follow after them. The law of equal freedom and equal justice knows none of them."

"Do you then condemn the use of force for all purposes?" asked Angus.

"Will you undertake to define for me the purposes for which I am and for which I am not to use force? For myself I fail to be able to do it. I cannot suppose that three men have power to compel two men in some matters without finding myself presently obliged to conclude that the three men must decide what these matters are, and therefore that they have powers of applying force in all matters. Between the some purposes and the all purposes I can find no settled boundary. You cannot draw, and no man living can draw, a force line. If you sat down with Mr. Gladstone today to do it, tomorrow his exigencies would have eaten out the line, and its authority would be gone, at all events for our planet. Do not let us play with these things, and build up pleasant fictions that are of no value. Either a state of liberty—that is, a state where no physical force is applied by man to man—is the moral one, or we must recognize force as rightly applied by those who possess it for all purposes that they think right."

"Now I become more and more puzzled," said Angus. "May not the majority employ force for what we call good, and not for bad purposes?"

"Please do define good and bad purposes. You will find that your definitions hold as much meaning as a sieve holds water. If you wish to see how hopeless is the task, read Sir F. Stephen's book, in which he tells us not to employ compulsion, even if calculated to obtain a good object, if it involves 'too great an expense.' What possible binding power is there in such a rule over the minds of men? Where is the common standard of measurement? Who sees with the same eyes the accompanying expense or the resulting good? It is far better to look the truth in the face and to say that when you sanction force for good purposes you sanction it for all occasions which the holders of power think good."

"But can one be sure that force is a bad thing in itself?" said Angus.

"Do you not see, first, that—as a mental abstract—physical force is directly opposed to morality; and, second, that it practically drives out of existence the moral forces? How can an act done under compulsion have any moral element in it, seeing that what is moral is the free act of an intelligent being? If you tie a man's hands there is nothing moral about his not committing murder. Such an abstaining from murder is a mechanical act; and just the same in kind, though less in degree, are all the acts which men are compelled to do under penalties imposed upon them by their fellow-men. Those who would drive their fellow-men into the performance of any good actions do not see that the very elements of morality—the free act following on the free choice—are as much absent in those upon whom they practice their legislation as in a flock of sheep penned in by hurdles. You cannot see too clearly that force and reason—which last is the essence of the moral act—are at the two opposite poles. When you act by reason you are not acting under the compulsion of other men; when you act under compulsion you are not acting under the guidance of reason. The one is a force within you and the other a force without. Moreover, physical force in a man's hand is an instrument of such a brutal character that its very nature destroys and excludes the kindlier or better qualities of human nature. The man who compels his neighbor is not the man who reasons with and convinces him, who seeks to influence him by example, who rouses him to make exertions to save himself. He takes upon himself to treat him, not as a being with reason, but as an animal in whom reason is not. The old saying, that any fool can govern with bayonets, is one of the truest sayings which this generation has inherited and neglected. Any fool can reform the surface of things, can drive children by the hundreds of thousands into schools, can drive prostitutes out of public sight, can drive dram drinking into cellars, can provide out of public funds pensions for the old, hospitals for the sick, and lodging houses for the poor, can call into existence a public department and a population of officials and inspectors, provided that he has the handling of money that does not belong to him, and a people not trained to inquire beyond the present moment, and ready to applaud what has a surface look of philanthropy; but what is the good of it all when he has done it? To be compelled into virtue is only to live in order to die of dry rot."

"I see the conflict between reason and force," said Angus; "still, I hesitate in the matter. Is it clear that I cannot use force to make people reasonable? Why may we not compel them to educate their children, to give up public houses, to only work a certain number of hours in the day, and many other things of the same kind? May not force be the instrument of reason?"

"It would be false to call such acts reasonable. You may use your own reason when you say that compulsory education, or compulsory temperance, is good for certain people, and proceed to carry it out; but in so acting you disallow the existence of reason in those whom you compel. You have placed them in a lower rank to yourself, you retaining and using your reason, they being disfranchised of it. Now this unequal relation between men, in which the reason of some is replaced by the reason of others, is one that reason acting universally rejects as a denial of itself. Why should your reason be recognized and not that of the man you compel? Moreover, from a reasonable point of view, can you not see that the very idea of force necessarily involves a fatal absurdity? If A has power over B, you must assume that in the first instance he has power over himself; no man can be master of another man and not master of himself. But if so, then B (unless you assume unequal rights as the basis of the social order) is also master of himself, which entirely destroys any rightful power on the part of A to be his master and to make him act against his will."

"I must confess, whether I agree or not with the abstract condemnation of force," said Angus, "that I sometimes regret to see the love of force and the belief in it growing so fast upon us. All our would-be reformers can only suggest compulsion of some kind. The word is always in their mouth."

"Yes, the mood is on us," said Markham, "and utterly debasing it is. We are filled with the Celtic spirit of wishing to govern and be governed; we creep into one pitiful refuge after another, as if anything could save us from our appointed heritage of the free reason and the free act. But I live in faith, Mr. Bramston. *Exoriare aliquis!* The time will come when some Englishman of sturdy common sense, a new *martellus monachorum*, will rise to rout these good gentlemen that wish to tie the English people to their apron strings, to smash these pagan revivals of Catholicism, this blind submission to authority, to strip these 'cloistered virtues' of their seeming excellence, and bid the people live in a free world, gaining their own good, trampling on their own sins, and making their own terms with their own souls. But let me ask you, Mr. Bramston, have you read Mr. Herbert Spencer's writings? We shall do little good unless you have done so. We owe to him the placing of this great truth, that man must be free if he is to possess happiness on its deepest and truest foundations. No discursive talk of ours will really help you until you have felt the marvelous power with which he has read the wider and deeper meanings of the world, and given order to our disorderly conceptions of it."

"I must confess with shame that I have never read his writings. I have always believed him to be the great teacher of laissez-faire, and everybody today supposes that laissez-faire lies on the other side of the horizon behind us."

"Ah," said Markham, "I fear that all you political gentlemen live in a greater state of ignorance than most of us. How can it be otherwise? With your committees and debates, and speeches to prepare, you have but little time for watching the graver discussions that are going on. Like lawyers in busy practice, you have no mental energy left to give to abstract questions; and yet I do not notice that any of you are wanting in courage when you come to deal with the very foundations of social things. So the world believes in the failure of laissez-faire? No, Mr. Bramston, it is not laissez-faire that has failed. That would be an ill day for men. What has failed is the courage to see what is true and to speak it to the people, to point toward the true remedies away from the sham remedies. But read Mr. Spencer and see for yourself. Believe me, you are not fit to be exercising power over others until you have done so. You had better leave some of your Blue Books unread than remain in ignorance of his work."

"What is that work as regards politics?"

"He has made the splendid attempt," replied Markham, "to give fixity and order to our moral ideas, and to place the relation of men to each other on settled foundations. The love of disorder is so great in the human mind that probably men will yield but slowly to his teaching, perhaps not till they have passed through many troubles. But it is along the track that he has opened out to them, and that track only, that every nation must escape anarchy and find its happiness."

"And the drift of his other work?"

"I should say that the result was to make the world, as a whole, reasonable to men. He has connected all human knowledge, establishing interdependence everywhere; he has taught us to see that everything in the world is part of a great growth, each part, like the different structures of a tree, developing to its own perfect form and special use, while it remains governed by the whole. He has helped us to rise everywhere from the reason that governs the part to the reason that governs the whole; and in tracing back this great growth of the past, compound form rising out of simple form, he has shown us the long, slow preparation toward perfection through which the world has traveled and yet has to travel. It is scarcely too much to say that he has given us a past and he has given us a future. In a time of sore need, when the old meanings were splintered to driftwood, he has seen that the true meaning of the world was to be found, and in finding it he has restored to us the possibilities of a higher religious faith. The influence of modern science has been to make men too easily satisfied with their own separate and fragmentary knowledge. Each man has settled down to his niche in the vineyard, and there labored industriously and successfully, but with his eyes closed for the wider meanings. To read a learned paper before a learned society, to be the highest authority on some special subject, have been objects which have unduly influenced our generation; and it is only such a work as Mr. Spencer's that recalls us to the truth that the use of knowledge is not simply to annihilate a rival on some particular subject that we look on as our private property, but to lead men to understand the great whole in which they are included—to bring that whole into perfect agreement with human reason. Specialism, however necessary, is not the end of science. The end of science is to teach men to live by reason and by faith, by grasping the great meanings of life, and by seeing clearly the conditions under which they can give effect to those meanings. How little science yet helps us in our general conceptions of life you can see by the quiet ignoring amongst politicians of the vital meaning which Darwin's discoveries have for them. And hence it is that, great as has been the multiplication of scientific facts, they have done but comparatively little to reform the ideas and reshape the conduct of men. Our intellectual life still remains thoroughly disorderly, notwithstanding stray patches of science and order introduced into it. It is here that we have so much to gain from Mr. Spencer. We owe to him our power to realize the harmony and unity embracing all things, the perfect order and the perfect reason, and thus to walk confidently with sure aims; and instead of being content to leave science as the technical possession of a few, he has, in a true sense, given it to the people by insisting on the universal meanings and making them accessible to all men."

"On what foundation does Mr. Spencer place political liberty?" asked Angus.

"He founds it on the right of every man to use the faculties he possesses. It is evident, as he insists, that all sciences rest on certain axioms. You remember Euclid's axioms, such as 'a whole is greater than its parts,' and you can easily perceive that any science, however complicated it may be, owing to its dependence on other sciences that have preceded it, must rest on its own axioms. Now politics are the science of determining the relations in which men can live together with the greatest happiness, and you will find that the axioms on which they depend are, (1) that happiness consists in the exercise of faculties; (2) that as men have these faculties there must be freedom for their exercise; (3) that this freedom must rest on equal and universal conditions, no unequal conditions satisfying our moral sense."

"Why do you insist on my treating these truths, if truths they are, as axioms?" asked Angus.

"Because you cannot contradict them without involving yourself in what is inconsistent and absurd, without giving up the belief that the world is reasonable, and, therefore, that it is worth our while to try to discover what we ought to do. Place before your mind the opposites of these statements, and try to construct a definite social system out of them. Happiness is not the exercise of faculties; men having faculties ought not to exercise them; the conditions as regards their exercise should be unequal and varying. Can you seriously maintain any of these statements? When you propose unequal conditions of freedom do you offer a standing ground which men universally could accept, which they could look upon as the perfect condition of their existence?"

"But might I not claim greater freedom for the abler and better man, for the more civilized race?"

"Why should you? What does any man or any race want more than freedom for themselves? Admit that any one may take more than his share; that is, in other words, that he may restrain by force the exercise of the faculties of others, and in what a sea of moral confusion you are at once plunged. Who is to decide which is the better man or the more civilized race, or how much freedom is to be allowed or disallowed? To settle this question men must sit as judges in their own case; and this means that the strongest will declare themselves the most civilized, and will assign such portions of freedom as they choose to the rest of the nation or the rest of the world, as the case may be. Are you prepared for this?"

"I agree in some measure," said Angus; "but how can you persuade the strongest not to use their strength?"

"Only by strengthening human belief in reason, by bringing men to see that the moral system regulating their actions toward each other is as true and fixed as the system of the planets, its parts as orderly, its whole as reasonable; and that force—I mean in every case physical compulsion of one man by another—has no possible place in it."

"But can men see this reasonableness, this orderliness, of which you speak?"

"Surely," replied Markham. "Is it not plain that between the world, the outcome of the highest reason, and the human reason as it evolves, harmony is ever growing? The evolution of the human mind means that its power increases to read order everywhere; and it is only as it perceives order that it can gain perfect confidence in its own conclusions. You must remember that a science is not a mere mass of separate truths or conclusions which may, so to speak, lie anywhere as regards each other in the same heap. As Mr. Spencer has so well pointed out, men at first begin by learning the detached truths, and then in later stages see that each truth has its own place in an indissoluble and reasonable whole, which whole, as we learn to perceive it, gives certainty to the separate truths. The separate truths are like beads before they are strung on a string, and which do not gain their full meaning until the string is there. Take Mr. Spencer's example of astronomy. By countless observations you learn that the orbits of planets are ellipses of a certain kind, and then presently you learn the great central cause in obedience to which these forms are what they are; you have gained a master key which, as you know, will unlock every fact, whether at present within or not within your observation, in the group that belongs to it. Hence it arises that a separate truth only becomes really known when you know the system of which it forms a part. Is it different in moral matters? Do you think that there are order and system for the facts that concern the planets and not for the facts that concern the human mind; for mineral and for plant, and not for the relations in which men are to live toward each other? Do you think that with order and system in every other part of the universe that here you suddenly enter a territory sacred to disorder and conflict, a sort of moral Alsatia, where alone the writ of the Great Power does not run? Surely you cannot defend such a belief. Surely you have some faith in the perfect reasonableness that underlies and overarches everything. To the politician it may be torture to believe that social and political questions are parts of a reasonable whole, and can only be rightly dealt with in strict obedience to that whole. His own course is just so much easier as he may disregard this reason of the whole, as he may by turns plead the law or the exception, as he may ignore all fixed moral relations of men to each other, as he may urge plaintively that all is so uncertain and subject to change, and claim permission to deal with the circumstances that exist as the light of the moment and the ever-urgent personal interest may direct. The world does not yet see the impertinence and the danger of such claims. It will do so as the consequences of existing mental disorder thicken upon it."

"But do you mean, the world being as it is," said Angus, returning to the old point of attack, "that we can get through it without force? Why, even a London street after dark may require one to use force to protect himself."

"I have not said that. Six months ago I knocked a scoundrel down who had snatched a lady's watch from her, and handed him over to the police. I do not say we can get through life without using force; but when we do so in the simplest and apparently most justifiable case, even to repel force, we are outside the moral relation, and are simply living again in that force relation in which man as half animal once lived, and in which the animals now live. Underneath all life lies the great law of self-preservation (a law which we may fulfill either by using force as the animals do, or by universally accepting the reasonable relation which, forbidding force, guarantees equal freedom to all), and those who use force may compel us to live toward them in the force relation; but the important thing is to see that it is only when we are living in the reason relation that we have distinct moral guidance to tell us what are right and what are wrong actions, and that in the force relation we must act often by guesswork and always without certain guidance."

"Why am I without moral guidance in the force relation? Were you not right in knocking the thief down?"

"My justification was, that he had established between himself and the rest of society the force relation, and therefore I had to deal with him as I should have dealt with a wild beast that had attacked me. The act on my part was so far a moral one, inasmuch as I obeyed the derived moral command to help my neighbor; but being an act done in the force relation, brute strength being simply opposed to brute strength, it is impossible that I should have that guarantee of certainty as regards right conduct, which can only exist where my actions are in harmony with the whole moral system. Mr. Spencer has stated this with his usual admirable force. 'Ethics, or the principles of right conduct, ignore all crime and wrongdoing. It simply says such and such are the principles on which men should act, and when these are broken it can do nothing but say they are broken.' Thus if there is a command that says, 'Thou shalt not lie,' you can have no certain guidance from that command or from any part of the moral system which is subordinate to it when you have once told a lie and choose to persist in it. It may be expedient to tell or not to tell another lie; many excellent secondary reasons, such as regard for your friend, may urge you to do so, but all fixed guidance is lost, for when once the coherence of the system is broken, the law of lesser authority being obeyed and the law of higher authority disobeyed, only conflict and contradiction can arise. To obtain certain guidance you must obey the moral laws in the order of their imperativeness; and while in my case I obeyed a derived law which bade me help my neighbor, I was outside the primary law which forbids the use of force. I did no wrong toward the thief, as far as I could judge, but I was acting on a personal judgment that might lead me right or wrong."

"Why do you speak of the act of helping your neighbor as a derived law, and that of not using force as the primary law?" asked Angus.

"Speaking rationally, do not honesty and justice precede generosity? To employ force to a man is to deprive him of what he rightly possesses, the freedom to use his faculties, and therefore is an act which I am bound not to do. To assist him by any gift or service of mine is an act which I am only bound to do in an inferior sense; it is but a development, important as it is, from the imperative command to respect a man's rights."

"Might not some persons try to make the laws change place, and insist that to help your neighbor was the primary law?"

"Yes," replied Markham, "if they had no fear of plunging into Serbonian bogs. Which neighbor am I to help, and in what fashion? Am I to help one at the expense of another? Am I, like Robin Hood of old, to take the purse of the rich man and give it to the poor? Try to construct a definite and certain system that is really to guide men in their dealings with each other on such a foundation. You may amuse yourself some day for half an hour, Mr. Bramston, by trying to do it, but you will hardly obtain any other result."

"I see the difficulty," replied Angus slowly. "To say we must do good to others means nothing unless there is some fixed system which allows us to define precisely the nature and conditions of this ever-elusive good."

"Exactly; there must be a fixed system, and that system must spring from rights. Without rights, no system; without system, no guidance. If you wish to realize the moral confusion that results where rights are neglected, glance at the world of today, and observe the good qualities which impede rather than assist the general cause of good. Do we not see nihilists and invincibles devoting themselves in the spirit of self-sacrifice in order to obey an order of assassination; slave owners showing kindness to their slaves; politicians carrying out what they believe to be useful measures for the people by appealing to selfish passions and infringing upon the rights of others; socialists hoping to regenerate the world by deciding in what way and to what extent men shall exercise their faculties. These and a thousand other examples show us that actions swinging from good qualities, but done in disregard of primary moral commands, may increase the sum total of unhappiness instead of happiness."

"What do you mean when you speak of primary and derived laws?" asked Angus.

"Necessarily at the beginnings of social life men's actions are confused and in conflict with each other. Presently a stage is reached at which reason asserts its claims to regulate these acts, and then, as we have already seen, it requires of men to respect each other's rights. This, though the necessary condition of all happiness, is not sufficient for the perfecting of it. A second command—inferior in authority and definiteness—succeeds to the first, and bids us not only respect rights but also feelings, so far at least as such feelings do not tend to restrict rights. There are many actions which we have, as far as the first command is concerned, a right to do, but which, as they cause unnecessary pain to others, we ought to abstain from doing. To these actions Mr. Spencer gives the name of negative beneficence. Again, succeeding to these acts of abstention are the acts of positive beneficence, the direct acts which men do for the sake of increasing the happiness of others; acts which, as human nature evolves, will become more and more a necessary and integral part of the happiness of each man. But you can readily see that to add to the happiness of our neighbor, or even to avoid giving him unnecessary pain, excellent as such acts are, are of little moral value unless you begin by respecting his rights. Except on such a foundation they cannot lead to the settled happiness of men; they can only lead to such confusion between good and evil as we see around us at present. And now observe a further development. From respecting rights we learn to recognize the self in each man as the true governing center of his actions. We learn to see the false side of those great systems which lower and debase a man by offering him comfort—whether it be intellectual or material comfort—at the price of liberty, which weaken his self-guidance and his self-responsibility, and make him but a semiconscious unit in churches and parties. We see that all social as well as political systems must be framed to make him not only in higher matters the possessor of his own soul, but in matters of everyday life the intelligent director of his own energies. Do you see how fruitful, how far-reaching, will be the influence of this recognition of the self in each man? For every act toward others will be shaped and determined by it. Is it a matter of helping some fellow man in distress, we shall ask, "Am I merely lifting the man by an external machinery out of a momentary trouble at the cost of depressing rather than increasing his own self-helping energies?' Of assisting masses of men to better their position, 'Can I rightly lighten the burdens of one man by increasing the burdens of another, to however small an extent, and however easily the latter may be able to bear it? Can I do so without weakening in all minds the sense of the universal agreement, and in the minds of those who are helped that self-respect which should only claim free play for the energies of each?' Of spreading opinion and bringing others within a church or party, 'Have I joined these men to myself by the true and pure conviction of each soul, or have I treated them as a mere crowd, to be moved as I wished by machinery, to be bribed and cajoled and driven toward the ends that I desired?' Of education, 'Am I mechanically impressing the self of my own opinions on another mind? Am I merely gaining the ends on which the world of the day sets store, and content for the sake of these to follow such lifeless and mechanical methods as promise the readiest success? Am I willing to make my own task easier by employing systems of bribes and threats, or is my one effort to develop another equal being that shall be strong in its own self-confidence and able by its own reason to make a life for itself?' There is no part of human life, no question of morality, that will not be illumined by the light thrown from that intense respect for each human self which in due time will succeed to the perfect recognition of each other's rights. The creed of rights leads as certainly to the elevation of the human race as the creeds of socialism, founded on force, lead to the degradation of it."

"Could you summarize for me what you said?" asked Angus.

"Using the fewest words, I should say all truths belong to their own system. There is not such a thing as a stray or independent truth in existence; and it is only as you know the system to which the truths belong, that you know with certainty the truths themselves. Moral truths, then, like physical truths, are united in a system, and as this system must rest on certain assured foundations, the question is on what foundations does it rest? The answer is, in Mr. Spencer's words, on the freedom of men to exercise their faculties. From these foundations arises a coherent and harmonious moral system governing our political and social systems, and illuminating the most complex questions of human conduct. Apart from this foundation, morality is a mass of indistinct and contradictory commands, men often obeying a derived command while they disobey a primary command."

"In all you have said you have only used a deductive

argument," said Angus; "will you not sacrifice to the gods of the present time by speaking inductively?"

"Ah! that greatest of all inductions! Some younger man with fuller stores of knowledge must give that induction to the world. It will be for him to follow the history of liberty as he would follow a great river in the East, whose banks are covered with rejoicing crops, while away from it all remains desert. You can see for yourself how vast is the material that it waiting to be used. Has any race of men ever fairly tried even the humblest experiment of freedom and found it fail? Have not the human faculties grown in every field just as freedom has been given to them? Have men ever clung to protection and restraint and officialism without entangling themselves deeper and deeper into evils from which there was no outlet? But tonight we cannot enter upon these wide fields. There is only one group of facts, those that belong to the history of plant and animal, at which we can glance. See how clearly under Darwin's revelations comes out the saving meaning that there is in competition, the destructive meaning that there is in protection. Protect the plant and animal by some mere external protection, as that of an island or an impassable barrier, and you reserve it for certain destruction when the day comes in which at last the life that has ranged over wider spaces and become adapted to the conditions of existence enters into competition with it. The very conditions that seemed to protect it have ensured its destruction. Had it not been protected it had passed through the same gradual adaptations that other life elsewhere has passed through. It was separation from the mainland that preserved the Australian marsu-

pials, that has made islands such as Madagascar the interesting relic houses of a life that had not been competent to
survive unless protected. So also has it been that the European plants, which by ranging over wider tracts have
more thoroughly undergone selection, have beaten the
native plants of La Plata, New Zealand, and, in a lesser
degree, of Australia, while speaking generally the plants
of these countries cannot obtain a footing in Europe; that
the intertropical mountains lost their true vegetation, and
accepted those hardier forms which in the glacial period
were able to reach them; that the wingless and defenseless birds, such as those of Mauritius, and Bourbon, and
Rodriguez, have only been found where beasts of prey
were absent. But why multiply examples? The history of
the world turns upon the fact of the hardier forms, per-
fected by a wider and sharper competition, inevitably
replacing the weaker forms. And do you not also see how
the lower kinds of self-protection die out before the
higher kinds? The huge armor plates and spikes that once
protected animal life are replaced by higher organizations,
better adaptations of bone and muscle, and therefore
quicker movements, by improved special organs, by increasing brain size. It is the same with men. The clumsy
restrictions and defenses which parliaments provide must
give place to those higher forms of self-protection which
depend upon mental qualities. Is it not plainly one and
the same sentence which nature speaks to plants, to animals, and to men, 'Improve in the true way or be destroyed?' She affixes everywhere her two great conditions
of improvement, variety (or difference)—that both in the
physical and in the intellectual world brings into exis-

tence the beginnings of higher life—and competition, that selects for survival these all-precious beginnings out of the midst of the lower forms; while outside these conditions she reserves no way of salvation. It is wrong and unfaithful to disguise or evade these truths. Whatever it costs, you must say plainly to all men that variety and competition are the only conditions of their advance, and that these conditions can only exist under a system of perfect liberty. All infringements of liberty sin in a twofold way. They tend to uniformity by excluding natural variety, and they give external protection at the cost of preventing the development of self-protection, saving the pain of the present by doubling it in the future. Does such a law seem hard to you? If so, remember that it is not a competition like that of animals and savages, to be decided merely by physical force or cunning, but one in which the more powerful brain, the truer perception, the more temperate habit, the more upright conduct, shall prevail in the end, and that thus the better type shall be always evolving, while the pain of the passage from the unfit to the fit grows less and less."

"And now," said Angus, "leaving further consideration of the principles, let me ask you for the net result. How would you give practical effect to such views?"

"The government, as pointed out by Mr. Spencer, must confine itself simply to the defense of life and property, whether as regards internal or external defense. You can defend neither of these systems, both of which involve the use of force, on true moral grounds; they can only be imperfectly defended under the law of self-preservation, which we extend to others beyond ourselves. But in the world as it is, those who use force must be repelled—and effectively repelled—by force. By their own act they place themselves in the force relation, and, barbarous as is the relation, we must accept it just so far as they thrust it on us. Farther the government must not go. It must not attempt any service of any kind for the people, from the mere mechanism of carrying their letters to that most arrogant and ill-conceived of all universal schemes, the education of their children. All services which the people require must be done by themselves, grouped according to their wants and their affinities in their own natural groups, and acting by means of voluntary association. The system would be one of free trade carried out logically and consistently in every direction. We should then be quit both of the politician, with that enormous bribing power which he possesses by offering services to one part of the people at the cost of another part, and of that fatal compression of ideas, energies, and experimental efforts which results whenever universal systems are imposed upon a nation. Those people who wish to make their fellow-men wise, or temperate, or virtuous, or comfortable, or happy, by some rapid exercise of power, little dream of the sterility that belongs to the universal systems which they so readily inflict on them. Some day they will open their eyes and see that there never yet has been a great system sustained by force under which all the best faculties of men have not slowly withered."

"As regards property, what would be the system which a government ought to defend?" said Angus.

"There is no choice except between an open market in all things—that is, free acquisition and complete ownership—or a more or less socialistic government. If government undertakes in any way the task of arranging and distributing property, it at once enters on the force relation. It presumes to set itself above all fixed moral relations of men, and to create for them out of its imagination the conditions under which they are to stand to each other. And notice that free trade and free acquisition of all property stand and fall together. Either a man may do the best for himself with his faculties, or he and his faculties may be sacrificed for the advantage of others. Our great effort at this moment should be to reconcile our people heartily to private property, whether in land or in any other thing (Mr. Spencer draws a line between the two, but I am unable to follow him), and to lead them to see that no nation can in any true sense be free which allows a government of the day to model and remodel that which touches a man's life so nearly as his property. That English land is not largely held by the small owners is a great public calamity, but it is not to be repaired by the greater one of small or big confiscations. Remove at once—as you would have done years ago, had the Liberal Party remained true to its traditions, and foregone popularity and sensation hunting, under Mr. Gladstone's leadership—all legal impediments that yet exist to free sale. Insist that the living owner should be the full owner in the sight of the law courts; avoid all ridiculous measures for patching up the present landlord and tenant system, and the land will soon naturally and healthily find its way into the hands of the people. Any way, it is better to bear the evils of delay than to demoralize a whole nation in their spirit and their aims by accepting

the bribes of the politician to take from the few to give
to the many."

"And taxes, Mr. Markham?" asked Angus.

"All taxes must be voluntary," said Markham.

"Voluntary!" said Angus, drawing the longest of
breaths.

"There is no moral foundation for taking taxes by
force. Those who pay taxes have not put themselves outside the reasonable relation and therefore you cannot
justly compel payment at their hands. The Dissenters
were on the right track when they refused to pay church
rates, and every measure to which a man objects is a
church rate if you have the courage and the logic to see it.
Your present plan, Mr. Bramston, is to tread men's objections as mere soil under your feet. It won't do. No plan by
which one man treads another man's freedom of action
underfoot will do. Besides, Mr. Bramston, can you not
see what lies before you in the near future? This unjustifiable power of taking money from others, even from
those unborn, has led to such extravagance, such waste,
and such heavy burdens that the people everywhere, improving upon the honest methods of the politicians, are
beginning to ask the question, 'Granted that, as you
teach us, our wishes are the law of right, why should we
pay debts we have never incurred?' "

"And what about the debt itself?" asked Angus.

"An upright people, not trained to juggling meta-
physics about the right and the convenient, will redeem,
and ought to redeem, every penny of it. But they must do
so voluntarily. The question has its difficulties, but I can
find no right to force payment from those who did not

contract it, great as I think would be the wrong toward the holders if it were not paid. I should give the holders a mortgage on all existing national property."

"And the franchise?" asked Angus.

"The franchise would depend on the payment of an income tax for which everybody, down to the lowest workman, would be voluntarily liable. Everybody, man or woman, paying it would have the right to vote; those who did not pay it would be—as is just—without the franchise. There would be no other tax. All indirect taxation, excise and customs, would be abolished, freeing the trading genius of the country with results that we can scarcely foresee."

"And could you ask the workmen to accept such a tax?" said Angus.

"If you wish to treat them as equal reasonable beings with yourself and to speak the truth to them, if you wish them to cultivate the highest kind of self-respect, to despise all favors and bribes, and to share power because they share burdens—yes," replied Markham. "If you mean to continue the politician's game, to trade upon the selfishness and the unfairness that are in human nature, to tread the principle of true equality under foot, and buy all those who can be bought for your side—no."

"And municipal government, with its care of streets?" asked Angus.

"You must let me reserve that matter for our next talk."

"And existing institutions—the established church, the House of Lords, the Crown—what would you do?" asked Angus.

"I fear that I must look upon them all as signposts that point the wrong way and condemn themselves. All privileged and artificial institutions, whether for the few or the many, are destructive and anarchical in their character, as they obscure our perception of the great and simple moral relations on which our dealings with each other must be founded. Our object is to teach the people to look on the equal and universal relations that are created by liberty as the most sacred thing in the world, and we must spare no darling institution of any class tending to perpetuate the idea of privilege."

"And Ireland?" asked Angus.

"Ireland must decide for herself," said Markham. "Why not grant its freedom for the sake of principle instead of for the sake of convenience, as you will do in a few years. But the landowners should be bought out; and if the northeast of Ireland elects to stay with England, let it do so."

"Would Mr. Spencer agree to such applications of his principles?" asked Angus.

"I fear that Mr. Spencer would dissent. You must not regard him as responsible for the corollaries which I have drawn. He would say that a truly equitable social system can be reached only as fast as men themselves become truly equitable in their sentiments and ideas, and in the meantime we must decide as well as we can on the relatively right, referring continually to the absolutely right, with the view of taking care that we move toward it, and not away from it," replied Markham.

"And now once more for the net result," said Angus. "What would be the effect of carrying out such a policy?"

"Why, such a lightening of the ship as would give her power to float in any weather. You are sadly weighting and crippling her now. You do not recognize how enormous is the amount of enterprise and energy that is restrained by this ever-encroaching matter of politics; not simply because whenever the state undertakes a great service even those who possess the most energy cease to think and to combine and to attempt for themselves, but by the sheer misdirection of effort. How many men there are who could give more time and thought to their own work—which is the true way of benefiting others—if they were not obliged to be politicians. You have made these bloated politics of such importance that the busiest workers can neither afford to follow them with any care nor yet to neglect them. To all such men they are a perpetual vexation and distraction. If you wish to economize the best brain energy of the country, reduce politics to the humble sphere that belongs to them, reduce Mr. Gladstone and Lord Salisbury to the smaller proportions for which two such men, highly gifted as they are, are fitted; disband this frightful standing army of politicians that, like other armies, eats up the people whom it claims to serve, and return it to useful occupations in civil life. Our great object should be not only to bring to an end the wasteful processes of government work—the overgrown departments, the official mismanagements, the heavy burden of taxation, the innumerable occasions of rivalry, of personal ambition, and corrupt uses of power— but to recall all human effort from a wrong direction and to put it in the one right track. We have to make each man a profitable worker by leaving him with undivided energies for his own work instead of letting him attempt to direct the work of others, and to place him under the one true and natural condition that his reward shall be all he can get in a free world, self-earned, and not adjusted for him by others. Achieve this great though simple result, and we should bring about a mental regeneration within a nation as great as if, in their external relations, nations were to abandon the idea of war. Of all perverted industries, that of accumulating force, whether in great bodies of soldiers or great bodies of electors, is the most wasteful and disastrous, not only because, as we have seen, the effort to obtain the possession of force is in itself an immense consumption of energy that should go for other things, not only because, so long as men are intent upon becoming the holders of power, they are blind to the true remedies; not only because systems founded on force are fatal to the two conditions of difference and competition, apart from which unfitness can never be changed into fitness; not only because all fixed laws of moral right and wrong disappear in the presence of force; not only because the world can find no repose or security as long as all the great matters of life are left in suspense, to be shaped and reshaped by those who have climbed yesterday or today to power; but because, so long as we live under force, compelling and compelled, so long the affections and sympathies of men for men— all that is lovely in human nature—must remain sealed from breaking into universal blossom, like the plants of the earth remain sealed so long as winter is with them. Man is predestined to find his complete happiness, as Mr. Spencer teaches, only when the happiness of others be-

comes to him an integral part of his own; but this development of his nature cannot take place unless he is living
under those true conditions which belong to a free life.
So long as force is paramount, so long must men stand
in hate and fear of each other, and the old saying, *homo
homini lupus*, remain true."

"And now, Mr. Markham, granting the force that there
is in much that you say, there remains the great question—is it possible to look on such a view as practical?"

"Practical!" said Markham, slowly shaking his head.
"And do you think, Mr. Bramston, that you politicians
are the practical people? Under the name of serving your
party you press on along an unknown road, no man really
taking the responsibility of his own actions, no man
knowing, or even trying to know, where he is going. How
would any politician of the day meet my demand if I were
to ask him to sketch the future of England as he desired
and as he expected to see it? Would he not excuse himself
from the task; or, had he the courage to attempt it, would
not his picture consist of a few incongruous conceptions
thrown together, some not possible, some not probable,
resembling in its want of definite idea an animal drawn
by a child, with the wings of a fowl and the legs of a
horse? And yet in the midst of such mental incoherence
you have the courage to act as if you were assured that
the power in your possession were a divine gift, and that
some shaping hand that you do not see would interpose
to give order and meaning to what you do. Practical, Mr.
Bramston! Is it practical to have created the relations that
exist between you and the people? You meet them, not to
speak the truth, not to confess real difficulties, not to try

to understand the real conditions under which men have to live, not to raise them in their self-respect, not to check the human tendency to selfishness and violence, and to bring out the reasonable self, but you speak to them as holders of power on whom power confers the right to be a law to themselves; and this you do in order that you may extract their votes from them. You are but courtiers of the people, as your fathers before you were courtiers of kings and emperors. If you call this practical, Mr. Bramston, I desire myself to have no share in what is practical. Practical! And do you think that when tomorrow succeeds to this reckless competition of parties, and you are called upon to deal with the greed you have appealed to, the expectations you have raised, the rash beginnings you have made, tomorrow, when the untruth, the weakness, and the personal rivalries of men who lead the people, not by real convictions but by beliefs assumed at the moment, when all these ugly things come home to roost, when that dangerous lust of power which is in all human breasts, and can only be conquered by the sense of the rights of others, has taken its full possession of us, do you think in that day of consequences that you will be satisfied that you were the practical people? Practical! And yet you do not see the meaning of the very things which you are doing. You call yourselves Tory, and Whig, and radical—there is as much meaning in the names of Shiite and Sonnite; there was more in those of Guelph and Ghibelline. Can you not see that there are only two creeds in the world possible for men; that there are only two sides on which a man can place himself? Are you for a free world, or for a world placed under authority? Are you socialist, a believer in the majority, a believer in force, or do you take your stand on the fixed and inalienable rights of the individual? These mixed and party systems, by which you set so much store, are only halfway huts in which the race sojourns for a day, and then burns behind it. Because you yourselves are confused, indistinct, and inconsistent in your ideas, do you think that the race, as a race, will stand forever, like recruits beating the ground in the drill yard, and march nowhere? Time is a great logician, and succeeding generations will either press steadily on to the system that is the perfection of force, socialism, or to the perfection of liberty, complete individualism. If men believe that they may rightly use force to gain any of their objects, they will claim in their supposed interest to use it for all their objects; if force is not a right weapon, then they will altogether abandon it. On which side then do you take your stand? I look at the parties of today and I can get no answer. Is Mr. Gladstone, with his many regrets and apologies, is Lord Salisbury, with his easy adaptiveness, for or against liberty? The one and the other seem to me equally ready to betray it for their necessities. But whatever be the issue of the present, that the world will remain in socialism—of that I can have no fear. The system is doomed by the great laws as inexorably as the Tower of Babel. I do not say it may not descend upon us for a time, like a great pall, blotting out all hopes of progress in our time. It may be that the race must pass through their season of it, as men pass through some delirious illness. After all it is only an old story repeating itself. Socialism is but Catholicism addressing itself not to the soul but to the senses of men.

Accept authority, accept the force which it employs, resign yourself to all-powerful managers and infallible schemers, give up the free choice and the free act, the burden of responsibility and the rewards that come to each man according to his own exertions, deny the reason and the self that are in you, place these in the keeping of others, and a world of ease and comfort shall be yours. It is a creed even more degrading than Catholicism, but it offers more tangible bribes for its acceptance. Still, Mr. Bramston, we must fight on. As the old darkness and mental cowardice come back upon us, we can only trust that the old light and courage and faith that protested may come back also. Mr. Spencer has set us a bright example of fearlessness in thought and speech. No man quite knows what that magical weapon, truth, can do when he sets himself resolutely to use it. I would rather choose it for our side than either Mr. Gladstone's eloquence or Mr. Chamberlain's organization. But the night is fast stealing away. I shall be glad to meet you again. Meanwhile study Mr. Spencer until his methods of order and reason become an intellectual necessity to you. And now, are you a reader of Browning? If so, repay me for my long talk by reading me *Galuppi* while I light my evening pipe."

"What a strange evening's work," said Angus to himself as his foot crossed the threshold. "Voluntary taxation, and ministers out of employment! How those dear wise fools in the House would shout at the idea; but then every fish believes in the swim to which he belongs. Ah!" he sighed as he walked along the Embankment, and the blue smoke of his cigar parted the fresh night air, "if this were the disentanglement of the mess—the perfect creed of liberty, the true acceptance by each man of the rights of the other, and yet——"

Note—Perhaps I should here point out quite distinctly that the proposal made by Mr. Markham, to place taxation on a voluntary basis, whether in itself a right or wrong deduction from Mr. Herbert Spencer's principle, has never received Mr. Herbert Spencer's approval; but, as I have some grounds for believing, would be looked on by him as an unpractical and undesirable arrangement.

ESSAY FOUR

THE RIGHT AND WRONG OF
COMPULSION BY THE STATE

*Published as a book by Williams and Norgate (London) in 1885,
this essay was based on a series of articles by Herbert which
had previously appeared in the* Newcastle Weekly Chronicle.

W e need not look for better words, than those used
by Mr. Herbert Spencer,* to describe the aim which

---

* It is to Mr. Herbert Spencer's clear and comprehensive sight that we owe so much in this matter of liberty. Mr. Mill was an earnest and eloquent advocate of individual liberty. He was penetrated with the leading truth that all the great human qualities depend upon a man's mental independence, and upon his steady refusal to let a church, or a party, or the society in which he lives think for him. His book on liberty remains as a monument of a clearer sight, a higher faith, and nobler aspirations than those which exist at the present time, when both political parties compete with each other to tread their own principles underfoot, and to serve the expediency of the moment. But Mr. Spencer has approached the subject from a more comprehensive point of view than Mr. Mill, and has laid foundations on which, as men will presently acknowledge, the whole structure of society must be laid, if they are to live at peace with one another, and if all the great possibilities of progress are to be steadily and happily evolved. We owe to Mr. Spencer the clear perception that all ideas of justice and morality are bound up in the parent idea of liberty— that is, in the right of man to direct his own faculties and energies—and that where this idea is not acknowledged and obeyed, justice and morality cannot be said to exist. They can only be more shadows and imitations of the realities. I should advise all persons to read Mr. Spencer's *Man Versus the State, Introduction to Sociology, Social Statics, Data of Ethics,*

we place before ourselves, as the party of individual liberty. That aim is to secure "the liberty of each, limited alone by the like liberty of all." Let us see clearly what we mean. Each man and woman are to be free to direct their faculties and their energies, according to their own sense of what is right and wise, in every direction, except one. They are not to use their faculties for the purpose of forcibly restraining their neighbor from the same free use of his faculties. We claim for A and B perfect freedom as regards themselves, but on the one condition that they respect the same freedom as regards C. If A and B are stronger either in virtue of greater physical strength or greater numbers than their neighbor C, they must neither use their superior strength after the simply brutal fashion of those who live by violence, to tie C's hands and take from him what he possesses, or after the less brutal but equally unjust fashion, to pass laws to direct C as to the manner in which he shall use his faculties and live his life.

I will explain yet more fully what I mean. Under a system of the widest possible liberty, each man thinks and acts according to his own judgment and his own sense of right. He labors as he will, making such free bargains as he chooses respecting the price and all other conditions that affect his labor; he is idle or industrious, he spends

---

and *First Principles*. I ought perhaps to add here that I have reason to believe that Mr. Spencer disagrees with the conclusions regarding taxation, which I have drawn from his principles. I have discussed this question of taxation shortly in the last chapter of a little book called *A Politician in Trouble About His Soul*, published by Messrs. Chapman & Hall, and would beg to refer any persons who may be interested in the subject to what I have said there. I hope soon to have ready a special paper dealing with this matter.

or he lays by, he remains poor, or he becomes rich, he turns his faculties to wise and good account, or he wastes possessions, time and happiness in folly. He is, be it for good or evil, the owner and possessor of his own self, and he has to bear the responsibility of that ownership and possession to the full. On the one hand he is free from all restrictions placed on him by others (except the one great restriction that he, too, in all his doings shall respect the like liberty of all men), and on the other hand he is dependent in everything on himself and his own exertions. He must himself meet and overcome the difficulties of life. Just because he is a free man, he must carry his own burden, such as it is, and not seek to compel others to bear any part of it for him. The really free man will neither submit to restrictions placed on himself, nor desire to impose them on others.

And here, it may be, you will ask, "Is it wise or right for men to claim so full a liberty? Is it not better for men not wholly to own and possess themselves, but to live under conditions which may save them, at all events to some extent, from their own folly and wrongdoing?"

To which question I first answer that to live in a state of liberty is not to live apart from law. It is, on the contrary, to live under the highest law, the only law that can really profit a man, the law which is consciously and deliberately imposed by himself on himself. As Emerson has said, "If any man imagine that this law is lax, let him keep its commandment one day."

Second, I answer that you will not make people wiser and better by taking liberty of action from them. A man can only learn when he is free to act. It is the consequences of his own actions, and the consequences of these same actions as he sees them in other persons, that teach him. It is not by tying a man's hands that you shall make him skillful in any craft, especially that difficult one of living well and wisely. It is true that by tying his hands you may, as long as your knots happen to hold fast, prevent his committing a murder or taking what belongs to someone else; but do not for a moment believe that in so doing you have made a better or more intelligent man of him. That can only come to pass, when, being a free man, he learns to choose the right for its own sake, and for the sake of the peace and happiness that, as he will slowly perceive, honest and wise conduct brings to him. It is impossible for us to make any real advance until we take to heart this great truth, that without freedom of choice, without freedom of action, there are not such things as true moral qualities; there can only be submissive wearing of the cords that others have tied round our hands. There cannot be unselfishness and generosity, there cannot be prudence and self-denial. For example, there can be nothing unselfish in a parent sending his child to school, because the law obliges him under penalties to do so; there can be nothing prudent and self-denying in a workman not getting drunk, because he cannot go into a public house and buy liquor. If a man is to be a really good parent, or a really thoughtful and self-directing man, it must not be because by law or by some other brutal force method you have tied his hands, but because of an inner sense in himself as to what is right, which he respects and obeys; and this inner sense tends only to survive in the free man. Nobody can say, as regards the man who has never been allowed to exercise a free choice, what are the real motives that direct him. It may be habit or submission to authority; it may be ignorance or superstition; it cannot be the free intelligent preference for what is right or wise, for he has always been in subjection to a power outside him, and has never looked the good and the evil fairly in the face, as a free man responsible to himself alone. His virtues, if we are to give them this name, are but the virtues of the cloister. His own self has never yet been brought into council, has never even been born into real life.

Third, even if you believed that you could make men wise and good by depriving them of liberty of action, you have no right to do so. Who has given you a commission to decide what your brother man shall or shall not do? Who has given you charge of his life and his faculties and his happiness as well as of your own? Perhaps you think yourself wiser and better fitted to judge than he is; but so did all those of old days—kings, emperors, and heads of dominant churches—who possessed power, and never scrupled to compress and shape their fellow-men as they themselves thought best, by means of that power. You can see as you read the story of the past, and even as you look on the world at present, what a mess the holders of power made of it, whenever they undertook to judge for others, whenever they undertook to guide and control the lives and faculties of others; and why should you think that you are going to succeed where they failed? On what reasonable ground should you think so? Why should you suppose that you have suddenly in this our generation grown much better and wiser and more

unselfish than they were? We have probably all of us
the same or nearly the same share of human nature as
they had. These rulers, whether of the past or present
time, under whose mistakes the world has so terribly
suffered, in many cases were not bad men; they were
simply "clouded by their own conceit," blinded by the
unquestioned belief that some men may exercise power
over other men. They did not see that the individual freedom of each man is the highest law of his existence, and
they thought, often honestly enough, that it was in their
power to give the mass of men happiness if they could
only have the restraining, and molding, and fashioning
of them after their own ideas and beliefs. And the worst
of it is that still in these democratic days we are all thinking the same thing. We are fast getting rid of emperors
and kings and dominant churches, as far as the mere outward form is concerned, but the soul of these men and
these institutions is still living and breathing within us.
We still want to exercise power, we still want to drive
men our own way, and to possess the mind and body of
our brothers as well as of our own selves. The only difference is that we do it in the name of a majority instead
of in the name of divine right. Radicals and republicans,
as we call ourselves, we too often remain Catholics, infal-
libilists and absolutists in temper.

Perhaps at this point you will interrupt me to say,
"Ah! but here is the whole difference. Today it is the
people who govern themselves. It is no longer emperors
and churches who decide and issue decrees. It is the
majority of the people who impose restrictions on them-

selves, who approve the laws, and construct the systems they live under."

If so, I must reply to you that your majority has no more rights over the body or mind of a man than either the bayonet-surrounded emperor or the infallible church. The freedom of a man to use either his faculties or his possessions, as he himself wills, is the great moral fact that exists in independence of every form of government. It is the moral law that, as we may believe, the Great Mind—in which we may trust, though we can neither know nor understand it—has placed as the foundation of human society, as the one necessary condition of all social happiness, to represent to us in the moral and intellectual order what gravitation represents to us in the physical order. We can see, when once our eyes have been opened to see clearly, that there is no other method by which it is possible to conceive of a man as arriving at his perfect development; that there is no other means by which he can even cease to be his own unresting tormenter. For think what human society must necessarily be without this law of individual liberty? If this law has no real existence, if the individual has no rights, then the larger or more powerful part of a nation may force upon the smaller or weaker part of a nation what they will. According to the ideas that prevail at the moment, they may dictate their religion or their philosophical creed; they may regulate their occupations, their labor, their amusements, their possessions; they may permit or refuse to permit them to marry; they may leave their children to dwell in their homes, or drag them away to be trained in state barracks. There is no matter, from the highest and most vital matters of life to the lowest trifle, that the stronger, the more aggressive, the more presumptuous-minded part of a nation may not decree and organize for the weaker part and compel them to observe, if this claim of some to direct others is once sanctioned. And if this be so, if this rule of the majority is the true rule for the guidance of the race, if each human being has in himself no rights of self-ownership, if to be the most numerous party in the state is to all effect to be the slave-owning portion of the nation—the portion which holds all others subject to its own ideas of what is best—think of the wretched future that by some cruel destiny would be reserved for all time for all men. In this case the possession of power would necessarily confer upon those who gained it such enormous privileges—if we are to speak of the miserable task of compulsion as privileges—the privileges of establishing and enforcing their own views in all matters, of treading out and suppressing the views to which they are opposed, of arranging and distributing all property, of regulating all occupations, that all those who still retained sufficient courage and energy to have views of their own would be condemned to live organized for ceaseless and bitter strife with each other. In presence of unlimited power lodged in the hands of those who govern, in the absence of any universal acknowledgment of individual rights, the stakes for which men played would be so terribly great that they would shrink from no means to keep power out of the hands of their opponents. Not only would the scrupulous man become unscrupulous, and the pitiful man cruel, but the parties into which society divided itself would begin to perceive that to destroy or be destroyed was the one choice lying in front of them. How true it is that the great evils under which men have suffered have always been those of their own invention; that man has been and still continues to be his own tormentor!

And here, perhaps, again you will say to me, "You are conjuring up mere phantom dangers. We are only inclined to give power to the majority for some things, not for all. There are many matters in which we would recognize the right of the individual to judge and to act for himself; while we allow society, organized as a whole, to decide such other matters as we are all pretty well agreed should be so decided."

I answer that when you use such words you are deceiving yourselves. You will find your position an impossible one. There never can be agreement amongst men as to what these things are. One person will wish to regulate the mass of men in matters of religion; another in education; another in philosophy; another in art; another in matters of trade; another in matters of labor; another in matters of contract; another in matters of amusement. One person will desire to regulate the people in a few matters, and give freedom in many; another to give freedom in few and regulate in many. There is no possibility of permanent human agreement in the matter, where once you have ceased to stand on any definite principle, where once you have sanctioned the use of force for certain undefined needs of the moment. And observe well what you are doing. Under this plea of the needs of the moment you are sanctioning not only the right

of some men to coerce others, but their right to decide
how and when and for what purposes they shall coerce
others. It is the power holders, freed from any general principle that controls and directs them, who have
to decide as to the limits and application of their own
power. For who else can do so? You have given this
right of using power into their hands because they are
the majority. You must also give this other right of determining and defining the application of power into their
hands, for there is nobody else to whom you can give it.
Nor is it reasonable to say that we may trust to the general good sense that exists amongst all men not to abuse
the power that is thus placed in their hands, and not to
stretch its limits to a dangerous and unjust extent. When
power is once given, it becomes impossible, in the absence of any general principle or fixed standard, to say
what is dangerous or unjust; because the danger and
injustice are involved in the very idea and the very fact of
some men—be they the many or the few—possessing
undefined power over others. I would urge upon all those
persons who hold this careless language—that power may
be justly used by the majority for some purposes and not
for others—that they have no right to sit down and take
their bodily and mental case, until they have distinctly
and definitely settled in their own selves what are the
purposes for which they are prepared to allow force to
be used and what are the purposes for which they are not.
Until they have done this, until they have found some
law by which they can distinguish the right from the
wrong use of power, by which they can justly satisfy not
only their own minds but the minds of others, they are

simply leaving in suspension the greatest matter that affects human beings; they are like men who start to make their passage over the wide seas, without chart or compass, and hopefully remark that the look of the waters, the face of the sky, and the direction of the wind will at any special moment tell them what course they ought to steer.

II

Do not let us flinch from probing this matter of compulsion to the core. If you really think that for some purposes we may rightly compel men, and for other purposes we may not, you are bound to arrange your perceptions on the subject and discover what is the dividing line between "the may" and "the may not." It is unworthy not to take your true position in this great matter—that of a human being whose reason can put all the facts of this world in order and subjection to itself, can become their intelligent regulator, by strenuously and resolutely seeking out the principle or law which underlies them—and simply to wait, as a slave instead of a master, to be swept in whatever direction the forces that are round you may happen to take. Let us grasp the great truth clearly. No man is acting consciously and with distinct self-guidance, no man possesses a fixed goal and purpose in life, until he has brought the facts of his daily existence under the arrangement of general principles. Until he has done this, the facts of life will use and command him; he will not use and command them.

I would therefore beg you to reject with scorn that

idle and unmeaning creed, which is so much in fashion today, of refusing to seek for general principles, and hoping to extract from the circumstances of the moment the right way of dealing with them. Think how utterly absurd is such a proposition. How could any astronomer conquer any problem submitted to him if you first told him he was not to trouble himself with the general principles of astronomy—if he was not to make use of the laws of gravitation, of inertia, or its derivative, centrifugal force? How could a physician hope to deal successfully with a case if he was told first to lay aside all the general principles of health and disease; the laws affecting the temperature and the nutrition of the body; the circulation; the general course of the disease, its accompanying and its resulting dangers? Both astronomer and physician possess their power, such as it is, simply in virtue of the laws which, as they have discovered, are invariably behind the facts. Facts not reduced to law can be of no practical service either to astronomer or physician. How can a politician dream that he exists in a different world from the physician and astronomer, and that it is given to him to use the facts which concern his trade, without understanding or caring to understand the laws of which they are but the expression?

We must—it is absolutely necessary—seek for law, or general leading principles, in politics. Until that is done there can be nothing rightly done; and the first great law which we have to seek out, is the law which determines the right of men to exercise power over each other. Have men any right to this power? If they have it, do they possess it for all matters? If not for all matters, for what matters? and in this last case how are we to tell what these matters are?

Now I do not hesitate to say that this question stands in importance far before all other questions which the human race has to answer. Indeed if we could see clearly, we should see that the decision of all these other questions is wrapped up in this one great decision; for I know of no question that would not be settled in one fashion by a free race and in another by a state-regulated race. But apart from this influence on character, which freedom and state-regulation must respectively exercise, the answer which every man finds it in his soul to make to this great question, "By what title do men exercise power over each other?" must decide for him the general course of his own life. In one of the two rival armies, which stand fronting each other today, as they have always done, and between which there never has been and never can be enduring reconciliation, whether he wills it or not, he has to take his place. All his hesitations, and inconsistencies and clever adjustments of opinion will not save his being enlisted in the one or the other cause. He must strike his blow and spend his small grain of life service either on the side of force, that is, of strong governments and interfering departments, of protection and regulation, of uniformity and system, of socialism and life divided between rulers and ruled, between slave owners and slaves; or on the side of liberty, that is, of self-dependence and self-responsibility, of free thought, free religion, free enterprise, free trade, of every free moral influence that grows where force is not, of all those countless individual energies and countless individual differences that arise where men are not constrained to live in imitation of each other, and of that natural selection that eventually preserves every improved form in other mental or material things, where these individual energies and individual differences are allowed to clash freely together. In other words every man has to decide for himself, as his creed in life, whether men are to be made happier by a system that rests on and believes in coercion, or a system of self-directed agencies and moral influences; whether their continual cooperation throughout life is to be voluntary or to be imposed; whether each is to take charge of his own existence and happiness, or those who can count most votes on their side are to take upon themselves, like a universal Roman Catholic council, to decide in what collective happiness consists, and administer it for the rest of the world. For strange as it may sound in some ears, these are the only two rival forces, the only two rival creeds that exist in the world. And whichever it is, liberty or force, that is to emerge as conqueror from the great struggle, by that one will the minds of men, their hopes, their fears, their pleasures, their pains, their beliefs and their systems, be molded and shaped.

And now let us look a little more closely into the rights of the individual. I claim that he is by right the master of himself and of his own faculties and energies. If he is not, who is? Let us suppose that A having no rights over himself, B and C, being in a majority, have rights over him. But we must assume an equality in these matters, and if A has no rights over himself, neither can B and C have any rights over themselves. To what a ridiculous position are we then brought! B and C having no rights over themselves, have absolute rights over A; and we should have to suppose in this most topsy-turvy of worlds that men were walking about, not owning themselves, as any simple-minded person would naturally conclude that they did, but owning some other of their fellow-men; and presently in their turn perhaps to be themselves owned by some other. Look at it from another point of view. You tell me a majority has a right to decide as they like for their fellow-men. What majority? 21 to 20? 20 to 5? 20 to 1? But why any majority? What is there in numbers that can possibly make any opinion or decision better or more valid, or which can transfer the body and mind of one man into the keeping of another man? Five men are in a room. Because three men take one view and two another, have the three men any moral right to enforce their view on the other two men? What magical power comes over the three men that because they are one more in number than the two men, therefore they suddenly become possessors of the minds and bodies of these others? As long as they were two to two, so long we may suppose each man remained master of his own mind and body; but from the moment that another man, acting Heaven only knows from what motives, has joined himself to one party or the other, that party has become straightway possessed of the souls and bodies of the other party. Was there ever such a degrading and indefensible superstition? Is it not the true lineal descendant of the old superstitions about emperors and high priests and their authority over the souls and bodies of men?

Let us look again at it from another point of view. You say a majority has a right to decide all questions. You perhaps do not like my words when I say, "to own the souls and bodies" of all who are outside that majority, but that is what is really meant; for once accept the doctrine that the bigger crowd is supreme over the smaller crowd, and you will find, as I have already said, that it is impossible to draw a line to limit the authority which you thus confer. But, now, let me ask this question. If the fact of being in a majority, if the fact of the larger number carries this extraordinary virtue with it, does a bigger nation possess the right to decide by a vote the destiny of a smaller nation? Such an exceedingly artificial matter as an invisible boundary line between two countries cannot suddenly deprive numbers of the sacred authority with which you have clothed them. Inside a country the bigger crowd is possessed of all rights, the smaller crowd is disfranchised of all rights; why not also outside a country? They are queer rights these, which appear and disappear, after the fashion of the supple articles which a conjurer orders into and out of existence.

Let us follow this same consideration a little further. A mass, as Mr. Spencer insists, can only possess the qualities that are possessed by its units. A mass of salt can only possess the qualities which are in the particles of salt. You deny the rights of the individual to regulate and direct himself. But you suddenly acknowledge and exaggerate these rights as soon as you have thrown the individual into that mass which you call the majority. Then you suddenly discover that men have not only rights to own themselves, but also to own their fellow-men. But where have these rights come from? By what hocus-pocus, by what magic have they been brought into existence? A man who makes one of the exactly equal half of a crowd has no rights, either as regards himself or as regards others; if he makes one in that part of the crowd which is larger by the tenth or the hundredth or the thousandth part, then he is clothed with absolute powers over himself and others. Did Central Africa ever produce a more absurd superstition?

Perhaps, however, you may say, "We do not pretend that a majority have any rights over their fellow-men. Still it is convenient to place power in their hands, and convenient not to define that power, but to leave the matter to be decided by their good sense."

Well, I am glad we have brought it to that point. You think then that convenience is the highest law in life. You think it convenient that one part of men—if larger in number—should own the souls and bodies of the rest of men. You think it convenient that there should be slave-owning, and that there should be no attempt to say where this slave-owning begins and where it ends. You think it convenient that all the old rights, freedom to think, to speak, to act, to possess, to labor, or to rest, shall be enjoyed at the discretion of those who today or tomorrow may climb to power. If those who have so climbed look with favor upon these rights, well and good; let the people enjoy them. If they look on them with disfavor, as inconvenient to the social whole, let them be abandoned as fashions that have ceased to be. We have plainly gone wrong in ever thinking that in the rights themselves there was anything sacred. Everything that men have striven for and suffered for, generation after generation, everything that the noblest men have placed before life itself, is to count for nothing in our more enlightened age, if the majority of the day or the morrow think that we can do better without it. There is nothing sacred except the convenience of the larger crowd dictating to the smaller crowd. Whatever is sacred in the world is to be found clinging to the skirts of the majority, is born with the majority, and dies with the majority. Please not to think that I am exaggerating in saying this. There cannot possibly be two supreme laws. Either the will of the majority or the rights of the individual are the highest law of our existence; one, whichever one it is to be, must yield in presence of the other. Now the question is, which is to be supreme? Which is to give way? Do not suppose that by any skillful arrangement you can ever reconcile the two as equal powers, or succeed in paying allegiance to both. You might as hopefully try to merge the two opposite poles into one; to be a believer in infallibility, and a soldier of free thought at the same time. Men once dreamed that the state could be a temporal and not a spiritual power. They can now see that they were only deceiving themselves by words. They can now see that wherever you exercise power over a man, whether it be in the matter of his education, or his labor, or any occupation of his life, you are as much constraining, molding, and forming him, you are as much his owner and possessor, as if you taught him a catechism and required him to accept a Thirty-nine Articles. The nature of man is indivisible; you cannot cut him across, and give one share of him to the state and leave the other for himself.

Now, perhaps you will turn round on me, and say, "Well, then, we understand you at last. Men have no rightful title to exercise power over each other. There can therefore be no government and no laws. The murderer and the thief are both to ply their trade unchecked, because men have no title to form a government and make laws.

I will answer as plainly and truthfully as I can. I do not think that it is possible to find a perfect moral foundation for the authority of any government, be it the government of an emperor or a republic. They are all of the nature of a usurpation, though I think when *confined within certain exact limits*, of a justifiable usurpation. I see that each man is, by virtue of that wonderful self which is in him, the owner of certain faculties and energies. I see that he, and none other, has the rightful direction and control of these faculties and energies. They are vested in him as an inseparable, inalienable part of himself; and I can see no true way in which they can be taken forcibly from him and owned by another. But I see that the exercise of these energies and faculties depends upon the observance of the universal law that no man shall by force restrain another man in the use of his faculties. The men who do so restrain their neighbor, who, being stronger than he is, break into his house, tie his hands behind his back, take from him what belongs to him, or compel him against his own consent to do certain actions, are men who disallow this universal law, and therefore lose the rights which they themselves possess under it. I can see in presence of such acts of physical violence that men are driven to band themselves together, and to form what are called governments, to restrain those who violate this law, and who, having disregarded it in the case of others, can no longer themselves claim to live under its protection. But it is also necessary to see plainly that governments, if they are to possess any moral justification whatever for their actions, can only use power over those who have thus lost their own rights; and that the justification which underlies this use of their power is solely that of self-preservation. Now, self-preservation is a plea of great authority, but an authority strictly limited by certain conditions. It justifies an action that is wrong in itself (as the employment of force) only because of the wrong which has been already committed in the first instance by some other person. I may preserve my life by taking the life of him who has attacked me, but I have no right to preserve my life by taking the life of him who is innocent of all wrongdoing toward me. And this is the position of all governments. Just as the individual has rights of self-preservation, as regards the special man who commits a wrong against him, so has a government—which is the individual in mass—exactly the same rights, neither larger nor smaller, as regards the whole special class of those who employ violence. We can justify the use of force by a government, its interference with the energies and faculties of those men who have themselves interfered with the energies and faculties of others, on the ground of our common self-preservation; but we cannot justify on this ground any interference on its part with the energies and faculties of innocent men, I mean, of those who have remained within their own rights. When governments do so act, when they interfere with the energies and faculties of innocent men—as the fact of their being a government cannot possibly place them in a different position from individuals as regards the universal laws of right and wrong—they simply join themselves to the already swollen ranks of the users of violence and the despisers of rights; and they lose all true title to be obeyed or respected by men. I would therefore say that where men commit acts of violence against each other, there lies in us all, whether, acting on our own behalf, or organized into a society, on the ground of self-preservation, the right to resist violence by violence; and that the most convenient form of such resistance is to make a government, elected by the whole people, the instrument of our resistance; but just as individually, for the sake of our own self-preservation, we have no right to sacrifice in any particular an innocent man, so also must the action of a government, which is merely built up from individuals, be bounded by exactly the same limits. It cannot aggress upon the rights of any innocent man; it can only restrain aggression upon such rights.

III

The man who believes in strong governments, and looks with a favorable eye upon socialism, may now say to me, "It is this very question of force that justifies us in what we are doing. We want to diminish the use of force in the world. The rich unscrupulous man is in reality the man who uses force, and it is the exercise of force on his part that we are seeking to restrain by force on our part. The capitalist who uses force toward his work-people, compelling them to accept his terms, is as much to be restrained by force, in our opinion, as the man who helps himself by violence or fraud to the property of other people."

To which argument I must reply that, notwithstanding your protestations against force, you are acting so as to establish force as the universal law of the world. When we propose to use force against the capitalist because he forces his work-people to accept certain terms, we are confusing the two meanings which belong to the word force. We are confusing together direct and indirect force. Where I directly force a man, I say to him, "You shall do a certain thing, whether you consent in yourself or not to do so." Thus, if I tie a man's hands and empty his pockets, or if I pass a law saying that he shall not enter a public house, or that his child shall be vaccinated or educated, or that he himself shall only labor eight hours a day, or shall only labor for the state and not for a private employer, I am using direct force against him. I say to him, "Whatever your own opinion is in these matters, whether you give or withhold your mental consent to the act that is in question, I require that the act shall be done." But when a capitalist says, "I offer employment on such terms," or a workman says, "I will only work on such terms," neither of them is employing direct force against the other. The employer may be indirectly forced to accept the workman's offer, or the workman may be indirectly forced to accept the employer's offer; but before either does so, it is necessary that they should consent, as far as their own selves are concerned, to the act that is in question. And this distinction is of the most vital kind, since the world can and will get rid of direct compulsion; but it never can of indirect compulsion, however much the growth of better influences may humanize and modify it. Direct compulsion, by whomsoever exercised, is only a remnant of that barbarous state when emperors and dominant churches used men according to their own ideas. Indirect compulsion is a condition of life to which we have always been, and always shall be, necessarily subject; it is inseparably bound up with our joint existence in the world. The richest and most powerful man lives under indirect compulsion as well as the poorest and feeblest. To use words which I have used elsewhere, "We may according to our character apply this indirect compulsion of each other kindly or harshly, scrupulously or unscrupulously; but from it there is no escape possible for us any more than from the atmosphere that surrounds us, both as regards compelling and being compelled. All life is subject to it. No man does and no child is born without in some way affecting the mass of indirect or conditional compulsion which weighs upon each of us individually."

Now let us see the mischief that arises when you make the existence of indirect compulsion a ground for employing direct compulsion. First, when you do so you at once destroy the immense safeguard that exists so long as one man cannot be compelled to accept another man's view as regards his own life or happiness—that is to say, that the person who knows most about his interest and cares most about it—I mean the man's own self—must give his consent to every action that he does; and you establish a system, founded on very puzzle-headed ideas, under which each man is not to be his own special guardian, but is to be put instead under the guardianship of (say) 10,000,000 of his countrymen and countrywomen. Second, observe, that in opposing such indirect force, as is tyrannously used, by the weapon of direct force, you fall into the same mistake as those do, who try to repress a crime by methods more brutal than the crime itself; or as those do who would forcibly repress teaching, such as that of the Roman Catholic religion, because they believe that the claim to possess infallibility tends to an intolerant use of power, whenever power and this claim happen to be joined in the same persons. But could such people have their way, they would immensely increase the intolerance that exists in the world by inducing all the tolerant—as well as the intolerant—persons to fight for their opinions by intolerant means. In exactly the same way he who uses direct force to combat indirect force only restrains one injury by inflicting another of a graver kind, places the fair-minded people as well as the unfair-minded people on the side of oppression, and, by thus equalizing the actions of the good and bad, indefinitely delays the development of those moral influences to which we can alone look as the solvent of that temper that makes men use harshly the indirect power resting in their hands. Do we wish to make men juster in their daily intercourse with each other? We shall certainly not succeed by acting more unjustly in return, for however unjustly a man may use the indirect power that he possesses, his injustice will always be surpassed by those who violate the universal rights of men by applying force directly.*

And now let us glance at another aspect of the question that must always discredit the use of force. Let us look at the machinery that is necessarily called into play, when you propose to give power to a majority, and make it supreme over individual rights. Consider what kind of a thing a majority is, by what means and in what way it is brought into existence. Look closely at any election that takes place, and see the process of management by which parties are got and held together. Try to separate yourself and your own interests from what is going on: climb if only for a few minutes to a height from which you can look critically and impartially at the ignoble and selfish scramble beneath you. Examine with a jealous eye the professional manipulation that goes on, the appeals made to this or to that section of the people, according as most votes are to be gained, the gross lesson of selfishness that is taught where the people are openly told to obtain the direct personal advantages that they desire by a skillful

---

* It must be borne in mind that the unfailing distinction between direct and indirect compulsion, as I have employed the words, is that in one case (indirect compulsion) the person in question gives his consent, in the other case (direct compulsion) his consent is not required from him. It is no answer to say that the weakness of men is such that their own consent is a mere form. Our effort in all cases must be to build up sufficient strength in the man so as to make his consent a real thing. To treat men as if their own consent were of no value or concern, is to treat them as the church in old days, the emperor, the slave owner, the force socialist have all treated or proposed to treat them—mere clay to be molded by some external process, not as individuals with separate minds and wills of their own. "The surest plan to make a man, is think him so.—J.B."

use of their votes, the personal ambition of the men who gain influence by making speeches that "go from the teeth outward," and by publicly lending themselves to causes which had remained untouched and uncared for by them till Doomsday, but for the politician's reward of popularity and influence which is attached to them. Remember that every politician has something to gain by his opinions, and that without and apart from these opinions he can rarely keep his place or succeed in his occupation. Very few men out of the whole number of us are strictly honest and truthful, but the politician has far greater hindrances in these respects than other men. He is bound to think as his party thinks; he is bound to think in such a way that he shall get a sufficient number of votes to give him the seat or the influence that he desires. He has mortgaged his own judgment and his own sense of what is right to the oppressive necessity that he shall be in agreemnt with others. If you who have the bestowal of a seat in Parliament in your hands, wish to be told what will please you, what will be in accordance with personal interests, with daily wants, with class hatreds and those prejudices that have grown with your growth and strengthened with your strength, if this is what you really desire, and what you honestly think will be the most conducive to your mental welfare, then I say, go in confidence to the first politician who is asking you to send him to Parliament, and feel assured that you will probably get from him all that you desire. If you wish to hear but the echo of your own voices, and see but the reflection of your own thoughts, and have no desire to be led out of and away from your own selves, imperfect as they must be, go and seek the politician. But if you have nobler desires than this, if you desire to see this world and its great conditions placed before you in their true light, if you desire to judge the questions that affect the future of society from a higher and truer standpoint than personal interests and the vote by which they may be secured, refuse to listen to any man as a guide who derives his success from simply pleasing you. The lips of such men are too smooth to help you in that which is the real struggle of life, the great search after truth. It is hard enough in this world to find anywhere those who are bravely searching for the truth simply for its own sake. Those who enter upon the search at all generally do so with the preconceived idea that the truth when they find it will be in exact agreement with their own personal wants and interests, and will conveniently supply them with a fresh stock of arguments on behalf of the causes to which they are already wedded. And although our own personal advantage may not wholly possess us, still there are plenty of snares and pitfalls left in our nature and in our inherited passions to hinder us from faithfully pursuing the search. We are, indeed, only too often destined to find that attainment is denied to us, even after long effort and long discipline of ourselves; but yet something—perhaps much—will be gained when we have learned to distinguish between the false guides and the true guides, between those whose success in life depends upon thinking in the same plane and in the same direction with ourselves, and those who are steadily desirous above everything else to be true to the light that is within them. Here and there you will find a man engaged in public life who, with courage to stand alone, strives to keep undimmed both for himself and others this inner light. Wherever and whenever you get such a man, stand by him and strengthen him. Do not let him be trampled underfoot by the impatient crowd of those whose opinions are shaped for them by the petty traffic of the hour, and who would have all others such as they are themselves. Remember that in the midst of the selfish scramble that we call politics, such as it is today, you may rarely hope to find a man with iron enough in his character to let him keep a true and dauntless self within him. The politician, as you may see him on any day, and at any hour, is a man bound by his own necessities. It is difficult for him to be anything but a retailer of borrowed convictions and imitated enthusiasms. In frankness I must say that it is in great measure your own doing. You make him your creature—and therefore worthless to you from every higher point of view—just because you are always requiring of him to preach the gospel of your own immediate interests.

IV

And now, if these principles, as I have tried to set them before you, are true; if men have no rightful claim to possess any sovereignty over the bodies and minds of each other; if that sovereignty only belongs to the man's own self; if the attempt to have and to exercise power over each other has been the most fruitful cause both of the past and the present misery of the world; if force has never permanently bettered and never can permanently better any of us, but only unfits us for our struggle in a world, where we must depend for our success, sooner or later, at some point or other, notwithstanding all ingenious systems of external protection, upon the selves that are within us, upon our own choice of what is right, and our own power to abide by that choice; then what is the practical aim we must put before ourselves in politics, what measures and what form of government will give the truest expression to these convictions?

First, we must establish a system of complete liberty under which no set of men should endeavor to force upon other sets of men their own view of what is right, as regards social conduct or fashions of living, as regards religion or education, as regards trade or labor of any kind, as regards amusements or occupations. The system must be a system of such complete freedom, of such perfectly free enterprise, free trade, and free action in all things, that under it, in industrial matters, men will be entirely content to further their own interests by means of their own efforts and their own voluntary and self-directed associations; and content in social matters to obtain acceptance for their views by such moral influence as each is able to gain in the universal moral conflict. There must be the complete renouncement of force—that force which all the present governments of the world employ without hesitation—as the instrument by which the condition of men is to be improved; and in its place the following out and perfecting by voluntary means of that good, whatever it may be, which seems to each man or each group of men the truest and highest. Second, governments recognizing that the only justification for their existence is to be found in the acts of violence and fraud

committed by men against each other, and in the right of
self-preservation in presence of such acts, must employ
the force which they possess for the one and single purpose of repelling force. They must simply defend the
person and property of all persons from attacks by whomsoever they are made. Private and personal property must
be fully and completely recognized, whether it be the
property of the rich or of the poor man. We must close
our ears to the careless and unthoughtful denunciations
of property, and see that without the fullest recognition
of property there can be no real liberty of action. It is idle
to say in one breath that each man has the right to the
free use of his own faculties, and in the next breath to
propose to deal by the power of the state with what he
acquires by means of those faculties, as if both the faculties and what they produced belonged to the state and
not to himself. Private property and free trade stand on
exactly the same footing, both being essential and indivisible parts of liberty, both depending upon rights, which
no body of men, whether called governments or anything
else, can justly take from the individual. Let us never
yield to the superstition of magnifying the governments
of our own creation. While we concede the power to governments to protect every man in his person and in his
property from the attacks of other men, rather than leave
this power in the hands of men individually, let me repeat
that it is a mere survival of old forms of thought to suppose that there is any odor of divinity about whatever
form of government it may be—imperial or republican—
that we set up. In presence of the necessities caused by
human wrongdoing, under the plea of self-preservation,

as the means of preventing aggressions upon liberty, we may pass laws and carry them into effect against those who disregard the rights of others, and in doing so we may commit no wrong against such men, seeing that they themselves have violated the universal covenant of rights. But let us, for the sake of keeping undimmed our own perceptions of what is true, frankly admit that the laws, passed in Parliament and administered in courts of justice, are really and essentially in the same class as those acts of earlier days, by which men with their own hand provided for their own safety. The act of Parliament may be as necessary for self-preservation in our time as the steel shirt, or the stone walls of the castle, or the body of armed retainers was in the Middle Ages, but both are expressions of force, both are the instrument of the strongest, both in a strict and true sense are outside morality, which only has to do with the free choice and the free action of men.

<h2 style="text-align:center">V</h2>

I will now sketch the practical measures by which, as it seems to me, we could give the best effect to a system of the widest possible liberty; our great object being to secure the limitation of services undertaken by the government. These services should be limited,

(A) *To the defense of men and women in their persons and property by means of a legal system which should be as simple, inexpensive, speedy and equitable as it can be made by a far greater concentration of public attention upon it than is possible in our present condition of over-*

legislation in all directions; (B) to the defense of the country and its dependencies from all enemies: and the carrying on of diplomatic intercourse with other nations.

The definition of offenses against person and property is so all-important a matter, that I must ask your attention to it before going further. It is a subject that will require very full and searching discussion, undertaken from the dominant point of view of a man's rights over himself and his faculties; and it is only wise to expect that some of the practical conclusions which we arrive at today, may, after fuller consideration, require modification. With a sense of many difficulties I offer my contribution to this discussion.

As the foundation of all morality is respect for the free choice and the free action of others, the essence of a true offense against person or property seems to be the violent interference with a man's faculties, the constraining of his will and actions. By constraining the will and actions, I mean either that a man is prevented (by physical coercion) from doing those actions which he is physically and morally competent to do; or that his will is constrained (without any acquiescence on his part) so that as a consequence his actions are constrained. I believe that no act should be treated as a legal offense unless such act is of a nature to constrain the will and self-dependent actions of another person.*

---

* I ought perhaps to give an example of acts within and not within a man's competency. Let me suppose that I grow lettuce to sell at market. If another man, envious of my success, destroys my lettuce, injures my cart or horse with which I go to market, he physically coerces me and prevents my doing an action—taking the lettuce to market—which I was

Let us take some instances. If I tie a man's hands, and take from him his purse, I evidently constrain both his will and his actions. If I sell a man a loaf professing to be made only of wheat, and in reality made partly of potatoes, I constrain his will so that his actions are constrained. My fraud is force in disguise. He intends to buy and consume a loaf made of wheat; and I, *against his own consent,* induce him to buy and consume a loaf made partly of potatoes. My conduct to him is nearly the same practically as if on his way home from market I had taken the loaf from him; the only difference being that in the case of the robbery I should have constrained both his will and his actions; in the case of the fraud I only constrained his will—his will being to buy a wheaten loaf— with the effect of constraining his actions.

If I let my sewage drain itself into another man's well, I thereby commit a damage upon his property by poisoning the water and making him incur the risk of illness. Now, a man's property is the result of the exercise of his faculties; is an inseparable part of himself and his faculties: and therefore, whenever his property is injured, his faculties are interfered with, and his will about himself, his faculties, his actions, and his property, constrained.

---

physically and morally competent to do. Let me now suppose that another neighbor, also observing my success, grows better lettuce than I do, and, by selling them at the same or a lower price, takes my customers away from me, can he also be said to have wrongly constrained my actions, since I am no longer able to sell my lettuce? No, certainly not; since the sale of my lettuce was not an action within my own competence. It depended upon the minds of my customers; and thus, though I may be suffering, no wrong has been done against me by my successful rival.

It is the same if I pour out noxious vapors into the air. The air which is polluted must be either private or public property, and in either case (I am supposing that the noxious vapors are created in the immediate neighborhood of others, and not in the center of my own ground) I have injured that which does not belong to me and have interfered with and constrained the faculties of those who are obliged to breathe the poisoned air against their own consent.

Let us take another instance of greater difficulty, on which I should only wish to write with reserve and suggestively. Can we look upon a case of really injurious libel, for example, where one man publicly and untruly accuses another man of being a thief, as a case of constraining a man's actions? I answer doubtfully, yes. Suppose I placed false weights in an honest tradesman's shop, and informed the police that he used them, I should certainly be constraining his will and actions. He having acted and wishing to act honestly would be publicly presumed to have acted dishonestly. I should, so to speak, have taken his own actions from him and substituted other actions. It is the same when, being in truth an honest man, I have libeled him by a public statement as a dishonest man. By my untruthful accusations I have taken his own actions from him and substituted other actions for them. I have, as it were, changed the weights behind his counter and publicly declared that he uses false weights.*

---

* I think it right to say that I do not feel satisfied with the reasoning used on this page as regards libel. The question is whether a real offense

If this is a true view of the nature of the offense of libel it is evident that the present law requires alteration, since untruth must in all cases be a necessary part of the offense; as it is the untruthful statement which, against the man's will, takes from him his own actions and substitutes others in their place.

Last, let me glance at another class of actions, which are a matter of local rather than central government. You may ask me, "Ought not such a thing as riotous or indecent behavior in the streets to be punishable; and if so, on what grounds?" To which I can only reply that we must not confuse those offenses which are rightly punishable by the law of self-preservation, because they are aggressions by one man upon the faculties and actions of another man, with offenses which are committed in disregard of regulations laid down by those who are holders of property. Those who own the streets, whoever they may be—private owners, companies, or municipalities— may in virtue of such owning lay down such regulations as they think right, just as the directors of a railway company issue directions as to where men may smoke or not smoke. These regulations may be unwise and vexatious, but there is no element of wrong contained in them, because they are the conditions under which a certain thing is allowed by its owners to be used. But let us be careful

---

is committed by A against B, by his having influenced the mind of C? I think it possible that another generation, bolder and more clear-sighted than we are in matters of liberty, may sweep away the law of libel altogether, and leave to each man the task of vindicating himself before the tribunal of public opinion. I should like to hear the subject fully discussed.

neither to assume ownership, where it does not rightly exist, as the result of acquisition under a free system, nor to create it by any act of force. No municipality should have the right to seize property, and then for such property make such public regulations as it chooses. The moment that it takes property by force, and sets itself above the rights of individuals, its action assumes the character of a very dangerous and unjust monopoly. In the case where it acquires property, either by purchase or by free concession, it may, like any other private owner, make such regulations as it chooses; and so long, as it is not clothed with greater powers than the individual, a guarantee of a certain kind exists that these regulations will not be oppressive on account of the opposition and competition that could be and would be called out in consequence. Given a free people accustomed to voluntary combinations, and I doubt if there is much cause for fearing the oppression of any associated body, if only no extraordinary powers have been given to it. The resources which created it, can generally call its rival or its superior into existence.*

The real danger begins where any body of persons, central or local, are armed with powers (I always except the powers necessary to protect person and property) which exceed those of the individual. Then we prepare for ourselves a formidable source of oppression, from

---

* All common property on a compulsory basis has this inherent defect, that two parties tend to be formed, and to intrigue against each other for the management of it. Under a perfectly free system this defect is reduced to its smallest proportions; under a compulsory system it becomes an evil of the first magnitude.

which, as time goes on, it becomes more and more difficult to escape. The question of local government, as it
stands now, is a very complicated one, municipalities
having already taken possession of many things by force;
and it will require much careful thought before we can
see the best way of harmonizing the old conditions of
force and the new conditions of liberty. One thing, however, is plain. No further powers should be allowed to
municipalities to take property compulsorily of any kind
or for any purpose, or to compel any citizen to consume
either its gas or its water or any other product against
their will, or to raise any kind of rate compulsorily. The
services it renders must be voluntarily rendered and voluntarily accepted. We shall gradually find our way out of
the tangle, in which we are at present, by steadily insisting that (with the one exception) no body of persons is
to be clothed with powers exceeding those of the individual; and by remembering that no momentary convenience can compensate for the mischief which arises
from our manufacturing little gods almighty, whether in
the shape of town corporations or central parliaments.

I cannot here enter fully into the many complexities
that surround this special question; nor can I here
undertake to show that, as in the case of the central
government, so also in the case of local governments,
compulsory powers have proved and must always prove
a curse and not a blessing. The compulsory powers of
municipalities have made it easy to carry out any great
work for a town without difficulty or loss of time, but
great works are a poor compensation for other serious
evils. Great debts have been accumulated; the burden of

rates has become grievous to be borne; possession of
power has become a matter of political party, with all its
innumerable evils; great monopolies are beginning to
occupy the ground—and let it be remembered that all
systems, once authoritatively adopted, stand in the way
of new discoveries and improvements—jobbery is said
to exist; the divine right of some to direct the manner in
which the resources of others shall be used has more and
more become a fixed national idea; and we have all, poor
and rich alike, been prevented from learning the fruitful
lesson of voluntarily combining to supply our own special
wants in our own special fashions. It is enough for our
purposes here to say that until the great principle of *no
compulsory powers* is carried out we cannot hope to discover the best form of local management. Where an existing body is clothed with compulsory powers there can be
no real competition between other forms and itself. To
discover what is really in the interest of men, there must
be free competition between all systems; and free competition there cannot be where one system can enforce
its own methods, and keep all rivals out of the field.

VI

And now, before leaving this part of the subject, I will
only glance at a large class of actions which, on the principles laid down, ought not to be treated as punishable
offenses, that is which have not the one element which
rightly makes a punishable offense—I mean the constraining of those actions of a man which are both within
his own physical competence, and within his own moral

competence, as far as the rights of others are concerned. Thus, there is no true authority in any person, or body of persons, to punish a man for getting drunk (setting aside offenses committed when drunk), or for indulging in vices in which, if others are concerned, they are concerned with their own consent; there is no true authority in any body of persons to say to a man "You shall only be allowed to make a contract concerning yourself and your labor in the form in which I direct you."* We can see at a glance that all such punishments or constraints are usurpations of power; are the mere forcible carrying out of their own views by those who happen to be the strongest; are, so far as they aim at bettering a man, examples of that legislation for the man's good against his consent which Mr. Mill so warmly denounced. His words ought never to be forgotten: "That the only purpose for which power can be rightfully exercised over any member of a civilized community, against his will, is to prevent harm to others. His own good, either physical or moral, is not a sufficient warrant. He cannot rightfully be compelled to do or forbear because it will be better for

---

* I do not wish to disguise the fact that the question of enforcing contracts is a most difficult and complicated one. The enforcing of contracts is in many cases the determination of the ownership of property; and unless such contracts were enforced, a man might obtain on loan his neighbor's property and refuse to return it. But it is possible, I think, that the state may greatly narrow its sphere of enforcing contracts. The springing up of voluntary courts of law outside the state courts points in this direction. This last experiment would be, I suspect, a far more fruitful one if these courts did not ask for state enforcement of their decisions. They should rely on their own conditions for this enforcement, and on refusing access to those who, they had reason to believe, might not abide by the decision.

him to do so, because it will make him happier, because in the opinion of others to do so would be wise or even right. There are good reasons for remonstrating with him, or reasoning with him, or persuading him, or entreating him; but not for compelling him, or visiting him with any evil in case he do otherwise."

We may now proceed to glance at some of the political measures which are implied in the limitation of state services.*

Class A—Removal of burdens of taxation

Examples—Abolition and reduction of state departments, and officials. Abolition of pensions after life of the present holders. Abolition of all custom and excise duties and assessed taxes, and establishment of complete free trade in all things. All government revenues (whether central or local) to be derived from *voluntary, not compulsory payments*. Payment as early as possible of national debt by sale of all such ecclesiastical property as may be adjudged to belong equitably to the nation, by sale of other national property, and by special fund raised by voluntary contributions; with mortgage of remaining national property to holders of debt, until payment is completed.

Voluntary taxation. Apart from the argument of convenience, which unfortunately governs us in so many

---

* Some small part of the following matter, relating to political measures, is given in Antiforce paper no. 1, published by Women's Printing Society, Great College Street, Westminster.

matters, it will be difficult, I think, to find any real justi-fication for the compulsory levying of taxes. The citizens of a country who are called upon to pay taxes have done nothing to forfeit their inalienable right over their own possessions (it being impossible to separate a man's right over himself and his right over his possessions), and there is no true power lodged in any body of men, whether known under the title of governments or of gentlemen of the highway, to take the property of men against their consent. The governments which persist in levying taxes by force, simply because they have the power to do so, will one day be considered as only the more respectable portion of that fraternity who are to be found in all parts of the world, living by the strong hand on the possessions of those who are too weak to resist them.

The more this question of taxation is considered, the more clearly I believe will the mischief of the present system come to light. So long as the political faction in power can decree the levying of what taxes it likes, it is unreasonable to hope that either the organized or the unorganized oppression of men by each other can ever be brought to an end. The conception of our true relations to each other is poisoned at an ever-flowing spring. Once give to me, or to any other man, the power to carry out our own ideas, and those of the majority to which we happen to belong, at the expense of all who are in the minority and who disagree with those ideas, and there and then the hateful state of oppressors and oppressed is necessarily established. There can be no true condition of rest in society, there can be no perfect friendliness amongst men who differ in opinions, as long as either you or I can use our neighbor and his resources for the furtherance of our ideas and against his own. The present power to levy taxes compulsorily seems to me the inner keep, the citadel of the whole question of liberty; and until that stronghold is leveled to the ground, I do not think that men will ever clearly realize that to compel any human being to act against his own convictions is essentially a violation of the moral order, a cause of human unrest, and a grievous misdirection of human effort. Of the immediate ill effects, of the waste, of the extravagance, of the jobbery, that are all born of the compulsory taking of taxes, I will not speak here. The first and greatest question is whether to help oneself to one's neighbor's property by force is or is not morally right.

In writing thus, I ought to say that on this point my view is, as I have reason to believe, opposed to the views of Mr. Herbert Spencer, without whose teaching scarcely any part of this paper could have been written. But I know so well his loyalty to truth, that I can differ from him almost without regret, feeling well assured that his one anxiety is that the truest application should be given to the principles he has laid down, and not that any special view of the moment as regards those applications should prevail. Even when we are convinced that his principle of "the widest possible liberty" is the true foundation principle of all human society, we must expect that differences will arise as to the truest application of the principle. Time, free discussion, and the aroused

interest of many minds in love with liberty, will bring us
to the right goal at last.

Class B—Abolition of monopolies and restraints which
prevent the people from gaining the full benefits of free
trade

Examples—Abolition of all legislation creating a monopoly in the liquor traffic; of state regulation of the
professions of law and medicine, with its resulting monopoly in each case; of legal impediments restraining the
free sale of land; of the state post office and telegraph
services. Such changes in the law of libel as would allow
the freest discussion to accompany all the developments
of free trade, while leaving men responsible for the truth
of their statements.

Changes in law of libel. It is the necessary comple-
ment of a free trade system and of open competition that
the most perfect freedom of discussion should take place
as regards all that comes into the market, and all methods
of carrying on business. It is in the vital interest of the
people that they should learn to appraise at his real
worth every seller in the market, and to understand every
method of carrying on business; and this they can only
do well by the habit of free discussion and of free interchange of ideas. No government inspection is of the least
real use in this matter. It is but a mockery and delusion,
disguising from the people the urgent necessity of watch-
fulness, a better understanding of their own interests,
and in some cases of defensive associations to secure the
full advantage of free trade. The free trade system de-

mands by its very nature a higher order of intelligence on the part of the people, and this intelligence cannot be developed unless the people can discuss freely, as well as buy and sell freely. At present the law of libel is of such a nature and is so mischievously interpreted, free criticism with all its valuable influences is so much hindered, that, to take a familiar example, a writer like Mr. Ruskin cannot speak without risk to himself of Mr. Whistler and his "paint pot."

Class C—Abolition of services done by the state, which if performed by those immediately concerned would result in

1. Greater independence of character, and greater sense of justice as regards placing burdens upon the shoulders of others.

2. Greater intelligence, enterprise, and fitness for voluntary association.

Examples—Abolition of all state education, established churches, poor laws, of state inspections, and regulation of factories, mines, railways, ships, etc.

State education and Poor Law. It should be observed that when taxes were converted into voluntary contributions, the great objection that now applies especially to such services as state education and Poor Laws—the injustice of *compelling* some to pay for others—would be removed, and when once that was the case, a state education or Poor Law system might be continued in certain places and under certain circumstances for a period, so as to give time to the people of each district to organize their own systems of dealing with these great matters.

But apart from the objection to compulsory taxation, we have to perceive that no universal system directed by an external and often remote authority can continue healthy or capable of continuous and sustained improvement. There is therefore a great need that state direction should gradually give place to the voluntary associations of men, working in their own self-chosen groups, and competing against each other to discover the best methods.

Class D—Abolition of restraints which give a character of infallibility to the state, replace the judgment of the individual as regards his own conduct and duties by the judgment of the state, and by the sterilizing effect of physical and external force prevent the development of self-protecting qualities and the transforming influences of moral force

Examples—Repeal of laws enforcing vaccination; directing the compulsory removal of the sick; imposing regulations as regards the labor or education of children on the whole class of parents (any person, whether parent or not, physically injuring a child either by overwork or in any other manner, should be punishable in ordinary legal course); attempting either to prevent or to impose certain opinions, such as the exaction of political or religious oaths from members of Parliament (oaths which led to the nationally disgraceful exclusion of Mr. Bradlaugh); impeding and harassing those who believe in or would examine the facts of spiritualism; enforcing a special observance of the Sunday; suppressing brothels; giving the police power to arrest women on the charge of prostitution, or, as regards the people, powers of other harassing interference; forbidding vivisection; restricting the stage and other amusements of the people; restricting or forbidding the liquor traffic; preventing divorce at the desire of either husband or wife; or enabling government (whether central or local) to take property compulsorily.

As regards this class it should be observed that the thing in question may be in the judgment of many of us a wrong thing, and yet at the same time one which ought not to be forbidden by the arbitrary power of the state. Speaking for myself personally I object strongly to vivisection, so far as it involves serious pain to animals, both on moral grounds and on grounds of public interest. On moral grounds I do not think we ought to purchase advantages—granting that they are advantages—at the price of deliberately inflicting great suffering; and on grounds of public interest I think (as I think Dr. Anna Kingsford and others have pointed out) that experiments on animals delay and impede improvement in the methods of observing human disease. They lead us in the wrong direction. I do not doubt that there is an utility of a certain class in vivisection, that experiments have been of service in confirming views already held, and that they often furnish simple and direct illustrations of such views; but in the general interest of society the method seems to me highly undesirable. It is against the public good that our doctors should train themselves to depend upon experiments upon animals. That which we desire for them is keener perceptions and more human sympathy with disease; and these qualities, as I believe, will not be fully developed until we have systems of closer observation of disease than those which exist at present, while at the same time I doubt if these qualities are reconcilable in human character with the reckless school of experiment which has grown up on the continent, and but for the present protests might grow up in this country. And yet, holding these views, I can find no true authority for enforcing them upon those who hold the opposite views in exactly the same good faith as myself. It is a matter of conscience on both sides, and must be left to be decided by discussion, and not by state decrees. Our effort, therefore, should be to persuade the antivivisectionists to abandon all agitation to obtain the passing of a prohibitory law. Such a law will be but of the smallest use to them, for it will not be respected or obeyed by the medical profession, and by its harshness it will still more unite the profession in their support of vivisection. That which we have to do is to create a state of freedom, as regards the profession itself, which does not now exist, as the only sure means of enabling the strong public feeling that has been called out against vivisection to produce a practical result. At present the profession holds to all intents a close position, which it is proposed to make by law still closer. If the regulation of the profession is left in their own hands, if only those can enter it who have passed through courses of teaching arranged and given by themselves, and through examinations of which they hold the control, so long the teachers will mold the taught, and the efforts of the antivivisectionists will be without any lasting result. In this case the simply professional view will dominate the profession, perhaps all the more strongly on account of the opposition outside. The profession must be thrown open, it must be made absolutely free, leaving to each medical school to choose and to follow its own course and methods. In such a case antivivisectionists would either get some of the hospitals with their schools of teaching into their own hands, or create new ones, and the matter would be brought to a practical test whether the more human and humane methods are or are not in the long run the best for men. There is no profession which seems to me to be greater or nobler in itself than that which is concerned with human healing, but I am convinced that its interests cannot and will not coincide with those of society, so long as any legal power or any kind of monopoly is left in its hands. Monopolies have always bred interests that diverge from those of society. It has been so with the church in all ages; it is so today with the professions of law and medicine; just as it also is, to pass to a lower level, with the trade of liquor selling.

Laws compelling the education of children. Here again the end is good, but the means are not good. Parents who are simply treated as so much material and summarily directed by a law to educate their children can never rise to an intelligent sense of their duties. Our wants, our family and social obligations, are our great moral educators in the world, but they can only do their work so long as we preserve free minds to listen to the moral appeal. The moment we begin to satisfy these wants by the machinery of external compulsion, all the good that would come to us from making the free effort is lost. He who voluntarily sacrifices his own interests to send his child to school is on the road to raise himself and the society to which he belongs, but he who simply pays mechanical obedience to a law, condemns himself—and all others, as far as his influence is concerned—to drowse on forever with unawakened senses.

Laws attempting to prevent vicious habits. All coercive interferences with vice end disastrously. They drive it out of the daylight into secret places, where it assumes lower and more degraded forms. They produce great hypocrisy, for none of us is sufficiently virtuous to act as the persecutor of others in these matters. They often inflict great cruelty by putting power into the hands of unfit instruments, a power, for example, so much dreaded in Paris that women have many times destroyed themselves rather than fall into the hands of the police. And, last, like all other employments of force, they prevent the growth of moral influence.

Laws regulating or forbidding the liquor traffic. There is much to be said on this subject. I can only say here that to forbid this traffic by law will be to destroy almost at a blow the moral energies which have been called out by the great evil of excessive drink. There has been a splendid energy developed by the antidrink party, which, with all its effects upon character, would be wiped out of existence whenever they begin to compel instead of converting the people. If there is any man who should pray and vote and fight against the permissive bill, it is the man who believes in abstinence. We ought to save the teetotal party from itself, as wise men would save a church from itself that asked to be turned into an established church and to be allowed to wield the power of the state.

Free divorce. Our marriage laws are another example of a good end sought through bad means. We have strong ground for believing that permanence in marriage relations is a mark of a higher civilization and higher type of character. But do not let us forget that the outward union must be based upon the inward union. If union be only the result of external authority, or pressure of any external kind, or obedience to fashion, it possesses no real value, it becomes a mere superstition, a fetter. There can be nothing which so lowers our view of marriage as the belief that, for the imagined good of society, two people, whose lives and aims are inharmonious, should by some sort of external coercion be bound together; as if society had ever been benefited by sacrificing the individual. Here, as everywhere else, freedom must be our guide. In all great matters of human feeling, not only the higher forms, but even the conception of the higher form, can only be reached through freedom. We bind men and women in order to save them from temptation, and we presently find that the effect of our binding is to make them slavish, mercenary, and untruthful in character, and to paralyze the upward tendency to good that exists in every free society.

I ought to add that some matters mentioned in Class D belong rather to the department of local than to central government; such as, powers entrusted to the police.

Class E—Abolition of restraints placed upon some for the benefit of others

Examples—Abolition of all special contracts forced upon either employers or employed, or landlord and tenant, in the interest of either party.

Class F—Constitutional and administrative changes

Examples—Abolition of privileges depending on birth. Abolition of the House of Lords; conversion of monarchy after present reign, and in course of time, into republic of simplest type. Manhood and womanhood suffrage. Ballot permissive individually. Proportional representation. Reference of measures passed by Parliament for ratification by the people, on demand of a certain number of members, according to the Swiss plan. Separation of Indian and home armies. Abolition of military life in barracks by placing soldiers on same footing as police. Commissions gained by service in the ranks, and as volunteers, and as result of special (qualifying, not competitive) examinations. Great development of volunteer system.

Conversion of monarchy into republic. This change is one that should not be forced upon a large and unwilling minority; but should be made with great consideration for those who, as the result of many past generations of inherited opinions, are strongly monarchical in feeling. The present queen has fulfilled her duties too faithfully toward the people not to make us heartily wish to see the undivided allegiance of the people remain with her until the end of her reign. It is possible that when the change takes place the appointment of the then reigning sovereign, as president for life, with no rights of succession, may greatly soften the resistance that must be expected to accompany this break in our national life.

Class G—Ireland

Ireland to choose its own government. The N.E. part to stay with England if it wishes to do so. Loan to be raised by Irish government to buy out at fair prices such landowners as desire to leave the country.

Class H—Colonies, India, Egypt, and Foreign Countries

Closer drawing together of mother country and colonies for purposes of foreign policy and defense. In every
case either a loyal and vigorous discharge of the obligations resting upon us, or a frank renunciation of such
obligations. It is of importance that confederation should
be constructed on such principles that any colony may
withdraw from it in the future, should it desire to do so.
We have no right to forejudge the future for these new
and growing countries. India to be ruled with a view to
its own approaching self-government, without any attempt at developing its civilization according to British
ideas and through taxation imposed by British force. No
government expenditure to be incurred except that which
is necessary for preserving peace and order. Egypt to
choose her own form of government under our protection for a time. Arabi and the exiles to be immediately
released.

Abroad a strictly nonaggressive policy. Our own assumed interests not to be placed before the rights of any
people. Support of principle of international agreement
in distinct and defined cases; but no wholesale placing of
our national judgment and action in the hands of unknown keepers. Influence of the nation to be steadily but
peacefully thrown on the side of those struggling for
independence, and against annexations made in disregard
of the will of the people.

Local or municipal government. The local governments
to exercise such powers of defending person and property,
and of preventing the molestation of one individual by

another, as may be given to them by general acts of Parliament. To have no powers of compulsorily taking of property, of levying a compulsory rate, or of compelling any person to take water, gas, etc., whether provided by the municipality or by a company. To have powers to regulate property of which they are the owners; provision being made (on the *ad referendum* principle) for submitting any regulation to those possessing the local franchise. If municipalities are to be owners of property (for example, of the streets), the impartiality and tolerance of these regulations must in a great measure depend upon the constant vigilance and love of liberty of the citizens; and it would probably be better for the central government to impose no hard and fast rules upon local governments as regards the management of property that is in their hands, but leave to the people in each district the duty of watching over their own liberties. Great battles for individual liberties have to be fought at present in the municipalities. All attempts to restrict rights of meeting and rights of procession, whether of the Salvation Army or of any others; to enlarge the powers of the police, to harass the people in their homes, to make sanitary matters an excuse for arbitrary regulations must be steadily and unflinchingly resisted. The *ad referendum* principle should be at once demanded by those locally governed as regards the provisions of local acts.

And now I have completed this slight and imperfect sketch of the measures which seem to be necessary to make liberty the foundation stone for men in all their dealings with each other. I can well believe that to many persons these proposals must seem of a wide and sweeping character. If they do, it is because they are so little accustomed as yet to the idea of liberty that they are like those who prefer the prison cell to the free sky. They have been so long bound hand and foot by state systems; they have been so long confined by rulers and churches, by sects and the narrow customs of the society in which they have lived, that they can only think of one part of men as placed in guard over the other part, and forever engaged in driving and compelling them to do what is right and reasonable and what their own interests demand. They can only think of improvements as presented to them by government officials, or of evils as warred against by police penalties. Innumerable education acts, factory acts, prohibitive liquor laws, sanitary decrees, form the joyless horizon with which most men bound the future of the human race, and are the materials out of which they construct their melancholy ideas of progress. If we can only have more prohibitions, more penalties, more departments, more ministers, more burdens of taxation, and more government of man by man, then, as they fondly believe, we shall at last begin to enter upon the long delayed millennium.

One further matter deserves brief attention. I would point out that none of the proposals that I have made are arbitrary in their nature. If they were arbitrary, if they were simply created out of the fancy either of myself or of any other man, they would not be worth the paper on which they are written. They are, as I believe, the necessary deductions from the great principle—that a man has inalienable rights over himself, over his own faculties and possessions—and those, who having once accepted this principle, who having once offered their allegiance to liberty, are prepared to follow her frankly and faithfully wherever she leads, will find, unless I am mistaken, that they are irresistibly drawn step by step to the same or to very similar conclusions. But perhaps once more you question if the principle itself is true? I affirm again that it is not only true, but that it cannot be challenged. If it is not true, what principle do you offer in its place to build upon? The principle that some men, according to their numbers, ought to own and possess the selves, the faculties and property of other men? But your justice and your good sense at once condemn that principle as absurd. It means, not order, but eternal anarchy and strife for the world. If then, you once agree with me in accepting this principle as the foundation law of human society, you will gradually feel yourselves constrained to lay aside all such special ideas and prepossessions as spring naturally from your personal or class interests, and instead of carving and clipping liberty, as you have hitherto done, to bring her to the image of your own minds, you will resolutely set yourselves instead to bring your creeds, your wishes, your efforts, into harmony with all her requirements. We must lay aside fanciful and merely speculative judgments of our own, and in each case simply seek for the truest and most faithful application of our principle. The worthlessness of ninety-nine out of a hundred human actions and opinions, in political life, arises from their arbitrariness. There are but very few men who loyally submit themselves to a great principle. We shall find many who will be willing to accept our principle in general terms, and yet will flinch from its universal application, because they want a saving clause inserted for some favorite institution of their own, either on behalf of a church, or of education, or labor laws, or poor laws, or some form of nationalization of land or other property, or laws affecting marriage, or the observance of Sunday, or the regulation of the liquor traffic. To all such men I can only say you cannot serve a great principle, and yet hope to drive your own little bargain with it, about some object of your special affections. You must be brave, and meet bravely the sacrifices which all great principles impose. Remember the loyalty of a student in science. Men do not accept gravitation as a principle, and yet claim that there is a special point at some special latitude at which its action is suspended. It may seem hard to you to give up the external protection which you at present enjoy for some darling interest or cause, to which your best energies are honorably given, but you will learn in time to see that if the great principle justifies itself anywhere, it justifies itself everywhere. All state protection is protection by external physical force, and those who choose the protection of external physical force must renounce the protection that depends upon qualities developed in the self and by the moral forces of freedom. Between these two kinds of protection, that from without and that from within, there is no alliance possible; for the one—whichever it be—fails and dwindles as the other grows and gathers strength.

VII

And now to conclude. With the exception of certain short notes attached to the legislative proposals, I have on purpose almost entirely confined myself in this paper to speaking of the fundamental moral wrong that is committed, where some men coerce other men, where some men forcibly and by means of the state power construct systems for the rest of men to live under. As regards the many practical evils that result from thus making other men accept our views of religion, or of education, or of the relation of labor and capital (remember that the wrong we commit in these cases is twofold, caused both by our prescribing the systems under which others shall live, and by our taking compulsorily from them, in the shape of taxes, the means by which such systems are supported) I must leave this branch of the great discussion for another occasion. I can merely point out here that all uniform state systems, excluding difference, excluding competition, mean a perpetual arrest at the existing level of progress. So long as great government departments (over which, be it observed, from the very exigencies of administration, the mass of the people can never have any real control) supply our wants, so long shall we remain in our present condition, the difficulties of life unconquered, and ourselves unfitted to conquer them. No amount of state education will make a really intelligent nation; no amount of Poor Laws will place a nation above want; no amount of Factory Acts will make us better parents. These great wants which we are now vainly trying to deal with by acts of Parliament, by prohibitions and penalties, are in truth the great occasions of progress, if only we surmount them by developing in ourselves more active desires, by putting forth greater efforts, by calling new moral forces into existence, and by perfecting our natural ability for acting together in voluntary associations. To have our wants supplied from without by a huge state machinery, to be regulated and inspected by great armies of officials, who are themselves slaves of the system which they administer, will in the long run teach us nothing, will profit us nothing. The true education of children, the true provision for old age, the true conquering of our vices, the true satisfying of our wants, can only be won, as we learn to form a society of free men, in which individually and in our own self-chosen groups we seek the truest way of solving these great problems. Before any real progress can be made, the great truth must sink deep into our hearts, that we cannot in any of these matters be saved by machinery, we can only be saved by moral energy in ourselves and in those around us. Progress, *or the education of men by the wants of life,* can have nothing to do with passing acts of Parliament; except so far as we pass them to break old fetters that still bind us. If civilization could be given by any government, as a royal present to a nation, the world had long since been civilized. One short session would be enough to decree all the new systems of education, and all the new dwelling houses, and all the new grants of land, and all the new penalties against vices, that are wanted. But at the end of it all the nation would be like a man who had dressed himself in a new suit of clothes. The man himself under all the new outward appearances would remain the same; only perhaps more hindered than before by the misleading belief that in some real way his clothes had transformed him. Civilization has never yet and never will be simply made by the fiat of those who have power. It must be slowly won by new desires arising in us individually and taking effect in new efforts. The common sense gained in daily life is quite sufficient to teach us that any number of brand-new splendid institutions cannot and do not alter men. To believe that they do we must go back to the fairy tales of our childhood. Nor does it require unusual intelligence to perceive that the real force of England has lain in the energy, the enterprise, the independence, the power of acting and thinking alone, that have belonged to the English character, and that it has not been her governing machinery, but these forces of character that have won for her the great peaceful victories of industry at home and of colonization abroad. These qualities form the true stores of her greatness and success, but they are qualities that are only produced by freedom in our life and constant responsibility for our actions. They cannot coexist— it would be contrary to the very nature of things—with great state systems and great governing departments, under whose direction men from day to day are controlled and cared for; I doubt if they can even long survive in presence of two powerful and highly organized political parties, whose members, giving up the attempt to see for themselves what is right and true, are content to act in a crowd and to follow their leaders in blind struggles to gain ascendancy over each other. These are the things which, as our political Marthas will presently learn, are not needful to a nation. We need not have great state departments, or great state systems, however splendid in their external appearance, we need not each of us be enlisted in a great army called Conservative or Liberal. But what is needful is that man should have a free soul in a free body; that he should hate the creeds of force and of regulation, that he should ever be striving to make his mind independent of the opinions of others, that he should ever be training it to form its own judgments and to respect its own sense of right. For a nation whose units are determined to keep their bodies and minds free, all progress is possible. For a nation whose units are willing to place their bodies and their minds in the keeping of others, there are no hopes of growth and movement. It is only reserved to them to fall from one depth to another depth of state slavery, while they live in the mocking dream that they are moving onward and upward.

There is very much more to be said as regards this matter of state power and state interference with the lives of men. I ought to point out the extravagance and bad management of state departments. It is not often that we see people spend the money that belongs to others either quite honestly or quite intelligently, and state departments are no exception to the rule. I ought to point out the jobbery and the stupidity that so often cling to state undertakings; the unfitness of the agents that governments are obliged to employ; the necessarily bad methods, whether by competition or official nomination, of selecting them; the unfitness of the universal systems which are applied to all parts of a nation, to those who ought by the very law of their being to be differing from each other, and yet are forced to be alike; the dull, heavy routine into which these undertakings fall within a few years after they have been commenced and have ceased to attract public attention—a routine only broken by the spasmodic revolutions in their management to which they are subject, when some flagrant abuse brings them now and again under the public eye. I ought to point out how reckless in all countries becomes the rivalry of the great political parties which hope to obtain the good things that go under the name of office; the increasing deterioration of the people when invited on all hands to judge everything from the one standpoint of their own immediate advantage; the inconsistency of what is said and done by each party, when acting as government or as opposition, and the hypocrisy that is begotten while they serve their own interests under the cloak of the interests of the people. I ought to point out how heavy and sore a discouragement for labor is the load of taxation, that is thrown upon the nation to support all the grand institutions, which politicians love to look at as their own handiwork; and I ought to show that the really successful nation in the industrial competition that is now springing up so fiercely between all nations will be the one that has fewest taxes, fewest officials, and fewest departments to support, and at the same time possesses the greatest power in its individual units to adapt themselves readily to the industrial changes that come so quickly in the present day. I ought to show you that all that encourages routine, dislike of change, dependence upon external authority and direction, is fatal to this habit of self-adaptation, and that this self-adaptation can only come where the free life is led. I ought to show that all great uniform systems—clumsy and oppressive as they must always be in their rude attempt to embrace every part of a nation—clumsy and oppressive, for example, as our education system and our Poor Law system are—are always tending (sometimes in very subtle and unsuspected ways) to stupefy and brutalize a nation in character; and, as far as the richer classes are concerned, to destroy those kindly feelings, that sympathy for the pains of others, and that readiness to help those who need help, which grow, and only can grow, on a free soil. If by official regulations you prescribe for me my moral obligations toward others, you may be sure that in a short time my own moral feelings will cease to have any active share in the matter. They will soon learn to accept contentedly the official limit you have traced for them, and to drowse on, unexercised because unrequired, within that limit. Indeed, I believe that if you only taxed us enough, for so-called benevolent purposes, you would presently succeed in changing all the really generous men into stingy men. Again I ought to show how all great uniform state systems are condemned by our knowledge of the laws of nature. It has been owing to the differences of form that come into existence that the ever-continuous improvement of animal and plant life has taken place; the better fitted form beating and replacing the less-fitted form. But our great uniform systems, by which the state professes to serve the people, necessarily exclude difference and variety; and in excluding difference and variety, exclude also the means of improvement. I ought to show how untrue is the cry against competition. I ought to show that competition has brought benefits to men tenfold— nay, a hundredfold—greater than the injuries it has inflicted; that every advantage and comfort of civilized life has come from competition; and that the hopes of the future are inseparably bound up with the still better gifts which are to come from it and it alone. I ought to show, even if this were not so, even if competition were not a power fighting actively on your side, that still your efforts would be vain to defeat or elude it. I ought to show that all external protection, all efforts to place forcibly that which is inferior on the same level as that which is superior, is a mere dream, born of our ignorance of nature's methods. The great laws of the world cannot change for any of us. There is but one way, one eternally fixed way, and no other, of meeting the skill, or the enterprise, or the courage, or the frugality, or the greater honesty that beats us in any path of life, whether it be in trade or in social life, in accumulating wealth or in following knowledge, in opening out new countries or in conquering old vices, and that way is to develop the same qualities in ourselves. The law is absolute, and from it there is no appeal. No Chinese walls, no system based upon exclusion and disqualification and suppression, can do this thing for us; can bring efficiency to a level with inefficiency, and leave progress possible. I ought to show how far more flexible, adaptive, and efficient a weapon of progress is voluntary combination than enforced combination; how every want that we have will be satisfied by means of voluntary combination, as we grow better fitted to make use of this great instrument; whether it be to provide against times of depression in trade and want of employment, of sickness, of old age; whether it be to secure to every man his own home and his own plot of ground; or to place within his reach the higher comforts and the intellectual luxuries of life.

And here let me point out that the money competition

of the world, against which men so often thoughtlessly
declaim, furnishes the soil, out of which that marvelous
system of insurance against the physical evils of life has
grown and is growing. Apart from profits and active competition in business, benefit societies and trades unions
would find no profitable investment for their funds; and
those, therefore, who would destroy or restrain the free
movement of capital are destroying the bird that lays the
golden egg. But the matter goes far beyond the range of
what exists at present. No man can foresee today the full
development in the future of the system of insurance.
If it is allowed to grow naturally, without disturbance
from the politicians, without impediment of any kind,
in response to the wants that are calling it into existence,
it is possible that in a certain number of years a man,
without taking on his shoulder any great burden, may
find himself sheltered, as far as shelter is possible, from
much the larger part of the world's material troubles.
But this development of voluntary protective organizations can never take place unless trade becomes wholly
free, having ceased to be half strangled by taxation and
official interferences, and unless personal enterprise and
voluntary associations of all kinds are allowed to mutually stimulate each other to the full, so as to produce
the richest results. Under such a competition we must
at the same time expect evils and frauds to show themselves, but we need have no nervous misgivings on this
account. The practical intelligence of the people, continually developed by a free system, will discover the
fitting safeguards. We must remember that the world
is still very young, as regards the application of voluntary

combinations for supplying our wants. It is only in the last few years that voluntary association has begun to disclose its great powers for good; and we have no right to expect that we shall suddenly become efficient masters in the use of so new and so great an instrument. Many high qualities in ourselves are required before this can be the case. You can regulate a mass of half-men half-slaves under government systems, under enforced association, almost when you choose, and as you choose; but it is only free men, with the qualities of free men, that can take their place in voluntary associations. When once our eyes are opened to this great matter, we shall see, perhaps with some indignation, that those who are constantly striving to extend the area of government management, and to make men do by compulsory association what they could learn to do by voluntary association, are pronouncing the doom of the race, and condemning it to perpetual inefficiency.

Passing on from the subject of trade to that of private property, I ought to show how freedom of action and inviolability of private property are inseparably bound up together. It is a great misfortune that property, especially land, is at present largely massed in few hands. Our need is that every man should be the owner of property; that the whole nation, and not a class, should be landowners. But strong as is our desire to see a state of things in which wealth will be far more widely distributed than it is at present, we must not sell ourselves into the politician's hands, and, taking the bribes that he offers, act unloyally to the principle of liberty and to all that it enjoins us. Make the people free from the many bonds that impede them—whether they are the indescribably mischievous legal complications surrounding land, that we have inherited from long ago, or the modern stupidities in the shape of compulsory agreements between landlord and tenant, just created (these share in the same vice as the old legal complications, since they tend to fix farms at their present size, by attaching a sort of tenant-right payment to each), release trade of every kind from regulation by the state, throw off the crushing burden of taxation, renounce the blinding and wasteful political struggle for power over each other, face the great truth and act on it, that in self-help, in the moral influences of example, of sympathy, and of free discussion, in leaving invention and discovery unimpeded to take their own course and to earn their full reward, and, above all, in voluntary protective associations of every form and kind, lies the method of progress; and you will find that with the outburst of intelligence and moral activity, which will come as we turn our faces resolutely toward freedom, that wealth and property will distribute themselves more widely and more deeply than by any revolution which either Mr. George, or those who succeed him, or imitate him, or outbid him, may be able to bring about. There are none of the good things of life, from the highest to the lowest, that will not come to the people when once they gain the clearness of mind to see the moral bounds that they ought to set to the employment of force, when they gain the loyally steadfast purpose to employ their energies only within such bounds. But by the wrong weapons and wrong methods nothing truly worth having can be won. The actual property gained by acts of expropriation would not be worth to them one-hundredth part of the property gained in a free market by free exertions, for the highest value of property results from the qualities of character that are developed in the gaining of it; and the moral curse that clings to all such acts would prove itself undying. If freedom of life, freedom to use one's faculties for the acquisition of property, and freedom of trade, are great moral truths, then each act of expropriation would lead us further and further into irretrievably wrong directions. We should pass from one period to another period of misdirected effort. Force would beget force; intolerance and suppresion would beget children after their own image and temper; until at last the burden placed by men upon themselves would become too grievous to be borne. Do not accept any words of mine in this matter. Let every man steadily think out for himself what the conditions of life must at last become when giving way to the temptation of rearranging existing property by the power of the majority, we place ourselves on the side of force, take it as our guide, and make it the regulator of all those things that most nearly touch our existence. Let every man follow out for himself in his own mind the growth of the system of force, until at last such perfection of it is attained, that no limb of his own body, no part of his own mind, no object within his household can be said to be wholly and entirely within his own direction, wholly and entirely his own. But further into this matter I cannot here go. There are many more points that belong to this vast and interesting discussion to which I ought to ask your attention, but they must all be reserved for other occasions. The leading intention in this paper has been to show—apart from all those practical evils which are the children of force—that there is no moral foundation for the exercise of power by some men over others, whether they are a majority or not; that even if it is a convenient thing to exercise this power, in so apparently simple a form as that of taking taxes, and for purposes which are so right and wise and good in themselves, as education, or the providing for the old age of the destitute, there is no true authority which sanctions our doing so; and therefore that the good which we intend to do will ever be perverted into harm. I have tried to show that this question of power, exercised by some men over other men, is the greatest of all questions, is the one that concerns the very foundations of society. Indeed, you will find, as you examine this matter, that all ideas of right and wrong must ultimately depend upon the answer that you give to my question, "Have twenty men—just because they are twenty—a moral title to dispose of the minds and bodies and possessions of ten other men, just because they are ten?" Is the majority morally supreme, or are there moral rights and moral laws, independent of both majority and minority, to which, if the world is to be restful and happy, majority and minority must alike bow? I invite you to give the deepest, the most honest, and the most unselfish consideration to this matter, and I bid you believe that no creed, religious or philosophical, no political party, no social undertaking will enable you to deal rightly with life unless you fairly grasp, with a grip from which there can be no escape until the answer is won, this great question, "By what right do men exercise power over each other?"

ESSAY FIVE

THE ETHICS OF DYNAMITE

This essay was published in the May 1894 issue of
Contemporary Review.

I hasten to reassure Mrs. Grundy as regards all her anxieties. I am happy to say, even at the cost of a dull article, that I am wholly orthodox on this question of villainous dynamite. I detest dynamite, my dear madam, for your own excellent reasons, because it is most treacherous, cruel—I should write scatterbrained, but some ingenuous person might accuse me of trifling with the English language—and altogether abominable; and I also detest it for other special reasons. I detest it, because I look upon it as a nineteenth-century development in the art of governing, and of that worthy art the world has had quite sufficient developments already. There is no occasion for adding one more experience to the long list. Perhaps I ought at once, for the benefit of some of my friends who are inclined a little incautiously to glorify this word "governing" without thinking of all that is contained in it, to translate the term, which is so often on our lips, into what I hold to be its true meaning: forcing your own will and pleasure, whatever they may be, if you happen to be the stronger, on other persons. Now, many worthy people are apt to look on dynamite as the archenemy of government; but remembering this definition, remembering that undeniably the great purpose of government is the compulsion of A by B and C to do what he does not want to do, it is plain that such a view fails to distinguish essence from accident, and to appreciate the most characteristic qualities that inhere in this new political agent. Dynamite is not opposed to government; it is, on the contrary, government in its most intensified and concentrated form. Whatever are the sins of everyday governmentalism, however brutal in their working some of the great force machines with which we love to administer each other may tend to be, however reckless we may be as regards each other's rights in our effort to place the yoke of our own opinions upon the neck of others, dynamite "administers" with a far ruder, rougher hand than ever the worst of the continental bureaucracies. Indeed, whenever the continental governments are reproached by some of us liberty folk for taking possession in so peremptory a manner of the bodies and minds of the people and converting them into administration material, they may not unreasonably remark—if they happen to be in a philosophic mood—that the same reproaches should be addressed, with even greater pertinency, to their enemy, the dynamiter, who dynamites us all with the happiest impartiality on the off-chance of impressing somebody or other with some portion of his own rather mixed views. Indeed, a touch of what is almost comic is introduced into the lurid matter by the fact that the views of the dynamiter, to which we are so unpleasantly sacrificed, are, as his best friend must admit, as yet very imperfectly arranged in his own consciousness. Although I am somewhat deficient in sympathy with most governments, yet I must confess that it is a little hard either for them or for us, the public, to be dynamited for not having already embraced theories which are still, intellectually speaking, in a half-born, unshaped condition—such as, for example, let us say, the gospel of anarchistic communism. Foreign governments have, however, as I think, an unavowed reason of their own for not loving the dynamiter, independent of any philosophical objections they may feel to the intellectual incoherences on his part. Conscience makes cowards of us all. Deep down in their consciousness lurks a dim perception of the truth, that between him and them exists an unrecognized blood relationship, that the thing of which they have such horror is something more than a satire, an exaggeration, a caricature of themselves, that, if the truth is to be fairly acknowledged, it is their very own child, both the product of and the reaction against the methods of "governing" men and women, which they have employed with so unsparing a hand.* Poor old Saturn, as he nods upon his seat, begins to feel that things are not quite so comfortable today as they were yesterday, that his family are not altogether at one with him, and that his own power has been suddenly brought face to face with a new power, which

---

* The two things often run into each other; each generation, for example, being both product and reaction in its relation to the preceding generation.

possibly may prove the stronger of the two. Our good
rulers are right to have their misgivings. We live in an
age of active evolution, and the art of government is
evolving like everything else round us. Dynamite is its
latest and least comfortable development. It is a purer
essence of government, more concentrated and intensified, than has ever yet been employed. It is government
in a nutshell, government stripped, as some of us aver,
of all its dearly beloved fictions, ballot boxes, political
parties, House of Commons oratory, and all the rest of it.
How, indeed, is it possible to govern more effectively,
or in more abbreviated form, than to say: "Do this—or
don't do this—unless you desire that a pound of dynamite should be placed tomorrow evening in your ground-
floor study." It is the perfection, the *ne plus ultra*, of
government. Indeed, if we poor liberty folk, we voluntaryists, who are at such intellectual discount just at present, and at whom none is too mean to fling his stone—
if we, who detest the root idea at the bottom of all governing—the compelling of people to do what they don't
want to do, the compelling of them to accept the views
and become the tools of other persons—wished to find
an object lesson to set before those governments of today
which have not yet learned to doubt about their property
in human material, where could we find anything more
impressive than the dynamiter, with his tin canister and
his supply of horseshoe nails? "Here is your own child.
This is what your doctrine of deified force, this is what
your contempt of human rights, this is what your property in men and women leads to."

About the actual character of those who throw bombs

there are two very different versions. To some persons they simply represent a childish, theatrical, vain type of men and women, who, endowed with more than their share of animal ferocity, and having exhausted the pleasures of living, wish to flutter some small bit of the world before they leave it. The *Times* correspondent wrote (February 26): "Ravachol was a . . . brute, resembling a hyaena rather than a man . . . . Vaillant an odious malefactor, impelled by hatred and passion for notoriety." To their own friends the bomb throwers appear in a very different light. They are heroes, devoted to their ideas, equally ready to sacrifice themselves and everybody else to those ideas. A correspondent writes:

> Vaillant was a real student. His authors were Darwin, Spencer, Ibsen, etc. During the short time between his arrest and his trial he devoured no less than seven solid scientific works. When will "society" understand that these acts of warfare are almost invariably undertaken by persons of exceptional mental power and moral grit; never by the ignorant rough, the commonplace assassin, the homicidal maniac, or morbid sentimentalist, desirous of posthumous notoriety? The thought which, at a certain stage, and conditioned in a given way, issues in this action is far away too big and all-powerful for minor motives and selfish considerations. One hears it said, right from a full heart, now and again: "Though nothing but infamy cover my name now and for all time, yet let me do the utmost that I can." They are none of them moral cowards.

Continuing, about Ravachol, my correspondent writes:

> I thought all that vilifying by the newspapers of one of the finest, tenderest, most social creatures might be allowed to go for what it is worth. This is what his personal friend ——— says of him: "Chivalrous to women, infinitely, pitifully loving

to children, an honest, steady workman, a brave struggler against the unemployed difficulties, and, at last . . . a soldier against what he had bit by bit come to see as the root cause of his fellows' misery." He hated no person. They never do. His throttling of the aged usurer was almost an accident. He meant to have his stolen money for . . . propaganda expenses. . . . The old chap surprised him at his appropriation . . . and he stuffed his handkerchief into his mouth; and as he was ninety, he was too old to bear the gagging.

Some of us might remark that if you undertake to gag old men of ninety—well, well, we will let the writer continue:

> Ravachol had not homicide in his mind or direct purpose ever, only protest and seizure (for moral use) of stolen money. Ravachol was at one time an ardent Christian, seeing in that doctrine social hope and a message to the poor. He kept his principles, but changed their form. One day Ravachol was walking with ——— through the slums of Lyons. A little neglected baby sat barefoot in the gutter. Ravachol stooped, lifted it up, pressed it to his breast, like any mother, and the tears came. "Can any revolt," he said, "be unjustifiable against a society that treats its little children in this way?" He then became taciturn and absent-minded through the rest of the walk.

There are the two pictures as regards the character of the men. We must each strike the balance for ourselves. For myself, I have no hesitation in saying that men may have great devotion, and may possess the most admirable qualities, while they serve their causes with the most detestable weapons. History crowds its pages with illustrations of this truth: Marcus Aurelius, who permits the Christian persecutions; the chivalrous Louis

IX, who considers "three inches of steel" the best method of converting heretics; Sir T. More, who superintends the ghasty torture chamber. But when we have admitted in the frankest way this truth, there is another greater truth to be placed by the side of it. All this use of bad weapons is one of the most fatal curses that afflict the world. No good cause—however good in itself—is worthy of bad weapons. If ever the world was presented with a saying of the highest wisdom and deepest truth, it was when we were told not to do evil that good might come. All the fighters, from the unscrupulous politician of a low type, who consents to trick or flatter for the advantage of himself or his party, up to the dynamiter, who seeks to terrorize society for the sake of views of which he himself has but a slight understanding, are all fighting together in one vast army to render true progress impossible. Progress can never be won by the weapons of trickery, flattery, or terrorism. The use of all such weapons only means the wearisome passage from one set of evils to another.

There are some reformers by dynamite who imagine that they are on the side of liberty. Poor liberty! As if liberty, that moves by the path of moral evolution, that moves so slowly, just because she cannot be created out of hand by those forms and systems which are established today and swept aside tomorrow—liberty, that depends upon inward processes in the consciousness of men, upon the gradual recognition by every person in every other person of his inherent inalienable right to be himself and lead the self-chosen life—as if liberty, in this one true sense, could have anything to do with a tin canister filled with blacksmith's nails and flung into the

midst of a body of old and middle-aged gentlemen, industriously playing at the nineteenth-century game of inventing rewards and devising restrictions for their fellow
men, or of peaceful citizens sipping their coffee! Friends
of liberty! No. Even the most clear-headed of the believers
in St. Dynamite understand as little of liberty as they
understand of themselves. Inventors of improved and
expedited processes of government perhaps they may be;
or avengers they may be, avengers as fungi are avengers,
when we establish the conditions that favor decay; or as
disease may be, when we recklessly depart from the conditions that maintain health; but don't let them dream
of themselves as friends of liberty. To be a friend of
liberty is one thing; to be a half-automatic reaction from
a bad system is another thing. It was necessary, it was
written in the Sibylline books, it was predestined of long
ago, that they should presently appear upon the world's
stage; it was inherent in the order of things that the
offense should come; and—we may add, as of old—woe
to them through whom the offense cometh! How could
you build up these lawless, irresponsible, all-grasping
governments, and not expect to see some dark shadows,
some grotesque imitations, some terrible caricatures, begotten of them? How could you deify force in one form
before the eyes of all men, and not expect sooner or later
to see other deifications set up at its side? And now that
at last in the fullness of time the thing, which was to be,
is amongst us, that the rival force deity has appeared and
is fighting for his throne, it is hard to restrain a somewhat bitter smile, as Europe looks on in utter bewilder-

ment at what is to it a very ugly as well as a very unaccountable phenomenon.

In truth, the new deity is not in the least unaccountable. He is only too easy to account for. Both his moral and his physical genesis lie at the door of the European governments. To almost all of them, we may in turn say: "Tu l'as voulu, Georges Dandin." In their different degrees they are, nearly all of them, alike; for long years they have plowed and sown and harrowed the soil; and lo! the crop is here. If any government thought that it could indefinitely go on turning men and women into administration material, fastening its grip closer and closer on their property, their lives, and their beliefs, until the chief purpose of human existence became—half-unconsciously, perhaps—in the eyes of these governmentalists, to supply a state revenue out of blood and sweat, while, fed and nourished by this state revenue, the grandeur of the governments was ever growing and growing, with officials magnified into creatures of a semidivine order, and a splendid and highly exciting game carried on by means of all this annexed property, and all these annexed lives, against other governments, equally engaged in playing the same splendid and exciting game— if they thought that this life of the gods ruling at their ease in the empyrean would flow on forever in a happy and unbroken stream, that nations, made of living men and women, might be turned wholesale into low forms of government property, without some strange phenomena, without some startling products and reactions breaking through the calm of the surface, we can only say of them, that, true as ever to the bureaucratic tradition, they were not in contact with the realities of flesh and blood—that they were, in an old phrase of Mr. Gladstone, "living up in a balloon." Two things were sure to arise, and they have arisen. In the moral world some men would begin to look at these gigantic structures of power, to ask questions about them, to finger them, and to probe deep to see on what moral foundations they rested; while in the world of daily life some men, less patient than their fellows, would be maddened by the close painful grinding of the wheels of the great machines, left wholly to the control of officials, and would become the right stuff for the wildest counsels to work in. Let us first take the moral genesis of the dynamiter.

In old days few questions were raised about power. The hurly-burly was universal. Whoever could get power got it, and those who could not went without it. But, in the due course of things, the time came when, with many flourishes of trumpets, the people were invited to take part themselves in this thing called power, to build it up with their own hands, and to look upon it—at all events on political platforms—as their own special property. Then came a great development of government—popular government it was called; and government undertakings and departments sprang up in their multitude, just as we have seen on occasion bubble companies spring up on all sides, when some wave of financial excitement ran through society. But the devil, as usual, drove his trade in the night season. He came and sowed just one of those little seeds, which for a time seem so utterly insignificant, and yet out of which grow in their season such big consequences. How much of this devil's seed was sown by Mr. Herbert Spencer, with his almost unique power of seeing the whole where other men see only the part, by Emerson, by Mill, by W. Von Humboldt, by Buckle, by Bentley, by Dumont, and by other fellow-laborers; how much of it was sown, quite unconsciously, by Darwin, who shattered the idea of artificial protection; how much of it was sown, at least in its potentialities, by a long line of predecessors of these writers, running back, if we choose, to Milton himself, it is not for me to inquire here; it is enough that the seed did get into the world after the fashion of all other devil's seed, and the consequence was that a time came when the well-known phrases "the power of the people," "the will of the people," "the will of the majority," which had so often been spoken *orc rotundo*, with a real sort of thunder of their own, when directed against things still more unreal than themselves, began to ring a little hollow, and to provoke critical inquiry into what was the true substance underlying these mighty oratorical expressions. What is this power? it was asked by the critical philosophers. What are the foundations on which it rests? What are its limits? Are there then no rights, no moral conditions, superior to this voting power; or is this power a sort of divinity come into the world, supreme beyond all question and challenge, illimitable in its desires and its will, before whom all men are to fall down and worship? Do individuals, then, come morally naked into the world? are they without choice and will as regards their own faculties, without authority and power of consent as regards their own actions, in presence of this vague, half-known, shifting,

impalpable thing—the will of the majority? Have they
ever consented to render this fealty? Have they ever
affixed their seal to a charter—a charter of lost rights—
signing away possession of body and soul? And what sort
of a philosophical doctrine is this—that numbers confer
unlimited rights, that they take from some persons all
rights over themselves, and vest these rights in others?
Are not rights—things equal, universal, immutable, as
long as their own conditions are preserved? How, then,
can the rights of three men exceed the rights of two men?
In what possible way can the rights of three men absorb
the rights of two men, and make them as if they had
never existed? Rights are not things which grow by using
the multiplication table. Here are two men. If there are
such things as rights, these two men must evidently start
with equal rights. How shall you, then, by multiplying
one of the two, even a thousand times over, give him
larger rights than the other, since each new unit that
appears only brings with him his own rights; or how, by
multiplying one of the units up to the point of exhausting
the powers of the said multiplication table, shall you take
from the other the rights with which he started? Now
look a little more closely at the matter, continued the
philosophers. What are these rights which—as we must
assume, if the world is not to be given over to a blind,
trackless, moral confusion—each possesses? Must they
not be rights, in the case of each person, over his own
body and mind? Is it possible to suppose, without absurdity, that a man should have no rights over his own
body and mind, and yet have a $\frac{1}{10000000}$th share in unlimited rights over all other bodies and minds? If he does not

begin by possessing rights over himself, by what wonderful flying leap can he arrive at rights over others? yet, if
he once possess these rights over himself, how can he
ever be deprived of them, and become the statutable
property of others? and again, where can a crowd of
individuals get rights from, unless it be from the individuals themselves, who make up the crowd? and yet, if
the individuals possess these rights over themselves, as
individuals, what place is left for rights belonging to the
crowd, as a crowd? You may appoint a committee, a
government, or whatever you like to call it, and delegate
to it powers already possessed by the individuals, but
by no possibility can this delegated body be seized with
larger powers than those possessed by the individuals
who called it into existence; by no possibility can the creature possess greater authority than those who created
it. It is easy to understand that an individual can delegate
full powers—powers of life and death—over himself; but
how can he delegate powers, which he himself does not
possess, over another individual? You may give your
own rights away, but you cannot possibly give away,
however generous your mood, the rights of your fellow-
man. If, however, you persist in attributing such powers
to the delegated body, please say exactly whence—from
what human or superhuman source—it has drawn them,
since it is plain that it has not drawn them from the
individuals. Nor is it possible to escape from the difficulty by denying human rights, and declaring that rights
are only imaginary things, for, in that case, government
itself has no rights. By such sweeping and reckless denial
of rights you make of government the very outlaw of out-

laws. All that it has done or is doing would then be absolutely void of moral foundations. All its regulations, its takings, its compulsions, would then simply rest upon what is convenient in the opinions of some persons, and what could be enforced by their superior strength; and, therefore, of course, it would be liable, as the mere product of convenience, to be removed in any way, or by any weapon, that is convenient and superior to itself in strength.

The was was also carried on from other less abstract points of view, and in less internecine fashion. The nation is divided, say, into two equal halves; can it, then, be maintained, it was asked, with due respect to mental sanity, that "the odd man"—that most remarkable production of parliamentarism—should be competent to assign all lives, all property, to one half or the other? Moreover, if the majority is the chosen vessel of power, if it is the instrument of human redemption, if rightly it holds the minority in the hollow of its hand, still, as a matter of fact, it is hardly ever the majority that does govern. Majorities are great, sluggish, inert bodies, made to be tricked and captured by enterprising spirits, and necessarily moved and directed by minorities within themselves. Moreover, the tendency of modern governments is more and more to fall under the rule of these active groups, one group fetching and carrying for another group, on condition that it shall be fetched and carried for in its own turn.

It must be frankly admitted that the liberty philosophers only acted directly upon a small group of minds outside themselves. Popular government was a new play-

thing in the world, and to an immense number of persons of very various kinds, who were pursuing very
various objects, it offered almost irresistible attractions.
But the ferment of new ideas works in strange and un-
expected ways. While the mass of those who enjoyed
playing the great game, as a sort of perpetual boat race
or cricket match *in excelsis,* and the still greater mass
of those who hoped to better their condition in life by
employing the huge hundred-handed machine, with its
inexhaustible resources, to do services for them, refused
to consider what right three men possessed to take over
by some voting process the lives of two men and convert
them into their own property; still "the divinity that
doth hedge" a state was shaken, and the revolutionary
forces no longer simply consisted of those who wished to
turn us into a condition of all-state, but also of dissidents
who believed in the unorganized individual, and without
any clear definition even to themselves of their own
views, wished to make a clean sweep of the state as it
exists today. The liberty philosophers had but slightly
affected the rich, and the more or less well-to-do classes,
or the mass of the workers, but their word had fallen
into patches of revolutionary soil, and the crop was growing strongly and quickly. The revolutionists have their
function in this world equally with the rest of us—although it is seldom what they themselves believe it to
be—and it was in their case, as in other cases, to force
upon the attention of the world a truth, a deeper, wider
truth than their own, with which, at all events until the
stimuli became slightly painful, our governing friends
had very little intention to concern themselves.

Of course answers were made to the philosophers who had attacked the moral foundations of power. It was asked in reply, which was most fitting, that three persons should govern two, or two should govern three? To which pungent question the philosophers again replied, that in all ordinary matters there is no right on the part of the three to govern the two, or of the two to govern the three. Both must be content to govern themselves. Self-ruling, not each-other-ruling, was the goal in front of the world. It is merely, as they contended, one of the assumptions of governing pedantry to suppose that the whole five ought to be made to walk in the same path and wear the same intellectual uniform.* In this world our function is not to make people do, but to let them do—especially, be it said, by removing impediments of our own clumsy invention. Next it was urged in defense of power that the part which falls to discontented minorities is to turn themselves into majorities. The remedy has the slight defect of drawing upon an imagined future and ignoring

---

* Of course the difference between two separate groups of cases should be clearly seen. Where there is a bit of property which belongs to the five collectively (the five agreeing to regulate it on the majority principle) and which does not belong to the five separately, as individuals, there, in such case, the rule of majority and minority is devoid of injustice. It may be a harsh rule, which hereafter we may see our way to soften and modify, but it calls for no moral lightning directed against its head. A bit of common property must be dealt with on some plan; and for the moment the minority and majority system, even if it have certain defects, may serve. But the usual application of the majority and minority system is for the purpose of dealing with the faculties and property of individuals, which, except so far as the *whole* body of individuals, as individuals, consent, by no moral process whatsoever (the great process of force appropriation always excepted) can be made to fall under the control of the majority.

a real present. I am walking along a road, and some one stronger than I knocks me down and begins to cudgel me about the head. I call to a passer-by to help me and to drag the villain off. He stands, however, with his hands in his pockets, and cheerfully tells me that it is all right; that I ought not to object. If I only practice the use of a cudgel myself with sufficient zeal for a month, or perhaps a year, I shall then be in a position to cudgel my assailant quite as effectively about the head as he is now cudgeling me. I reply that I don't believe in cudgeling heads, whether it is my head or the head of somebody else. The passer-by, however, merely shrugs his shoulders, by way of telling me that it is idle to object to what is so excellent a custom, and one which is universally practiced in the district. Thereupon I find nothing more to say, and have to endure my cudgeling as best I can. Of course, the retort, however good as a bit of rhetoric, is of small value as regards its logic, for, in addition to the pleasant irony of telling an insignificant section, who are aggrieved, that they are presently to govern the country, there are many injuries which the majority of the future, however much it may approach to omnipotence, can with difficulty redress. It can hardly unhang a man, or wipe out of existence the weeks he has spent in prison, or give back property that has been taken from him and spent, or build up some great voluntary institution which has been destroyed, or invent redress for restrictions placed upon the facilities of an individual during the best years of his life, or remove the twist it has given to national character by unwise and harsh measures.

Then came the national-life or national-unity argument, and we were told in a rather vague and specious manner that we were all bonded together in one society, and that it was needful that the one society should grow together in the same way and under the same influences, which perhaps it might not do, if we did not freely compel each other. That argument was more flowery than convincing, since in all the other forms of daily society men live together fairly well without establishing a system of compulsion, and no one had yet ventured to get up and propose that, for the sake of improving the general good temper and happiness, we should vote upon the practices and habits which make up the daily life of each of us. Moreover, it was pointed out that it was the spirit of respect for, and concession toward, each other, not the minute regulation of innumerable acts, which made life pleasant and enjoyable. Let a man keep the unwritten law, Emerson had said, if he really desires to fulfill his duty to his neighbor. It was, however, a truth taught by Mr. Herbert Spencer that most effectually withered the rhetorical foliage of this particular argument. When he wrote "progress is difference," he wrote the doom of many pretentious state undertakings, whether systems of religion, education, trade, poor relief, insurance, or any other member of the same unprosperous family. In those three simple words, a revolution, mental and material, lay enfolded; and it would be hard, I suspect, to place by their side any other three words in our language that have ever been so charged with deadly force, as regards the human institutions into the midst of which they have been flung. Those three words always seem to me a very fine example of the dynamite which it is worthwhile carrying in your coat pocket and chucking about in the midst of society. Then there were the state-morality people, and they were nearly as flowery in their language as the unity people. The state was father, mother, or goodness knows what, controlling with its superior wisdom the rash impulses of the children. It was replied that the state was not father or mother, but it was only one rash set of the children—and perhaps not the best set—controlling for their own purposes another set of the children; that there was nothing very moral in controlling other people—the worst rulers had always been glad to perform that office for others; that what was moral was self-control; and that there was no possibility of the compelled man becoming a moral man, for he was reduced to the position of a person with his hands tied, from whom had been taken the power of choosing the good thing for its own sake. In fine, that as you extended the area of compulsion, the practice ground of morality shrank in proportion, until at last morality itself, or the free choice of good and the free rejection of evil, would become as extinct as the iguanodon. Then there were the laissez-faire objectors. They cried, half in contempt and half in exultation, "Poor laissez-faire is dead." It seemed enough to reply, *Si quaeris rationem, circumspice;* to ask what profitable material thing, what invention, what addition to the comforts and refinements of the race, what work of art, what scientific discovery, what moral idea, what destructive criticism, was a product of the governments and not of the individual; what improvement in their own work had not been forced on the governments from outside, or borrowed from some example given by free enterprise; and what would be the prospects of the race, if the governments could no longer count upon the services of those brains which had been formed in a free world, but must wholly depend upon the brains formed in the petty and contracted world of their own official departments? Then the deadly waste of compulsion was insisted on. Which was most profitable, it was asked, to employ one-half of the race in perpetually tying the hands of the other half, or in leaving all hands free; which was the most hopeful process, to leave every man uninterfered with to do his own work with his whole heart and soul, or to make each man the supervisor of his neighbor's work? Next came the shortcut men, the hard-headed, practical men, as they rather ostentatiously called themselves, who were for doing what was wanted with the easiest instrument that came to hand. In reply to their appeal to dismiss all discussion as regards theory, and to push on with the work itself, it was pointed out that what educated men and developed strong qualities of character was the doing of a thing rather than the thing done, that the doing of a thing by free men and women, without compulsion, without officialism, with much experiment and comparison of method, so that the better methods gradually disclosed themselves out of the resulting failure and success, with strong interest evoked on all sides, and with friendly cooperation and friendly ties created between those directly and those indirectly concerned, formed the true education, intellectually and morally, of the individuals of a nation. Apart from this practical education, all progress would be partial, lopsided, disappointing, and even dangerous; that the very ease with which official power created huge systems was an evil and not an advantage, since they were created with insufficient discussion, experience and knowledge, as well as insufficient effort on the part of the individual, and each huge system so created not only involved terrible financial burdens but stood in the way of the future introduction of better systems. About this stage, however, of the argument, the good Giant Power's temper began to grow a little short. "Why should he argue any more," he asked with much logic, "when the fact was patent to all that he was Giant Power?" and in his impatience with the philosophers and their questions he dashed his great club on the ground. Unfortunately the club landed on his favorite great toe which was just recovering from one of those attacks of gout to which well-fed giants are subject, and that exhausted the last remnant of his patience. Then I am sorry to say he took to using strong language, crying out in his pain: "What the ——— does it all signify? What do you want reasons for? I am Giant Power, and that's reason enough. I choose, and you must."

Then it was, as we may fondly imagine, that took place the clarifying of certain minds. Then it was that all verbiage and rhetoric were thrown on one side, and it was plainly said: "We, the majority, intend to govern. We care nothing for abstract reasoning or imaginary human rights. We are the strongest, and in virtue of that fact we will govern just as we choose. There shall be no law except our will," then it was that the gathering mental reaction against governments came to a head, and the dynamiter with his creed of unorganized force against organized force was born. Then it was, while the great mass of the modern world waked and slept, toiled and feasted, in their unconsciousness, that the pains of travail began, and a new thing, hideous and terrible, came to the birth. From that hour, and thenceforth, the governments of Europe were face to face with a rival who should dispute with them their rights and their powers. The new claimant for the government of men was not impeded by any diffidence or modesty of temperament. He saw no reason why he should not rule as well as any other Giant Power. With a hideous leer upon his face, he turned to the governments and said:

> You govern, you do what you choose, you take possession of body and mind, you wring from this subject human material all that you imagine that you want for your own purposes, you send men hither and thither to be shot for the quarrels that it amuses you to make, you burden them with all the restrictions and vexations that in your belief can add some little thing to your own security or convenience or dignity, and you do it just because you are strong enough to do it—because you have discovered and perfected the trick of the majority. You say that you have a majority on your side—that this majority is strong enough to inflict its will upon all others. Let it be so; I make no pretense to possess a majority; a minority is good enough for me—a small minority of desperate reckless men, believing in their ideas, and not caring much for their lives. But such as we are, we, too, have power. It is not like your power, disguised under innumerable forms and ceremonies; it is just what it professes to be—power, brutal, naked, and not ashamed. Come now, let us reason for a moment together. Where, after all, is the difference between us? We both of us are believers in power; we both of us desire to fashion the world to our own liking by means of power. The only difference between us is in the form of the power which we each

make use of. Your power depends upon clever electioneering devices, upon tricks of oratory, upon organized wealth and numbers; mine is the power that can be carried in the pocket of any ragged coat, if the owner of the ragged coat is sufficiently endowed with courage and ideas. We are both seeking to govern. Why, then, do you turn your faces from me, flout me, and disown me? I am your brother, younger, it is true, than you, a little down in the world and disreputable perhaps, but for all that, child of the same family, equal in rank, and claiming by the same title deeds as yourselves. True, I am not magnificently equipped as you are; I have no court as you have, no army, no public institutions, no national treasury, no titles, no uniforms resplendent with decorations; I have only a few fanatical followers; and yet, perhaps, as regards the true test of power, I can command the fears of men and possess myself of their obedience quite as effectually as you can. Let us greet each other and shake hands, even if we are opposed. Believe me, though you shrink from recognizing me, I am in very deed your own brother, your coequal, flesh of your flesh, and spirit of your spirit. Henceforth from today we divide the government of the world between us. You are the force of the majority; and I am the force of the minority.

On some such wise, morally speaking, was the birth of the dynamiter. We need not inquire how many of the party had studied Herbert Spencer, had found a corner for *On Liberty* in their bookshelves, had made extracts from Emerson in their notebook, or were penetrated either by the subtleties of Proudhon or the passion of Bakunin. It was sufficient that the philosophers had scattered their devil's seed, and the wind had carried it, as it listed, to the highways and byways of the world. A disintegrating influence was in the air, and the state superstition—if I may speak so irreverently of what most of my friends so industriously cultivate—was powerless to resist it. A search had been made for the foundations on which the state power and its dominion over the faculties of men rested, and unless it were the bare material fact that a majority of three men were stronger, more capable of imposing their will, than a minority of two men, no foundations were forthcoming. But the moment that this truth—that no moral foundations for unlimited and undefined power could by any intellectual ingenuity be discovered anywhere—that if the world rested upon the elephant, and the elephant upon the tortoise, still the tortoise rested only in space—the moment that this truth was grasped in all its significance by the quick perceptions of the nineteenth century, the moment that all rhetorical sophistries were swept aside, and it was seen that, morally speaking, three men had no better right to govern two men than two men to govern three, then at once it became open to any revolutionary section of the minority, who considered that war was to be met by war, and were not impeded by any moral scruples as regards the use of means, to equalize or reverse the conditions of power by finding some new agent which had "governing force" in it. This new agent was supplied by dynamite, and from that day it has become war—war between those who govern openly by majorities and those who govern secretly by dynamite. I am content to undertake the defense neither of the one nor of the other.

As regards the material genesis of the dynamiter, few people in this country—where we are only at the beginning of bureaucracy—realize what the working of the great official machines has been—the pedantry, the cruelty, the maddening influence. Take a few stray examples from France that occur to me as I write, not collected with any care, but mere samples drawn from the bulk. Do you remember the terrorism that existed a good many years ago in a well-known provincial town where some men personated officials, and a number of women—*not daring to protest*—fell into their hands? Have you ever read Guyon's account of the Police of Morals? Heaven save the mark! Or to pass to much less serious examples, do you remember the graphic account given in the *Times,* perhaps three years ago, by a lady who, recovering from an infectious disease, was sent to a special hospital in Paris—the filth, the discomfort, the no responsibility, the no management? There would be a long chapter to write about the state hospitals of Europe; let us hope someday, for the good of the world, it may be written by one who has not learned to look at these things with official eyes. I will give only one experience. A well-known English surgeon visited a famous hospital in ——— and found a certain operation being performed upon a woman. It is a very painful operation, especially when certain precautions are not observed, and, according to some English surgical ideas, it is an obsolete operation, which ought never to be performed. In this case it was being performed without the precautions that would have rendered it less painful, and without chloroform. Why? Simply because there was a classification of operations, and this operation was not considered of sufficient dignity to be placed amongst those for which chloroform was used. The wretched woman was shrieking and imploring help from all the saints, with the effect upon the Englishman that, *unused as he was to pain in his own hospital,* he could with difficulty remain through the operation. Take the case of the religious sisters driven out of the French hospitals, as was distinctly stated, against the wishes of the medical staff, for the mere sake of a bit of odium antitheologicum, and the patients handed over to an altogether inferior set of nurses. Take the exemption of officials from ordinary jurisdiction as regards their official acts.* Take the theatrical bullying of the accused in court, or the extortions of confessions in the prison cell, or the power of the magistrate to examine the accused "personally, and in private," and to send him back "into solitary confinement for an indefinite number of times," recalling him for examination when he chooses; ". . . there are said to be cases of prisoners wrongfully confessing to a charge in order to put an end of the worrying torture of private examination" (*Paris Law Courts*, pp. 4, 5). Take the system of ubiquitous official spying, constantly on the edge, as it is believed, of provocation to crime; or take again the case that lately excited such unfavorable comment in England—the two Englishmen

---

* Professor Dicey writes (*The Law of the Constitution*, p. 184): "If we take France as the type of a continental state, we may assert with substantial accuracy that officials—under which word should be included all persons employed in the service of the state—are, in their official capacity, protected from the ordinary law of the land, and subject in many respects only to official law administered by official bodies." Speaking of our own country (p. 183), he writes: "With us every official, from a prime minister down to a constable or a collector of taxes, is under the same responsibility for every act done without legal justification as any other citizen." So in *The Paris Law Courts* (p. 2), Mr. Moriarty writes: "In France, these actions (to which a government official is a party) are tried in special administrative courts, and by special administrative rules," and he adds later (p. 7) "that these courts have a strong official bias, and actions laid by private individuals against state officials rarely succeed."

wrongly accused of picking pockets on a race course, arrested, and not allowed to communicate with friends; or the account that was published by an Englishman in the *Pall Mall Gazette* of his arrest and imprisonment in Paris, with the little incident, that reads as if taken from the last century, of the rats and mice that shared his cell— an incident that one is the more inclined to believe from the facts which were reported in our English papers, and which, if true, reflect very unfavorably upon prison management, that one of the first outbreaks of cholera in the suburbs of Paris in the recent attack took place in one of the prisons; and again that typhus broke out last year, not in one, but in several Paris prisons (*Westminster Gazette*, April 8, 1893).

No fact, however, that I know tends to show more vividly the official contempt which grows up in bureaucratic countries for the accused, and the official cynicism and arrogance with which the law is administered, than certain facts recorded in the book from which I have already quoted, *The Paris Law Courts*. This book, which has been translated by Mr. Moriarty, is written by different writers who each take a special part of the subject. Speaking of civil cases, the writer says:

> There is hardly a lawsuit in Paris, even among those classed as summary proceedings, which does not last a year. For ordinary cases a much longer space of time must be allowed. . . . I know of few which have not lasted for two or three years. In the first chamber of the tribunal one must no longer count by years but by lusters [p. 17].

But, grave as is the condemnation of the civil side of the system contained in these words, a far darker shadow rests upon the administration of the criminal side. There are three grades of criminal courts: (1) The court of simple police, where infractions of police regulations (legal peccadilloes) are tried, or, if tried is an inappropriate word, are at all events punished. The fines range from one franc to fifteen francs (or five days' imprisonment). The defendants often do not appear. "In the majority of cases the delinquents prefer to suffer judgment by default," which is hardly to be wondered at, since, "as a rule, the court of simple police decides cases summarily without listening to any defense" (see pp. 140 et seq.), dispatching them as if "by electricity." There is but one police court (i.e., court of the lowest grade) for the twenty arrondissements of Paris. About two-hundred cases are taken at each sitting, which lasts "from an hour and a half to three hours. This only gives about one minute per each case" (p. 141). This lightninglike or electrical dispatch of business is secured by putting the delinquents into batches, according to the nature of their offense. (2) Next come the correctional courts, in which misdemeanors are tried. In these courts, again, the same vicious principle exists. In one of these courts we are told that the president pushed through seventy-four cases in two and a half hours (p. 152). In another of these courts, "between noon and five o'clock sentence is passed upon a herd of 108 wretches arrested by the police, some in one place, some in another. . . . They are brought into the dock in batches of ten, taken at random" (p. 164).

It is not, however, simply in criminal matters, it is almost everywhere that you find examples of official arrogance, cruelty, and incapacity, not arising, as I hold, from bad intention, but from the corrupting effect of power which is uncontrolled—all power, remember, being necessarily uncontrolled where the area of officialism is large. It is plain that, just as this area of official management is extended, so all effective control on the part of a busy public must necessarily grow weaker and weaker. I call to mind that many years ago the *Daily News* published (from an occasional correspondent, I think—not its own) an account of how stray dogs in Paris were destroyed after being captured. They were simply thrust on to great hooks, which pierced the throat, and were so left to die as they could. The thing impressed me a good deal as a young man, and, having to go to Paris, I saw a gentleman who was interested in the matter, who told me, rather despondingly, that they had not succeeded as yet in getting it changed, and spoke but doubtfully of their being able to do so.* There, in miniature, is the exact picture of the bureaucratic state. In this instance, dogs; in the next instance, men and women. Any cruelty, any stupidity, any incapacity, may go on indefinitely, just because there is no living, acting public opinion to scorch the thing up into tinder. There can't be such public opin-

---

* I cannot, of course, say that the matter was reported correctly and without any exaggeration. The *Daily News'* account seemed to me, at the time, simply and circumstantially given. I mentioned the affair to a French minister, who was good enough to promise to inquire into it. The latest exploit of the authorities, in tying a number of dogs to posts in order to rehearse upon them the effect of such bombs as are used by the dynamiters, is another example of the stupid cruelty which we have gradually learned to expect from those who believe that they civilize— well, if not themselves, at all events the public—by their methods of thinking and acting for it.

ion where people are unceasingly administered. There may be revolutionary forces smoldering at the bottom, but the living, healthful opinion of every day, acknowledging its responsibility for what is officially done, cannot exist among the timorous, compressed self-distrustful human particles who live under the heel of the officials. Now take other matters, none of them, perhaps, in itself inflicting a grievous burden, but still expressing significantly enough the oppressive and vexatious whole of which they form a part.* Take the ludicrous prohibition about sea water. An unfortunate seaside resident may not go and dip his bucket into great Father Ocean and carry off water for his bath, as such liberty might interfere with the revenue derived from salt. I would commend this fact to any innocent-minded land nationalizer as a trifling but significant example of the spirit in which governments deal with so-called national property. So, too, if I am rightly informed, no ordinary person is allowed to fish in the sea within the three-mile limit—that ordinary right of the citizen being turned into a bit of state property and reserved for special classes of persons; again I bespeak the attention of the innocent-minded land nationalizer. So also notice the petty tyranny which

---

* The cases which I have quoted I think are accurately given; but it is very easy to miss changes in the laws or in the administration of another country. One has also to bear in mind that, in the rapid provision of daily news, facts cannot be always quite correctly reported by foreign correspondents, and wrong impressions once given are not always subsequently corrected. Being away from home, and not in possession of my notes and papers, I have been obliged to trust to memory, and I have not given the dates of the cases referred to; but I could do this later in almost all, if not all, cases to any person desiring it.

forbids a child being called by a new name, requiring, I believe, that the name given should be one that has been already in use; or the stringent rules affecting joint-stock companies, rules which, in the opinion of the *Economist*, would in this country prevent the best men from acting as directors or the vexatious formalities that have surrounded public meetings; or the perfectly absurd extension of the law of libel—already most absurdly exaggerated with us—under which, for example, a Paris firm that retailed a newspaper published in America was recently held responsible for the contents; or the liberty of the press itself, which is occasionally conceded in moments of indulgence, like sweetmeats to a child, then snatched away again by the rude hand of the state. Referring to this matter, Professor A. Dicey writes (*The Law of the Constitution*, p. 256): "To sum the whole matter up, the censorship (of the press) though constantly abolished has been constantly revived in France, because the exertion of discretionary powers by the government has been and still is in harmony with French laws and institutions." The recent exaggerated and unreasoning legislation passed in a panic after the bomb explosion in the Chamber is a striking example of this tendency to fall back into the arms of government and to renounce vital rights whenever there is public alarm. In another passage Professor Dicey says, that notwithstanding recent legislation in favor of a free press, the notion (in France) seems still to exist that press offenses "require in some sort exceptional treatment." To continue the list of petty vexations—the suppression (before trial in court) of an ingenious person who discovered a way of cleaning and renovating playing cards, his machinery being seized, and his trade stopped, because he might have diminished the profits arising from the card tax; or the harassing proceedings lately instituted against aliens; or the law under which persons who have been detected committing adultery (*in flagrante delicto*) may be hauled off by the police before the correctional court; or the disregard of truth in official matters, and the suppression of inconvenient facts, such as those relating to the existence of cholera: or the quite incredible official persecution, resembling a legend imported from Timbuctoo, of a most eminent man like Leroy Beaulieu—it was fully described in the *Times* and the facts are given in a special pamphlet—because the government was afraid of his entrance into the Chamber; or the panic-begotten law that was lately passed, making it a crime to disturb confidence in the government savings banks; or the still worse mixture of timidity as regards free speech and blind belief in punishment which led— on the charge of defaming the army—to the imprisonment of a man for declaring that the army was a school of licentiousness and most corrupting to young men in its influence; and the last piece of quite unnecessary intolerance which compels those preparing for the priesthood (I think it was also reported as regards those who had actually become priests) not simply to serve in the ambulance corps but in the ranks. Well, this is but a part, a small part, of the black list which might be drawn up against official France, as indeed it might be drawn up against official Germany, Austria, Italy and Spain—I need not perhaps include Russia or Turkey. I could myself extend it to many pages, and those who know France really well could extend it so as to fill a volume. Is there any occasion for wonder at such a state of things? It will always be so, say we liberty folks, wherever the spirit of administration, the spirit of officialism, takes strong root in a country. Like the rest of us, the French people have their faults—their grave faults—but left to themselves, freed from this vexing and maddening rule of the officials, they would be, as I believe, a gay, friendly, bright-tempered people, charming Europe with their quick perceptions, their ingenuity and resource, their strong family instincts, their love of the bright side of things. But officialism is destroying that pleasant side of their character. It has entered like iron into their souls. It has developed envy and jealousy and fear and hatred of each other, while it makes of their country the dangerous explosive spot in Europe, because passions are so strong, and self-control—the child of liberty—is so slight.

What I have said of France might be said, with the necessary difference, of other European countries—each country being vexed and harassed by its bureaucrats, and each being affected in its own way according to the genius of the people. But in each country the general effect is the same. Almost every European government is a legalized manufactory of dynamiters. Vexation piled upon vexation, restriction upon restriction, burden upon burden, the dynamiter is slowly hammered out everywhere on the official anvil. The more patient submit, but the stronger and more rebellious characters are maddened, and any weapon is considered right, as the weapon of the weaker against the stronger. It matters little that a great deal of what is done is done in the alleged interest

of the people themselves. I myself have seen in England
a clever industrious workman driven to the edge of revolt
by the persecuting character of our education laws, and
changed from a man ready to fight within the law to one
who was almost ready to fight outside it. There are men,
not bad parents, who have passed from town to town to
avoid this persecution; these are families who have
broken up their homes and lived as they could, in their
detestation of it. It is time that we laid aside this odious
weapon of compulsion. More and more bitter will be the
fruit of it as the years go on. Compulsion everywhere is a
brutalizing weapon. The English, with their faults—and
there are plenty of them—are, I think, the most tender-
hearted people anywhere on the earth. That tender-
heartedness, both to each other and to animals, arises, as
I believe, mainly from their past free life. They have
never as yet been officialized; they have never as yet been
turned into government material. Recently we have been
reversing our traditions; but it is not yet too late to step
back from the mire and the slough which lie in front of
us. As yet we have only soiled our ankles, where other
nations have waded deep. We inherit splendid traditions
of voluntaryism, which hardly any other nation has inherited; and it is to voluntaryism, the inspiring genius of
the English character, that we must look in the future, as
we did in the past, for escape from all difficulties. If we
cannot by reason, by influence, by example, by strenuous
effort, and by personal sacrifice, mend the bad places of
civilization, we certainly cannot do it by force. Force is
the very weakest and most treacherous of all human im-
plements. The history of force is the history of the con-

tinuous crumbling away of every institution that has rested upon it. The irony of history has never faltered for a single generation. It is no mere paradox to say that to be strong with the world's strength is to be weak. Whatever on the one day looked to the eyes of men as if it could defy all attack, towering above subject things in its magnificence, and resting on what seemed its immovable and almost eternal foundations of force, on the morrow has gone to pieces as if it had been wholly built of rubble and clay. It would seem as if every institution possessed of overweening power—material power—has been pitilessly selected for destruction. The jealous gods have hated it, and ever since the days of Horace have aimed their lightnings at its head. There has been a curse pronounced against force, as force, which knows no exceptions in any country, in any time, or as regards any cause. The only thing that lasts through it all, that endures while the other perishes, is moral force—the word, the conviction, which attempts to bind no hands but acts only on the soul. As Emerson said—I don't remember his exact phrase—there is only one victory worth winning, the victory of principle, the victory over souls. To that belief we have to return, if we have ever held it; or to ascend to it, if it has never yet been counted amongst our intellectual possessions; and blessed, thrice blessed, will be the dynamiter, with all his cruelty and with all his insanity, if in his distorted features we learn to see as in a mirror a reflection of our own selves, and thus are compelled to recognize the true character of the odious force weapons with which we have warred against each other. If we cannot learn, if the only effect upon us of the presence of the dynamiter in our midst is to make us multiply punishments, invent restrictions, increase the number of our official spies, forbid public meetings, interfere with the press, put up gratings—as in one country they propose to do—in our House of Commons, scrutinize visitors under official microscopes, request them, as at Vienna, and I think now at Paris also, to be good enough to leave their greatcoats in the vestibules—if we are, in a word, to trust to machinery, to harden our hearts, and simply to meet force with force, always irritating, always clumsy, and in the end fruitless, then I venture to prophesy that there lies before us a bitter and an evil time. We may be quite sure that force users will be force begetters. The passions of men will rise higher and higher; and the authorized and unauthorized governments—the government of the majority and of written laws, the government of the minority and of dynamite—will enter upon their desperate struggle, of which no living man can read the end. In one way and only one way can the dynamiter be permanently disarmed—by abandoning in almost all directions our force machinery, and accustoming the people to believe in the blessed weapons of reason, persuasion, and voluntary service. We have morally made the dynamiter; we must now morally unmake him.

ESSAY SIX

SALVATION BY FORCE

*This essay and the next, "Lost in the Region of Phrases," were
the last two articles in the published debate between
Herbert and J. A. Hobson which took place in the pages of* The
Humanitarian: A Monthly Review of Sociological Science.
*Herbert's "A Voluntaryist Appeal" (May 1898) called forth
Hobson's critique, "Rich Man's Anarchism" (June 1898). Herbert
replied in this essay (October 1898) and in "Lost in
the Region of Phrases" (May 1899).*

My criticism upon Mr. Hobson's recent paper in defense of socialism must be that he takes much trouble to prove that which is not in dispute, that which almost all of us, I presume, are ready to admit, and which, when admitted, can be of no use as regards the defense of the socialist position, while he altogether passes by the real point at issue—the crux of the whole question— by which socialism has to stand or fall.

Now let us get to business and see how the matter stands. Mr. Hobson justifies socialism—or the compulsory organization of all human beings—by the fact of our social interdependence. In many forms of words he returns again and again to the same point of view. Psychology brings, he tells us, "a cloud of witnesses to prove the direct organic interaction of mind upon mind"; society is "an organic system of the relations between individuals"; "the familiar experience of everyone exhibits thoughts, emotions, character as elaborate social prod-

ucts"; "minds breathe a common atmosphere, and habitu-
ally influence one another by constant interferences."
We are not, as he says, to look at "numbers," but rather
at "the action of the social will." Without examining
critically these metaphors, that he employs, we need not
so far have any quarrel. We are all agreed probably that
we are subject to innumerable influences, that we all act
and react upon each other in the great social whole, that
the environment constantly affects and modifies the individual. Marvelous indeed is the great subtle web of relations in which we are all bound together—man and
nature, man and man, body and mind, nation and nation, each forever interacting on the other. But what in
the name of good logic and plain common sense have
this universal interaction and interdependence to do with
the fundamental dogmas of socialism? Socialism rests
upon the assumed right of some men to constrain other
men. It naturally exhibits several varieties; but all the
thoroughgoing forms of it are so far alike that they depend upon universal compulsory organization. It must be
always borne in mind that socialism differs from other
systems in this essential, that it recognizes, and, so to
speak, sanctifies compulsion as a universally true and
proper method; and the compulsion, which it sanctifies,
must for practical reasons, as well as for the assumed
virtues in compulsion itself, be left undefined and unlimited in extent. It represents the belief that prosperity,
happiness, and morality are to be conferred upon the
world by force—the force of some men applied to other
men.

That may be, or may not be. Force may be the greatest and most far-reaching thing in the world; or it may be the weakest and most contemptible. But before we discuss the strength or the weakness of force as a reforming instrument, before we decide what force can or cannot do on our behalf, we have to consider, first of all, if we have a moral right to employ force. The socialist assumes—he is obliged to assume for the sake of his system—that men have a right to use force for any purpose and to any extent that he desires, in order that he may be enabled to restrain men from using their faculties for their own individual advantage. If you ask which men are to be the depositories of force, he can only answer, the biggest number of men; or if not the biggest number, then such a number of men as by efficient organization can succeed in obtaining possession of power and in retaining it.

I need not spend time in proving this point. Every thoroughgoing socialist, who is willing to deal frankly in the matter, will admit that socialism rests on the cornerstone of force. Private property is by force to be turned into common property; and when that has taken place, no individual will be allowed to acquire private property or to employ it for his own purposes, except to a very small extent, and under strict regulations. John Smith could not be allowed to work for Richard Parker, as this would be a return to the system of free labor, and must necessarily endanger the system of state labor. Richard Parker could not be allowed to open a shop and sell his wares to John Smith, for this would be to allow free enterprise and the individual acquisition of wealth once more to reappear in the world. The whole meaning of socialism is force, applied in restraint of faculties. For good or for evil, it is the attempt to place all men and all human affairs under a compulsory system; and to allow no free system to exist by the side of its own system, which would be necessarily endangered by such rivalry. It differs from every free system in this essential particular: that under liberty, you may give away your own liberty, if you think good, and be socialist, or anything else you like; under socialism, you must be socialist, and may not make a place for yourself in any free system.

Now we can all see that any writer, with the literary abilities and instincts possessed by Mr. Hobson, who under these circumstances proposes to plead the cause of socialism, finds himself involved in considerable difficulties. He has to apologize for and to defend a system of universal force, and he instinctively dislikes the task. Of course he might openly take force under his protection, declare that it was the reformer's true weapon, and glorify the whole business of compelling all dissidents. But the systematic glorification of force is an awkward piece of work; for as it is generally conceded for good and for evil that we are all to be free and equal in forming our opinions, so as a necessary consequence it must be conceded that we are to be free and equal as regards the methods of advancing our opinions. A method that is good for one must be good for all; and in accepting the method, we must expect to find that, here too as in every other human matter, considerable differences will exist as regards the application of the method. *Tot homines, tot sententiae.* Tastes must vary. Some men will prefer the confused mixture of force and liberty that usually prevails under the system of party government; some men will prefer the stronger article of compulsory social-ism; some men will prefer military despotism; and some the force of the anarchist, who employs dynamite as a social corrective. On what ground can the believers in force quarrel with or even very seriously criticize each other? They are all fellow worshipers in the same tem-ple, and at the shrine of the same principle. Once admit that force is right in itself, and then you cannot pick out any special sect or party, confer special privileges upon them, and declare that they alone, and nobody else, are entitled to use force. That would be a mere arbitrary and fanciful selection, as arbitrary and fanciful as picking out certain opinions, and declaring that these opinions are orthodox, and that all other opinions are heterodox. If force is good in the hands of some men, it is good in the hands of other men; if it is a good instrument to serve some causes, it is good to serve other causes. You can't have a monopoly in the use of so valuable "a resource of civilization." If the socialist with his compulsory system can succeed in justifying his use of force so also can the ordinary politician, or the military despot, or the dyna-miting anarchist, with his newly awakened perceptions that force can be applied in very uncomfortable fashions, without any machinery of government, or policemen, or soldiers. Having once arrived, after much searching of heart, at the belief that we must concede to all men the right to think as they like, and having got rid of the Old World idea that we can authoritatively pronounce some opinions to be good and some to be bad, we must take the further step, and admit that every holder of opinions has an equal right to use the same methods of advancing his opinions. In a word, we must concede equality as regards the method of advancing opinions, just as we have conceded equality as regards the holding of opinions. We must therefore choose between either altogether rejecting force as an instrument for advancing our opinions and our interests, or recognizing equality in the use of method—accepting, so to speak, free trade in force, even if this last alternative is not altogether reassuring as regards the peaceful and friendly relations of men to each other. This difficulty therefore confronts the socialist. If he is resolved to employ a frank and consistent logic, he must admit that force is a good instrument in the hands of all who can possess themselves of it; or employing the defective and halting logic that all his predecessors in power have employed, he must try to persuade us that force is good for him, but not for the rest of his fellow men, and claim, in common with the other worshipers of force, that there exists a mysterious dispensation given from some unknown quarter in his own special favor.

But the literary difficulties of those who plead for the compulsory organization of all men, under the name of socialism, do not end here. I will not touch now upon the difficulties of conceiving that you can organize society upon the principle of dividing every five men in the nation into two groups—a group of three men, who have all rights, and a group of two men, who have no rights, of turning the three men into those who own others, and the two men into those who are owned by others. Apart from the verdict, which reason and morality if fairly

questioned, must pass upon every system which splits
the nation into a crowd that owns, and a crowd that is
owned, into a conquering and a conquered faction, the
socialist, who plainly and frankly invites men to banish
freedom of action from the world, will find himself
opposed by a large number of persons who, as the result
of living in a fairly free country, and who, guided by
their feelings and daily experience, have a strong moral
and intellectual dislike to force. It is only a few persons
as yet amongst us who consciously submit themselves
in this matter to the discipline of first principles; but
there is a large number of persons whose general habit
of thought and whose instinct tell them that force is the
wrong method, and that discussion, persuasion, the light
of reason and the attraction of example, are the right
method. They see that force is at best a clumsy and
brutal argument. They remember the wise saying: "Any
fool can govern with bayonets." They see that those
who use force most freely are as a one-eyed race, with
very limted perceptions, able to perceive dimly the immediate consequences, but not the more remote consequences of what they do. And just as these disbelievers
in force see that those who accustom themselves to the
use of force grow stupid, and not only stupid but brutal,
so they see that those, who are subject to force, also grow
stupid in their own way, indifferent, apathetic, and generally revolutionary in temper. They see that mistakes
made under force systems are apt to persist, that they
are not easy to discover or remedy, when you have dis-
couraged the growth of all systems by their side. They
see that every force system requires a great complicated

machinery, and that this machinery always eludes popular control, and falls under the management of some not
very intelligent or disinterested clique. They see not only
that every act of force requires continual new extensions
of force, but also that force breeds many forms of intrigue
and deception. Even when you have force in your hands,
it is not an easy task to compel a great number of persons to do what they don't want to do—it is much like
the labor of making water flow uphill; and force, therefore, naturally allies itself to trick and to management.
The moral transition is always an easy one.

Those persons who have taken the one shortcut readily
persuade themselves to take the other shortcut. No believer in force truly respects his fellow-men. He always
slightly despises them, even while he serves them. They
tend to become to him mere material for carrying out
his views. His views may be honestly and sincerely held;
they may be excellent in themselves; but when he uses
force on their behalf he commits the capital mistake of
exalting himself and his views into the first place, and
of degrading his fellow-men, with an intelligence and
conscience like and equal to his own, into the second
place. Thus it comes about that the user of force loses
all hold on moral principles; he becomes a law, and a
very defective law, to himself; and thus it comes about
also that politics—which are simply the method of force
—are in every country not only the battlefield of opposed
fighters, but the hotbed of intrigue and corruption. The
career of a politician mainly consists in making one part
of the nation do what it does not want to do, in order
to please and satisfy the other part of the nation. It is

the prolonged sacrifice of the rights of some persons at the bidding and for the satisfaction of other persons. The ruling idea of the politician—stated rather bluntly—is that those who are opposed to him exist for the purpose of being made to serve his ends, if he can get power enough in his hands to force these ends upon them. Is it wonderful then, if trick and intrigue grow rank and fast in the garden of politics; or that amongst the many things which you may find there, you will rarely find flowers that are fragrant, and fruits that are clean and wholesome?

And again, men see another evil, which arises where the use of force is admitted. So long as we remain in the region of discussion and persuasion, so long there is a sure guarantee that the truest view will gradually prevail. The truest view necessarily commands the best arguments, just as it gradually attracts to its side the higher class of minds; and therefore having the best arguments and the best fighters on its side must win in the free open field, sooner or later. But when we abandon the free open field, in which reason and persuasion, the appeal to reason and the appeal to conscience, are the only admitted weapons, and allow force to be recognized as an equally righteous method, then this certainty of ultimate victory for the truest view entirely disappears. Why? Because force enlarges and degrades the issues. It adds inducements of an effective, if of a very coarse kind, in order to win men over to its side. As long as we are only seeking to persuade, we can only offer the fruits of persuasion. We can promise men that they shall be better, happier, more prosperous, by certain changes in their conduct, but we cannot promise that they shall find tomorrow or the next day five shillings or five pounds, magically placed in their pocket, without any effort of their own. But this is exactly the kind of promise that force can make; indeed, not only can make, but must make. From the nature of things, force cannot fight a pure battle, or appeal simply to pure motives. There is nobody amongst us who can become possessed of force, unless he can first of all induce a very large number of persons to fight on his side. To be the possessor of force you must possess a force army; and your force army must be larger than the force army of any of your rivals. How are you to collect together and keep together such a force army? You cannot do it by appeals to reason and conscience, for that is a slow affair, which wins its way by influencing individuals, and these individuals, who are influenced, are influenced by the same appeal in very different degree and fashion. To obtain a force army, capable of defeating another highly organized force army, you must bring in the recruits in shoals and masses, you must bring them in on a given day, at a given spot, you must bring them in in such a state of discipline, that they will all keep step together and follow their leader like one man. But if appeals to reason and conscience, being, as I have said, essentially individualistic in their action, cannot produce disciplined masses on the given spot and at the given moment, force has a store of arguments exactly suited for the purpose. Give me force enough, and I can promise you almost any material prize for which your heart lusts. If you are a poor man, I can promise you three acres and a cow, gratuitous education, state pensions, and state insurance, novels provided at the public expense, and taxes thrown upon your richer fellow citizen; or better still, all private wealth converted at a touch of my wand into public wealth; if you are a rich man, I can promise you bigger armies and fleets, more territory, more glory, and many noble opportunities of making a splash before the eyes of the world; and if you are nervous about the safety of your possessions in these socialistic days, I can turn the nation into an army for your convenience, and submit it to military discipline—an excellent way, as some persons think, of conjuring away, at all events for some twenty-four hours, all socialistic dangers. Give me force enough, and I can offer every kind of glittering ware for every class of customer. In this way, if I am only a skillful buyer of men, I can recruit my force army; and when I have recruited them, I can pay them out of the prize money which I employ them to win.

From certain practical points of view the system is excellent, as the politicians have discovered, only you must not ask from it, what it cannot pretend to offer— any test as regards the moral and intellectual value of conflicting views; or, if does offer you such a test, it can only offer it by the rule of contraries. If we wished to be ingenious, we might perhaps say that the moral and intellectual value of the views, which are backed by force, is generally in inverse proportion to their momentary attractiveness. The more any particular kind of political prize money attracts, the less clean, and sound, and wholesome, and really desirable in itself, it will probably be discovered to be under searching criticism. I do not know if the philosophers will someday be able to extract a more definite moral canon for our guidance as regards the attractions of force, but meanwhile, we may content ourselves with certain homely but useful truths. You cannot possess force, without first recruiting a force army; you cannot recruit a force army, without the free use of prize money; and you cannot offer prize money without putting the prize money in the first place, and the appeal to conscience and reason in the second place, with a very large interval disclosing itself between the two classes of inducements.*

I have dwelt at some length on this question of force, because it is *the test question*, by which socialism has to be tried. Socialism undertakes to save the world from all its sorrows by a greatly extended use of force, a use of force, far exceeding the force which even emperors and despotic governments employ; and what the philosophical and literary defenders of socialism—I do not mean the mere promisers of prize money—have to do is to convince us first of all that force is a right weapon in itself—that we are morally justified in using it against each other; and second, that it is likely—as far as we can judge by past experience—when applied in this new universal fashion, to make men better and happier. Social-

---

* A qualification ought to be made here. Where force has inflicted much suffering on a people, in such cases, as crushing taxation, protection, restriction of faculties, military despotism, etc., the sense of wrong may be quite sufficient *without prize money* to make a nation remove the cause of its suffering, and to undo what force has done. But apart from such cases, the present race of politicians cannot reasonably hope for place and power except by the generous use of prize money. Force armies, like all other fighters, must be paid.

ism intends to found itself upon force; and therefore
we stand upon the threshold, and call upon it, before it
goes any further, to justify force. Does Mr. Hobson do
this? Does he lay any moral foundations for the use of
force? Does he satisfy us that three men may rightly do
whatever they please with the minds, bodies and property
of two men? Does he satisfy us that the three men can
produce any lawful commission for saying to the two
men: "Henceforth your faculties belong to us and not to
you; henceforth you are forbidden to employ those faculties for your own advantage, and in such fashion as you
choose; henceforth they are to be employed for what
we are pleased to call the public good." In another paper,
I hope to follow Mr. Hobson's argument, and see how
far it is suited to remove the hesitations and scruples of
those who believe that every man and woman is the true
owners of his or her own faculties, and that every forcible
annexation of these faculties by others has prevented the
world from discovering the ways of true happiness.

ESSAY SEVEN

LOST IN THE REGION OF PHRASES

This and the previous essay, "Salvation by Force," were the last two articles in the published debate between Herbert and J. A. Hobson which took place in the pages of The Humanitarian: A Monthly Review of Sociological Science. *Herbert's "A Voluntaryist Appeal" (May 1898) called forth Hobson's critique, "Rich Man's Anarchism" (June 1898). Herbert replied in "Salvation by Force" (October 1898) and in this essay (May 1899). This essay especially responds to Hobson's organicism and his attack on metaphysical individualism.*

I owe many apologies both to the editor and to Mr. Hobson for the long delay which has taken place as regards this discussion. I can only hope they may both be willing to forgive me. And now to our business in hand. I tried in my last paper to show that while Mr. Hobson had written with much literary skill an interesting paper about socialism, he had left the great fortress untaken, even unbesieged, which stands in the way of the advance of socialism. He made a delightful excursus into the region of metaphor and literary imagination, but he never troubled himself to convince us that force was a weapon which the larger number are morally justified in using against the smaller number, or that, when used, is likely to produce the happiness which we all desire. But if Mr. Hobson did not raise this all-important question, but passed it by, as skillful leaders sometimes pass by strong positions, which threaten heavy loss for those who attack them, he tried to open out a new road toward his end with no little literary ingenuity. By the way of metaphor and abstract conception he sought to steal our senses from us, inspiring us with the socialistic temperament, and leading us along pleasant and flowery paths toward that new form of Catholic church, in which he invites us to find our rest. Some of his readers probably felt much the same influence gently stealing over them as they have felt in listening to some of the great Jesuit teachers. In both cases the real issues are passed by, and side issues, sentimentally and artistically tricked out, are skillfully put in their place. It is only natural it should be so. Our socialist friends and the Jesuits plead for their own causes in much the same spirit. They both believe absolutely in great external organizations; they each put their own external organization above and before everything else; conscience, judgment, and will are, on a fixed system, bent and bowed before it; and reason and individual judgment, who always demand to stand at the gate with erect head, become to both of them as the voice of the Evil One moving man to his ruin. If I remember rightly, even Luther spoke of reason as "the harlot"— I presume because reason requires that every claim put forward by authority should first pass before its own tribunal.

Now let us examine Mr. Hobson's apology for socialism, and see how far it carries us. I think I am right in describing his paper as an attempt to reduce the individual to nothingness, and on the ruins of the individual to exalt and glorify "the social organism." The individual deserves no thought or consideration at our hands; he is the product of the social entity; all that he is and all that he has are borrowed from the social entity; not only his material possessions, but his very qualities and thoughts—just as a flower, we might say, contributes nothing of its own, but borrows all its beauty and fragrance from the air and the soil on which it feeds. To which little parable—which I freely offer to Mr. Hobson for his acceptance and use—I must, however, attach the individualist's comment—that it is the skillful chemistry of which the flower is master that turns these contributions of a lower order to its own profit; and that it is just on account of this marvelous vital power that the flower is far higher in rank than the elements which it transmutes into color and fragrance.

Now let me ask, is there any solid reality in this view of the social entity, or must we treat it as a mere literary creation? When we oppose the social entity to the individual, are we not tricking ourselves with words; are we not simply opposing some individuals to other individuals? If the individual is molded and formed by the social entity, it can only mean that he is molded and formed by other individuals. If John Smith's thoughts are formed for him, it is as the result of what other John Smiths have spoken or written. If you like to christen all these other John Smiths by the rather fine name of "social entity," there is no great objection, perhaps, provided only you keep the simple truth in view that it is the individuals who act on each other; and (setting aside the action of the forces of nature and the existence of higher beings than man) that in no conceivable way can we think of influence as passing except from individuals to individuals. So also with our material debt to each other. If in an expanding community A.X. grows rich, because, as a doctor, he has more patients to look after, or as a tradesman, because he has more customers to serve, or as a landowner, because he has more persons to whom to sell his land, it is in every such case the result of the actions of some definite individuals affecting other definite individuals. If the individuals who come to reside in a place increase the prosperity of (a) the lawyer, (b) the doctor, (c) the tradesman, and (d) the landowner, so in return do these four persons increase the prosperity of those for whose wants they provide in their different ways. It is the exchange of services and useful commodities by which each benefits the other, and each in turn is benefited. The increase of prosperity simply results from the interaction of the individuals amongst themselves. It seems cruel to break butterflies on logical wheels and to deal harshly with Mr. Hobson's poetical creation, but outside and beyond this action of the individuals there is no place left of any kind for the action of the social entity. Like so many other things of imposing pretensions, it fades into nothingness at the touch of simple analysis. Again, even if Mr. Hobson could make good the existence of his social entity, as distinct from the action of individuals, would he be any nearer the object that he has in view—the investment of the social entity with supreme importance, and the reduction of the individual to insignificance? If the social entity—supposing that such a thing existed apart from the individuals—acts upon the individual, so beyond dispute must the individual in his turn, as regards the work that he does and the thoughts that he thinks, act upon the social entity. What therefore might be claimed for the one must also be claimed for the other. The two factors, being placed in opposition to each other, would then simply cancel each other—would "go out," as schoolboys say about opposed factors in a sum of arithmetic. What then is left of the supremacy of the one, and the insignificance of the other? The truth is that the contrast that it is attempted to draw between the individual and the social entity is a wholly unreal one. You might as usefully contrast pence and pounds. The social entity really means: some individuals; nothing less and nothing more.

And here it may be useful to follow Mr. Hobson a little further in his adventurous attempt to get rid of the individual. Many things have been dared and attempted by philosophers in their day; but the elimination of the individual out of the social system is an undertaking that throws into the shade most other philosophical exploits. Mr. Hobson writes: "The modern man, at any rate, is a highly social product; his thoughts, feelings, the skill with which he works, the tools he employs, all essential to his effective labor, are made by society." Again: "The so-called individual mind is distinctly a social product, made, maintained, and constantly influenced by other minds." "Other minds," I think, must be a slip of the pen, for that is simply to make the plain and matter-of-fact statement that individuals influence each other. Mr. Hobson should have written "influenced by the social entity." Again he writes: ". . . the conception of a society which is not the mere addition of its individual members, but an organic system of the relations between individuals." So, we poor mortals are evidently greater than we know. John Smith, like most of us addicted to the prose of everyday life, has probably looked on himself hitherto as an individual, possessing a distinct separate body and mind of his own, not in any way to be confused with the body and mind of his neighbor Thomas Robinson. At the same time John Smith is quite aware that he shares, in common with Thomas Robinson and his other neighbors, a certain number of thoughts, feelings, and interests; he knows that he agrees with them on some points, while he disagrees with them on other points. But no amount of such agreement has hitherto affected John Smith's conviction that his individuality is one thing, and the individuality of Thomas Robinson is another thing. At last, however, better days are coming for good John Smith. The new knowledge and the new gospel have abolished his old status. Henceforth he is invited to exchange his prose for poetry, and to look upon himself, not as an individual, but as part of the social entity, as a something included in "an organic system of the relations between individuals." It sounds grand, even if it is a little difficult to understand. Let us piously hope that John Smith will not only understand, but will also profit by his newly acquired dignity, if not mentally or morally, at least by finding more bread and cheese in his cupboard.

Then Mr. Hobson illustrates his idea of the individual who is lost in the crowd (I am afraid that this is a very homely presentment of the fact, which Mr. Hobson himself would express by speaking of a man's inclusion in the "organic system of the relations between individuals") by appealing to the state of a nation at war. "Can a national enthusiasm for war," he asks, "be resolved into the desire of individual American citizens to fight

individual Spaniards, or vice versa?" Even a crowd, "the
simplest form of social organism," is something more
than a large-scale copy "of the feelings and conduct of
its constituent parts." Now, how much of this will bear
analysis? Is it not all conceived in the dangerous region of
metaphor and abstraction, and, I must add, of exaggeration? If a crowd, a town, a nation, is not in each case a
collection of individuals—more or less acted upon, it is
true, by certain common feelings, more or less possessing
certain common interests—what can it be? That when
you bring men together for any purpose, either for the
purpose of listening to speeches or for some common
undertaking, such men act upon each other in a very
marked manner, both for good and for evil, sometimes
heightening the good that is in their nature, and sometimes heightening the evil, is what we all daily know
and experience; but I cannot see how this heightening of
emotion can in any way affect the fact that those who
thus influence and are influenced are individuals, each
with his own set of feelings, each with his own separate
body and mind, and each with his own responsibility (to
which Mr. Hobson must very much object) for what he
does with that mind and body. Because John Smith and
Richard Parker are under the influence of the same class
of feelings, or are engaged in seeking the same ends, that
does not in any way get rid of the individuals John Smith
and Richard Parker, or put in their place a new sort of
being made up half of Smith and half of Parker, or—to
state the case of the social entity even more exactly—
made up of some twenty or thirty millions of Smiths and
Parkers. But why should we create this monster, simply

because men under certain states of feeling act powerfully on each other? A man, I presume, still remains a
man, and a woman a woman, even when their feelings
are so heightened by the words and actions of others,
that they are, as a consequence, more ready to die for
each other, or to cut each others' throats—as the case
may be. There at the bottom of it all—whether it is a
crowd shouting for war, a political party rejoicing over
an election victory, a body of schoolboys triumphant
over the victory of their eleven or their eight, a professional body clamoring for some professional interest,
a clerical meeting denouncing some heresy, a socialist
congress rejoicing in the onward march of universal
coercion, a trades unionist body denouncing nonunion-
ists, or a gathering of capitalists drawing tighter the
bonds of their organization—there in every case are the
individuals sharing in some common aim, and therefore
sharing in the same feelings—the John Smiths and the
Thomas Robinsons, exciting both themselves and their
fellows by the old love of strife, or the old craving for
utopia, and borrowing what is both good and bad—
sometimes ugly passions, and sometimes splendid devotion, from each other.

This, then, is the first point to notice—that no literary
phrases about social organisms are potent enough to
evaporate the individual. He is the prime, the indispensa-
ble, the irreducible element in the whole business. The
individual has a far too solid and matter-of-fact existence
to be eliminated by any arts of literary conjuring. Now
take the second point. Is there a resemblance, on the one
side, between the individual and certain social wholes, in

which he is included, and on the other side, between an organism and its component parts? The answer must be: yes. All parts included in wholes have a generic likeness to each other of a certain kind. A brick in a house, a muscle in a body, have each of them relations to their own whole (the house and the body) which may be compared to the relations existing between an individual and the various social bodies in which he is included. But if there is a certain resemblance, there are also striking differences. The life of the muscle exists simply for the sake of the organism. Taken out of the organism it dies, and has no further use. So with a brick. Like the muscle, it does not exist (excluding, perhaps, the case of a certain town in the Midlands on election days in the old times) for its own sake. It has no use or purpose apart from the building in which it is to form part. It is not an end in itself. In these cases the organism is greater than the part; but with the individual it is not so. He is included in many wholes—his school, his college, his club, his profession, his town or county, his church, his political party, his nation; he forms part of many organisms, but he is always greater than them all. They exist for him; not he for them. The child does not exist for his family, the boy does not exist for his school, the undergraduate for his college, the member of a church or club, or trades union, or cooperative society, or joint-stock company, for his church, club, society, trades union, cooperative society, or joint-stock company, the member of a village or town does not exist for his village or town, or the member of a nation for his nation. All these various wholes, without any exception, in which an individual is included—these so-called organisms of which he forms part—exist for the sake of the individual. They exist to do his service; they exist for his profit and use. If they did not minister to his use, if they did not profit him, they would have no plea to exist. The doom of any one of them would be spoken, if it were found to injure, not to benefit, the individual. He, the individual, joins himself to them for the sake of the good they bring him, not in order that he may be used by them, and be lost to himself, as the brick is lost in the house, or the muscle in the organism. The individual is king, and all these other things exist for the service of the king. It is a mere superstition to worship any institution, as an institution, and not to judge it by its effects upon the character and the interests of men. It is here that socialist and Catholic make the same grand mistake. They exalt the organization, which is in truth as mere dust under our feet; they debase the man, for whose sake the organization and all other earthly things exist. They posit *a priori* the claims of the external organization as supreme and transcending all profit and loss account, and they call upon men to sacrifice a large part of their higher nature for the sake of this organization. They both of them sacrifice man, the king, to the mere dead instrument that exists for man's service. But why is a man to be sacrificed to any organization? How can any organization stand in front of, stand higher than, man? Test the matter by mere common sense. Could we go to a man and say: "You will be so much worse off materially, mentally, morally, by joining such and such an association, but for the sake of the asociation itself I entreat you to join it."

Does not every person, who pleads for an association, take pains to show that in some way, materially or morally, the individual will be profited by joining it; and in so speaking he bears evidence to the simple truth that the association—whatever it be, church, nation, or penny club—exists for the individual, and not the individual for the association.

There is another striking example of this tendency to put phrases in the place of realities in Mr. Hobson's paper. We all of us depend, says Mr. Hobson, upon services rendered by and to each other; we are all of us influenced by the thoughts and actions of each other; therefore—so the argument seems to run—we can have no individuality of our own, we can have no private possession of our own faculties (still less, of course, of the property won by faculties); no rights over ourselves; being parts of the social whole, and not in reality separate individuals, we cannot own ourselves, we can only be possessed in common; we can only share in owning all our fellow-men, while at the same time we ourselves are owned by our fellow-men. Humanity, in the socialist view, cannot be divided up into such valueless and insignificant fractions, as individuals; it must be treated in a more dignified manner—wholesale, in the lump.

Now let us put these curious abstractions into more concrete form. My baker and I everyday exchange services. He leaves me so many loaves, and I put into his hand so many bits of money. We are both of us quite content with this arrangement; but because I depend (in part) upon his bread, and he depends (in part) upon my shillings, given in payment, therefore for the sake of this common dependence we are both to be bound up together, whether we wish it or not, in Mr. Hobson's universal compulsory organization. How little, during our simple and innocent transactions, did either of us realize the yoke, which we were silently and unconsciously forging for our own necks and for the necks of the rest of the world. Because quite voluntarily and for our mutual convenience one of us bought, and the other sold, therefore henceforward all our relations are to be regulated by an all-embracing compulsion. That may be literature, but it is not logic, and it is not reason. The syllogism, I presume, would run: We all depend upon the exchange of voluntary and mutually convenient services, arranged according to our own individual likings and requirements; *therefore* we are to be placed, as regards our material wants, under the system of universal compulsion, which has been amiably devised for us by Mr. Hobson's friends in their spare moments of abstract contemplation, and which may not in any way correspond to our own individual likings and requirements. Take, now, the case of the intellectual services which men perform for each other. I read the writings of certain authors and am influenced by them; and perhaps in my own turn try to influence others; therefore, as a penal consequence of this intellectual influence I am to be placed under a universal compulsory system which is to undertake the regulation of my mind, and of all other minds. This syllogism again, I presume, would run: We all influence each other by our words and our writings; *therefore* we are all to be yoked together under a system of intellectual compulsion, chosen for us by others. Literature apart, I think Mr. Hobson will admit that it is a bold transmutation of unlike things unto each other—voluntary service and the free exchange of influence, passing into the universal compulsion of each other, worked by the votes of a majority. If he has not as yet hit upon the alchemist's stone, he has at all events discovered the secret, that lies at the opposite pole, of degrading gold into lead.

In all the annals of reasoning—and they are many and strange—was there ever such a perverse method followed of reaching a conclusion? And to what is it due? It is all due to the fact that the socialist is under the unhappy destiny of having to plead for an impossible creed—a creed founded on Old World reactionary and superstitious ideas, that are only waiting half-alive to be decently buried forever by the race that has suffered so much and so long for them. The socialist, as an individual, is often infinitely better than his creed of power worship. You can't read the papers of Mr. Hobson or of some other socialistic writers without feeling that generous impulses and desires, and in a certain sense large ideas, run through them; but unfortunately all these generous impulses and large ideas turn, like fairy gold, to dust and ashes, because they are wedded to compulsion, which degrades all that it touches. What can be pettier, narrower, more reactionary, more superstitious and irrational, than the worship by the socialist of majority rule—the crowning of every three men, because they are three, and the moral and material effacement of every two men, because they are two; or the building up of a gigantic fabric of unlimited power, with the arbitrary suspension and limitation of the faculties of the individual in every direction? What moral or intellectual redemption can possibly be found for such a system? It would be as narrow and stifling as a prison cell; as full of trick and intrigue as the inner council chamber of the College of the Jesuits; as timorous and despairing as the creed of the ascetics, who pronounced the world to be evil and the cloister to be the only safe place in it; as brutal as the politics of a Napoleon or a Bismarck. Is there any reason, then, to wonder that men, with the literary tact and ability of Mr. Hobson, seek, almost unconsciously to themselves, to cover up the dead bones of their system with metaphor and abstract conception, and to ask us to admire the something of their literary manufacture, which has as little to do with the real thing, as hothouse flowers have to do with the poor decomposing remains that lie inside the coffin on which the flowers are flung. The highest art in the world cannot gild socialism. It is impossible to make beautiful the denial of liberty. To slightly alter a famous saying—socialism is the negation of all personal rights, erected into a system; and literature, even in the hands of a master, is powerless to make us look with anything but scorn on that negation. The bones and the bare skull grin through all the false decorations that you hang about them, making them only more the ghastly, the more skill you expend in trying to adorn them. I would suggest to Mr. Hobson whether it would not have been truer art to have left on one side the plaster and stucco work of literature, and to have simply said: "Our creed is a brutal and stupid one—all compulsion is brutal and stupid—but the world is an evil one, and its evils must be pounded with cudgel and club, just in such fashion as we can most easily get at them."

And here, in conclusion, I am tempted to say a rather unkind thing. Is not our friend the socialist the very one special person in the world who is unfit to preach the doctrine of his social entity? Granting its existence—where is the social entity to be found? Our answer must be that it can only be found in the whole mass of individuals— in the whole nation, with all its many differences, freely allowed to find their own expression; and not in that mock imitation of the nation, a majority worked by the politician's machinery. There is, as I believe, a something which we may rightly call the social entity, but Mr. Hobson and his friends skillfully contrive to turn a blind eye in its direction, to pass it by on one side, and thus conveniently to miss it altogether. They do not see that it is vain to look for it in any faction or part of a nation overriding other factions or parts of a nation; that it is vain to look for it in a handful of men sitting in a council chamber and fondly imagining themselves to be the nation; that it has nothing to do with laws and regulations, and the effacement of the individual by a system of huge and complicated state machinery; but that it can only be found where all bodies and minds are free, and each individual gives his contribution of bodily or mental labor voluntarily, after his own kind and his own fashion. Clearly the social entity must embrace the whole, no part excluded; otherwise the very idea of unity—of organic oneness—at once disappears. Freedom is the only one thing that offers a possibility of such unity, because under freedom no man can place another man in subjection to his views, and because unrestrained difference offers the nearest and truest approach to true unity which this world allows. The unity of unrestrained difference is a far truer unity than the unity of compulsory sameness. Let us take a simple example. Suppose a country, where education is free, in the true sense, free from all possibility of government compulsion and authoritative direction. Then, in every effort and every experiment made, in every joining together for practical purposes of those who are in sympathy with each other, in every formation of cooperating groups, in every discussion of the truer meanings of education, in every meeting called, in every book or letter written, you have the real expression of the social entity. Whatever force of conviction, whatever practical energy there is anywhere in the great mass of individuals, these find their outlet and their own method of working, and represent the social entity for exactly what it is in its reality. The social entity must be represented by free contributions of mental and bodily labor, for only in such a way is it possible for every individual, without exception, to take part in the expression of the common life and work. It cannot be represented where there is an effacement of minorities by majorities, where there is a cooked-up thing, called representation, which simply means the utterly false and artificial merging of thousands of persons into one person, and where one faction imposes its will on another faction, while the great mass of individuals simply look on, and a handful of self-seeking and self-glorifying persons act in their name. What is there of "entity" and what of "social" in such systems? The truth is, that the socialist, unknown to himself, is the most antisocial of all human beings, and, if he had his way, would render all true social action impossible. His creed of universal compulsion and wholesale effacement of the individual is the very essence of antisocialism. The true social life is the sum of all individual differences and energies; and if these component elements are to be suppressed, the resulting whole, the entity, necessarily disappears. Mr. Hobson—will he forgive me?—is the deadliest enemy conceivable to his own creation, his well-beloved social entity, just because he makes war upon the individual. In slaying the unit, he slays the whole, that is compounded from the units. In truth, under his system the individual, who is the living active element of the social entity, and apart from whom the social entity is a mere phrase and nothing more, is not simply to be suppressed, but is sentenced to an even harsher and more ignominious fate. Hitherto, most of the tyrants and autocrats, who have tried the experiment of fashioning the world in their own image, have been content, like the present German emperor, with planting their imperial feet upon the individual, and so suppressing him; but it has been left for Mr. Hobson and his friends to discover a more subtle and deadly way of abolishing him. They have buried him alive in the social entity, and explained him away. Even the modest luxury of a theoretical existence is denied him at their hands. And what "plowing of the sands"; what good literary labor thrown away! For, as we have just seen, the more you suppress the individual, the further the possibility of the social entity, in its true sense, recedes. There is only one result you can get out of the suppression of the individual, and that is the organized dominant faction triumphing over the defeated faction. Every form of socialism only represents the dominant faction—that and nothing more; and if socialists wish to bring names and things into a true correspondence with each other, they should change their name and call themselves the anti-socialists. But that is to ask for much. For they are at present lost in the region of phrases, and have yet to learn the simple truth, that there is no real social life conceivable apart from the free movement of the individual—apart from the free play of the individual will and conscience.

ESSAY EIGHT

MR. SPENCER AND THE GREAT MACHINE

*Delivered as the Herbert Spencer Lecture at Oxford University
on June 7, 1906, this paper was published by Oxford
University Press in 1908 as part of* The Voluntaryist Creed.

I

I began my lecture at Oxford by expressing my sense
of the debt that we owed to Mr. Spencer for his
splendid attempt to show us the great meanings that
underlie all things—the order, the intelligibility, the
coherence, that exist in this world of ours. I confessed
that, on some great points of his philosophy, I differed
from his teaching, parting, so to speak, at right angles
from him; but that difference did not alter my view of
how much he had helped us in the clear bold way in
which he had traced the great principles running through
the like and unlike things of our world; and in which with
so skillful a hand he had grouped the facts round those
principles, that he always followed—might I say—with
the keen instinct of a hound that follows the scent of the
prey in front of him. Time, I thought, might take away
much, and might add much; but the effort to unite all
parts of the great whole, to bind and connect them all

together, would remain as a splendid monument of what one man, treading a path of his own, could achieve.

But today we are only concerned with his social and political teaching, where we may, I think, follow his leading with more reliance, and with but little reserve. I have often laughed and said that, as far as I myself was concerned, he spoiled my political life. I went into the House of Commons, as a young man, believing that we might do much for the people by a bolder and more unsparing use of the powers that belonged to the great lawmaking machine; and great, as it then seemed to me, were those still unexhausted resources of united national action on behalf of the common welfare. It was at that moment that I had the privilege of meeting Mr. Spencer, and the talk which we had—a talk that will always remain very memorable to me—set me busily to work to study his writings. As I read and thought over what he taught, a new window was opened in my mind. I lost my faith in the great machine; I saw that thinking and acting for others had always hindered, not helped, the real progress; that all forms of compulsion deadened the living forces in a nation; that every evil violently stamped out still persisted, almost always in a worse form, when driven out of sight, and festered under the surface. I no longer believed that the handful of us—however well-intentioned we might be—spending our nights in the House, could manufacture the life of a nation, could endow it out of hand with happiness, wisdom and prosperity, and clothe it in all the virtues. I began to see that we were only playing with an imaginary magician's wand; that the ambitious work we were trying to do lay far out of the reach of our hands, far, far, above the small measure of our strength. It was a work that could only be done in one way—not by gifts and doles of public money, not by making that most corrupting and demoralizing of all things, a common purse; not by restraints and compulsions of each other; not by seeking to move in a mass, obedient to the strongest forces of the moment, but by acting through the living energies of the free individuals left free to combine in their own way, in their own groups, finding their own experience, setting before themselves their own hopes and desires, aiming only at such ends as they truly shared in common, and ever as the foundation of it all, respecting deeply and religiously alike their own freedom, and the freedom of all others.

And if it was not in our power—we excellent and worthy people—fighting our nightly battle of words, with our half-light, our patchwork of knowledge, and our party passions, often swayed, in a great measure unconsciously, by our own interests, half autocrats, half puppets, if it was not given to us to create progress, in any true sense of the word, and to present it to the nation, ready-made, fresh from our ever-busy anvil, much in the fashion that kindhearted nurses hand out cake and jam to expectant children; if all this taking of a nation, ready-made, fresh from our ever-busy anvil, bewildered dream, a careless conceit on our part, might it not, on the other hand, be only too easily in our power to mislead and to injure, to hinder and destroy the voluntary self-helping efforts and experiments that were beyond all price, to depress the great qualities, to soften and break down the national fiber, and in the end, as we flung our gifts broadcast, to turn the whole people into two or three reckless quarreling crowds, that had lost all confidence in their own qualities and resources, that were content to remain dependent on what others did for them —ever disappointed, ever discontented, because the natural and healthy field of their own energies had been closed to them, and all that they now had to do was to clamor as loudly as possible for each new thing that their favorite speakers hung in glittering phrases before their eyes? I saw that no guiding, no limiting or moderating principle existed in the competition of politician against politician; but that almost all hearts were filled with the old corrupting desire, that had so long haunted the world for its ceaseless sorrow, to possess that evil mocking gift of power, and to use it in their own imagined interest—without question, without scruple—over their fellow-men.

From that day I gave myself to preaching, in my own small way, the saving doctrine of liberty, of self-ownership and self-guidance, and of resisting that lust for power, which had brought such countless sufferings and misfortunes on all races in the past, and which still, today, turns the men and women of the same country, who should be as friends and close allies, if the word "country" has any meaning, into two hostile armies, ever wastefully, uselessly, and to the destruction of their own happiness and prosperity, striving against each other, always dreading, often hating, those whom the fortunes of war may at any moment make their masters. Was it for this—this bitter, reckless and rather sordid warfare—

I tried to ask, that we were leading this wonderful earth-life; was this the true end, the true fulfillment of all the great qualities and nobler ambitions that belonged to our nature?

Now, whether you judge that I acted rightly or wrongly in thus yielding myself to Mr. Spencer's influence, you will not, I think, quarrel very seriously with me, if I say that between Mr. Spencer's mind and the mind of the politician there lies the deepest of all gulfs; and that there is no region of human thought which is so disorderly, so confused, so lawless, so little under the rule of the great principles, as the region of political thought. It must be so, because that disorder and confusion are the inevitable consequence and penalty of the strife for power. You cannot serve two masters. You cannot devote yourself to the winning of power, and remain faithful to the great principles. The great principles, and the tactics of the political campaign, can never be made one, never be reconciled. In that region of mental and moral disorder, which we call political life, men must shape their thoughts and actions according to the circumstances of the hour, and in obedience to the tyrant necessity of defeating their rivals. When you strive for power, you may form a temporary, fleeting alliance with the great principles, if they happen to serve your purpose of the moment, but the hour soon comes, as the great conflict enters a new phase, when they will not only cease to be serviceable to you, but are likely to prove highly inconvenient and embarrassing. If you really mean to have and to hold power, you must sit lightly in your saddle, and make and remake your principles with the needs of each new day; for you are as much under the necessity of pleasing and attracting, as those who gain their livelihood in the street.

We all know that the course which our politicians of both parties will take, even in the near future, the wisest man cannot foresee. We all know that it will probably be a zigzag course; that it will have "sharp curves," that it may be in self-evident contradiction to its own past; that although there are many honorable and high-minded men in both parties, the interest of the party, as a party, ever tends to be the supreme influence, overriding the scruples of the truer-judging, the wiser and more careful. Why must it be so, as things are today? Because this conflict for power over each other is altogether different in its nature to all other—more or less useful and stimulating—conflicts in which we engage in daily life. As soon as we place unlimited power in the hands of those who govern, the conflict which decides who is to possess the absolute sovereignty over us involves our deepest interests, involves all our rights over ourselves, all our relations to each other, all that we most deeply cherish, all that we have, all that we are in ourselves. It is a conflict of such supreme fateful importance, as we shall presently see in more detail, that once engaged in it we *must* win, whatever the cost; and we can hardly suffer anything, however great or good in itself, to stand between us and victory. In that conflict affecting all the supreme isues of life, neither you nor I, if we are on different sides, can afford to be beaten.

Think carefully what this conflict and what the possession of unlimited power in plainest matter of fact means. If I win, I can deal with you and yours as I please; you are my creature, my subject for experiment, my plastic material, to which I shall give any shape that I please; if you win, you in the same way can deal with me and mine, just as you please; I am your political plaything, "your chattel, your anything." Ought we to wonder that, with so vast a stake flung down on the table, even good men forget and disregard all the restraints of their higher nature, and in the excitement of the great game become utterly unscrupulous? There are grim stories of men who have staked body and soul in the madness of their play; are we after all so much unlike them—we gamesters of the political table—staking all rights, all liberties, and the very ownership of ourselves? And what results, what must result from our consenting to enter into this reckless soul-destroying conflict for power over each other? Will there not necessarily be the ever-present the haunting, the maddening dread of how I shall deal with you if I win; and how you will deal with me if you win? That dread of each other, vague and undefined, yet very real, is perhaps the worst of all the counselors that men can admit to their hearts. A man who fears, no longer guides and controls himself; right and wrong become shadowy and indifferent to him; the grim phantom drives, and he betakes himself to the path—whatever it is—that seems to offer the best chance of safety. We see the same vague dread acting upon the nations. At times you may have an aggressive and ambitious government, planning a world policy for its own aggrandizement, that endangers the peace of all other nations; but in most cases it is the vague dread of what some other

rival nation will do with its power that slowly leads up
to those disastrous and desolating international conflicts.
So it is with our political parties. We live dreading each
other, and become the reckless slaves of that dread, losing
conscience, losing guidance and definite purpose, in our
desperate effort to escape from falling under the subjection of those whose thoughts and beliefs and aims
are all opposed to our own. True it is that the leaders
of a party may have their own higher desires, their own
personal sense of right, but it is a higher desire and sense
of right which they must often with a sigh—or without
a sigh—put away into their pockets, bowing themselves
before the ever-present necessity of winning the conflict
and saving their own party from defeat. The stake is too
great to allow room for scruples, or the more delicate
balancings of what is right and wrong in itself.

Now let us look how that winning of the political battle
has to be done. Winning means securing for our side the
larger crowd; and that can only be done, as we know in
our hearts, though we don't always put it into words, by
clever baiting of the hook which is to catch the fish. It is
of little use throwing the bare hook into the salmon pool;
you must have the colors brightly and artistically blended
—the colors that suit the particular pool, the state of
the water, the state of the weather. Unless you are learned
in the fisherman's art, it is but few fish you will carry
home in your basket. So in the political pool you must
skillfully combine all the glittering attractions that you
have to offer, you must appeal to all the different special
interests, using the well-chosen lure for each. It is true
that there may be exceptional moments with all nations

when the political arts lose much of their importance, when some great matter rises above special interests, and the people also rise above themselves. But that is human nature at its best; and not the human nature as we have to deal with it on most days of the week. It is also true that the best men in every party stoop unwillingly; but, as I have said, they are not their own masters; they are acting under forces which decide for them the course they must follow, and reduce to silence the voice within them. They have gone in for the winning of power, and those who play for that stake must accept the conditions of the game. You can't make resolutions—it is said—with rose water; and you can't play at politics, and at the same time listen to what your soul has to say in the matter. The soul of a high-minded man is one thing; and the great game of politics is another thing. You are now part of a machine with a purpose of its own—not the purpose of serving the fixed and supreme principles—the great game laughs at all things that stand before and above itself, and brushes them scornfully aside, but the purpose of securing victory; and to that purpose all the more scrupulous men must conform, like the weaker brethren, or—as the noblest men do occasionally—stand aside. As our system works, it is the party interests that rule and compel us to do their bidding. It must be so; for without unity in the party there is no victory, and without victory no power to be enjoyed. When once we have taken our place in the great game, all choice as regards ourselves is at an end. We must win; and we must do the things which mean winning, even if those things are not very beautiful in themselves.

And what is it that we have to do? In plain words—
and plainness of thought, directness of speech, is the
only wholesome course—we must buy the larger half of
the nation; and buying the nation means setting up
before all the various groups, of which it is composed,
the supreme object, the idol of their own special interests. We must offer something that makes it worthwhile
for each group to give us their support, and that something must be more than our rivals offer. "Put your own
self-interests in the first place, and see that you get them,"
is the watchword of all politics, though we don't often
express it in those crude and unashamed terms. Political
art has, like many another accomplishment, its own refinements for half veiling the real meanings. If we wish
to do our work in the finer fashion, in the artist's way,
we must use the light and skillful hand; we must mix in
the attractive phrases, appeal to patriotic motives, bor-
row, a little cautiously, such assistance as we can from
the great principles—a slight passing bow that does not
too deeply commit us to their acquaintance as regards
the future—and throw dexterously over it all, as a clever
cook introduces into her dishes her choicest seasoning, a
flavor of noble and disinterested purpose. It is a fine art
of its own, to buy, and at the same time to gild and beautify the buying; to get the voter into the net, and at the
same time to inspire him with the happy consciousness
that, while he is getting what he wants, he is through
it all the devoted patriot, serving the great interests of
his country.

And then also you must study and understand human
nature; you must play, as the skilled musician plays on

his instrument, on all the strings, both the higher and lower, of that nature; you must utilize all ambitions, desires, prejudices, passions and hatreds—lightly touching, as occasion offers, on the higher notes. But in this matter, as in all other matters, underneath the fine words, business remains business; and the business of politics is to get the votes, without which the great prize of power could not by any possibility be won. Votes must be had— the votes of the crowd, both the rich and the poor crowd, whatever may be the price which the market of the day exacts from those who are determined to win.

II

So rolls the ball. We follow the inevitable course that seeking for power forces upon us. Politics, in spite of all better desires and motives, become a matter of traffic and bargaining; and in the rude process of buying, we find ourselves treading not only on the interests, but on the rights of others, and we soon learn to look on it as a quite natural and unavoidable part of the great game. Keener and keener grows the competition, more heart- and brain-absorbing grows the great conflict, and the people and the politicians cannot help mutually corrupting each other. This buying up of the groups is so distinctly recognized nowadays, that lately a *Times* correspondent—whose letters we read with much interest— speaking of a newly formed ministry abroad, wrote, with unconscious cynicism, that it would have to choose between leaning on the extreme right or the extreme left.

What then, you may say, are we to believe; that the

whole body of those concerned with politics—in which class we almost all in our degree are included—are selfish and corrupt, utterly disregarding and despising the just claims of each other? I hope things are not quite so bad as that. Human nature is a mixed thing, and many of us contrive to think in the nobler way and the smaller way at the same time. There is at least one excuse that may be pleaded for us all. What happens here—as happens in so many other cases—is that carelessly and without reflection we place ourselves under an untrue, a demoralizing and wrong system, that fatally blinds and misleads us, lowers and blunts the better part of our nature, and almost compels us, by the force that it exerts, to follow crooked paths and do wrong things. I have not time to illustrate this simple truth of the sacrifice of character to system; but let me take one instance of the injury that results, whenever we lose our own self-guidance under a system, that is wrong in itself, and, as a wrong system so often is apt to be, despotic in its nature.

I think many of us see the existence of this injury as regards character, when we watch that part of fashionable society which makes of organized pleasure-hunting the first occupation—I might almost say the duty—of life. Here also people construct a system which overpowers their individual sense of what is right and useful and fitting; they submit themselves to the tyrannous rule of follies of different kinds, as if they had no judgment, no discriminating sense of their own, and as a consequence become as a mere race of butterflies, losing the higher sense of things, and wasting their lives.

In all such instances, where lies the remedy? I think

both Mr. Spencer and Mr. Mill would have made the same answer—you can only mend matters by individualizing the individual. It is of little use preaching against any hurtful system, until you go to the heart of the matter, until you restore the individual to himself, until you awaken in him his own perceptions, his own judgment of things, his own sense of right, until you allow what Mr. Spencer called his own apparatus of motive—and not an apparatus constructed for him by others—to act freely upon him, an apparatus that tends sooner or later to work to the better things; and so detach him from his crowd, which whirls him along helplessly, wherever it goes, as the stream carries its unresisting bubbles along with it. There lies the great secret of the whole matter. We have as individuals to be above every system in which we take our place, not beneath it, not under its feet, and at its mercy; to use it, and not to be used by it; and that can only be when we cease to be bubbles, cease to leave the direction of ourselves to the crowd—whatever crowd it is, social, religious, or political—in which we so often allow our better selves to be submerged.

It was for this individualizing of the individual that both Mr. Spencer and Mr. Mill pleaded so powerfully; only in the free individual, self-restraining, self-guiding, that they saw, I think, the hope of true permanent good. They saw that nobody yet has ever been saved, in the best sense, or ever will be saved by vast systems of machinery; Mr. Mill, perhaps, especially looking from the moral point of view, and Mr. Spencer contrasting the intellectual and material consequences of the two opposed systems—self-guidance, and guidance by others.

And here, perhaps, I ought to add a few words. While we lay the heaviest share of blame upon the political system that takes possession of us, and leaves little room for self-guidance, are we to lay no direct blame upon ourselves, for being content to take our place in the system, that few, I think, in calm moments of reflection, can fully justify to their own hearts? Let us be completely frank in this great matter. Is the system of giving away power over ourselves, or seeking to possess it over others, in itself right or wrong? If it is wrong, don't let us make excuses for acquiescing in it; don't let us sigh and feebly wring our hands, confessing the faults and dangers, but pleading that we see no other way before us. Where there is a bad way, there is also a good way, if men once resolutely set themselves to find it.

But you may, perhaps, doubt if the system *is* wrong in itself; if it is not merely perverted and turned from its true purpose by our human weaknesses. You may be inclined to plead: "It is true that politicians must suppress a part of their own opinions; it is true that there is a sort of bargaining that goes on among the groups, that in order to gain their own special end, they have to act with other groups—groups which may differ strongly from themselves on some important points; it is true also that the leaders of a party must take all these groups into their calculations and, as our American friends say, placate the interests; but there is not necessarily anything corrupt in such action on the part of either the groups or the politicians, or their leaders, at least so long as we can fairly credit them all with desiring the common good, at the same time as they pursue their own special interests, and doing the best that the situation allows alike for these two ends; even if these ends may occasionally diverge somewhat from each other.

"Of course we admit that men may be easily tempted to overstep the just and true line, may be tempted in the rivalry of parties, in the strife for power, in the desire to seize the glittering prize, to forget for a while the common good, to push it back into the second place, to be overkeen about their own interests; no doubt the possession of power has its dangers, and tempts many men to say and do what we cannot defend; but we must trust to the general better and wiser feeling of the whole people, or of the whole party, to hold in check these aberrations of some of the fighters, and to strike the balance fairly between the two influences. We must remember that all action in common demands some sacrifices; has its disabilities, as well as its great advantages. We cannot act together, unless there is a considerable, sometimes a large, suppression of our own selves. We must accept that bit of necessary discipline; we must be prepared to keep step with the marching (or ought you to say the maneuvering) regiment, if we are to achieve anything by united action, and not to remain as separate sticks, that no bond holds together. All through life the same principle runs. In every club, society, joint-stock undertaking, we submit to guidance; we give up a part of our views and desires to gain the more important object. Yet when we do so, nobody accuses us of sacrificing our own guiding sense, or of being corrupt, or of entering into a hurtful and dangerous traffic."

Yes, I should reply, but in all these voluntary asociations you retain your own free choice; you can enter into them or leave them, as you think right; and that free choice in all these cases is the saving element. But I ought to ask pardon of our friend, the apologist, for interrupting him.

"Even if our political system" (it is our friend who is again speaking) "has its defects—grave defects if you like—still after all, it is the instrument of progress, and we know of no other to take its place. Surely it is more profitable to try to mend its faults than to quarrel with the whole thing, for which we can see no substitute."

That, I think, is a fair representation of the way in which many of us look at political life, a way that perhaps supplies us with some momentary consolation, when our minds are troubled with what we see passing before us; but how far, if we try to see quite clearly, can we accept such reasoning, as giving any real answer to the graver doubts and hesitations? Is it not only a bit of agreeable sticking plaster, laid over the sore place, an opiate-like soothing of troubled consciences, hardly intended seriously to touch the deeper part of the matter? Let us now try to look frankly beneath the surface, and do our best to see what is the true nature of the system in which we so easily acquiesce.

What does representative government mean? It means the rule of the majority and the subjection of the minority; the rule of every three men out of five, and the subjection of every two men. It means that all rights go to the three men, no rights to the two men. The lives and fortunes, the actions, the faculties and property of the two men, in some cases their beliefs and thoughts, so far as these last can be brought within the control of machinery, are all vested in the three men, as long as they can maintain themselves in power. The three men represent the conquering race, and the two men—*vae victis* as of old—the conquered race. As citizens, the two men are decitizenized; they have lost all share for the time in the possession of their country, they have no recognized part in the guidance of its fortunes; as individuals they are deindividualized, and hold all their rights, if rights they have, on sufferance. The ownership of their bodies, and the ownership of their minds and souls—so far as you can transfer by machinery the ownership of mind and soul from the rightful owners to the wrongful owners—no more belongs to them, but belongs to those who hold the position of the conquering race.

Now, that is, I believe, a true and uncolored description of the system, as it is in its nakedness, as it is in its real self, under which we are content to live. It is not an exaggerated description—there is not a touch in the picture with which you can fairly quarrel. It is true that the real logic of the system does not yet prevail. It is true that a certain number of things may for a time modify and restrain the final triumphs of the majority. In some parliamentary countries, the majority tends to be more composite in its character than with us, and therefore tumbles more easily to pieces. On the other hand, with us at least, whatever it may be in some other countries that have parliaments, minorities may rend the air and reach the skies, if they can, with their cries and complaints, and so to a certain extent may raise difficulties—a method of warfare in which all minorities grow more or less skillful by practice—in the path of the majority; with us also there still exists happily a friendlier, more genial spirit between all parts of the people than prevails in other countries. Thanks to the fact that the great serpent of bureaucracy holds us as yet less closely in its folds; thanks to the still lingering traditions of self-help and voluntary work; thanks to the good humor and love of fair play, which is to some extent nursed by our fellowship in the same games that all classes love—games that I think have redeemed some part of the politician's mistakes—the rule of the majority is with us as yet more tempered, less violent and unscrupulous, than it is in some other countries; but give their full weight to all these modifying influences, which *as yet* restrain our system of the conquering and the conquered races from finding its full development—still they do not alter the main, the essential fact, that we are content to live under a system that vests the rights of citizenship, the share in the common country, the ownership of body, faculties, and property, and to some extent, the ownership of mind and soul, of, say, two-fifths of the nation in the hands of the three-fifths. Such is the system in which we think it right and self-respecting to acquiesce—a system which, in the case of every two men out of five, wipes out at a stroke, so far as the duties of citizenship are concerned, and even to a large extent as regards their personal relations, all the higher part of their nature, their judgment, conscience, will—treating them as degraded criminals, who, for some unrecorded offense have deserved to forfeit all the great natural rights, and to lose their true rank as men. They tell us that nowadays men are not punished for their opinions. They succeed in forgetting, I suppose, the case of every two men out five.

Plead then, if you like, on behalf of such a system all the expediencies of the moment, all the conveniences that belong to power, all the pressing things you desire to do through its machinery, plead objects of patriotism, plead objects of philanthropy; yet are you right for the sake of these things, excellent as they may be in themselves, to acquiesce in that which—when stripped bare to its real, its lowest terms, is—the words are not too harsh—the turning of one part of the nation into those who own their slaves, and the other part into the slaves who are owned?

You may say, as a friend of mine says, "I feel neither like a slave owner nor like a slave," but his feelings, however admirable in themselves, do not alter the system, in which he consents to take part, of trying to obtain control over his fellow-men; and, if he fails, in acquiescing in their control over himself. He may never wish or mean to exercise unfairly the power in which he believes, should it fall into his hands; but can he answer for himself in the great crowd, in which he will count for such a minute fractional part, for what they will do, or where they will go?

III

My friend is quite aware, I think, that power is a rather dangerous thing to handle; but he will handle it with good sense, in the spirit of moderation and fairness, he will not suffer himself to let go of the great principles;

he will not cross the boundary line that divides the rightful from the wrongful use. Well, moderation, and fairness,
and good sense are excellent things, not in this matter
alone, but in all matters. And so are the great principles;
that is to say, if you see them in all clearness and are
determined to follow them. But the saving power of the
great principles depends upon how far we loyally and
consistently accept them. They can be of little real help
and guidance to us if we play and trifle with them, accepting them today, and leaving them on one side tomorrow,
making them conform, as occasion arises, to our desires
and ambitions, and then lightly finding excuses for deserting them whenever we find them inconvenient. Let us
once more be quite frank. When we talk of fairness and
moderation and good sense, as constituting our defense
against the abuse of unlimited power, are we not living
in the region of words—using convenient phrases, as
we so often do, to smooth over and justify some course
which we desire to take, but about which in our hearts
we feel uncomfortable misgivings? Let us by all means
cultivate as much fairness and moderation as possible—
they will always be useful—but don't let our trust in
these good things lead us away from the question that,
like the Sphinx's riddle, must be answered under penalties
from which there is no escape: Is unlimited power,
whether with or without good sense and fairness, a right
or wrong thing in itself? Can we in any way make it
square with the great principles? Can we morally justify
the putting of the larger part of our mind and body—in
some cases almost the whole—under the rule of others;
or the subjecting of others in the same way to ourselves?

If you answer that it is a right thing, then see plainly what follows. You are putting the force of the most numerous, or perhaps of the most cunning, who often lead the most numerous—which, disguise and polish the external form of it as much as you like, will always remain true to its own essentially brutal and selfish nature —in the first place, making of it our supreme principle; and if unlimited power—remember it is *unlimited* power; power to do whatever the governing majority thinks right—is a right thing, must you not leave it, whatever may be your own personal views, to those who possess it to decide how they will employ it? You can't dictate to others, in the hour of their victory, as to what they will do or not do; and they can't dictate to you, in the hour of your victory. Unlimited power, as the term expresses, can only be defined and limited by itself; if it were subject to any limiting principle, it would cease to be unlimited, and become something of a different nature.

And remember always—when once you entered into the struggle for the possession of this unlimited power— that you sanctioned its existence, as a lawful prize, for which we may all rightly contend; and if the prize does not fall to you, it will only remain for you to accept the consequences of your consent to take part in the reckless and dangerous competition. By entering into that conflict, by competing for that prize, you sanctioned the ownership of some men by other men; you sanctioned the taking away from some men—say two-fifths of the nation—all the great rights, and the reducing of them to mere ciphers, who have lost power over themselves.

Once you have sanctioned the act of stripping the individual of his own intelligence and will and conscience, and of the self-guidance which depends upon these things, you cannot then turn your back upon yourself, and indignantly point to the mass of unhappy individuals who are now writhing under the stripping process. You should have thought of all this before you consented to put up the ownership of the individual to public auction, before you consented to throw all these rights into the great melting pot. In your desire to have power in your own hands, you threw away all restraints, all safeguards, all limits as regards the using of it; you wanted to be able to do just as you yourself pleased with it, when once you possessed it; and what good reason have you now to complain, when your rivals—or shall I say your conquerors—in their turn do just what they please with it? You entered into the game with all its possible penalties; you made your bed, it only remains for you to lie on it.

Let us follow a little further this rightfulness of unlimited power in which you believe. If it is a right thing in itself, who shall give any clear and certain rule to tell us when and where it ceases to be a right thing? Is any right thing by being pushed a little further, and then a little further, and yet a little further, transformed at some definite point into a wrong thing, unless some new element, that changes its nature, comes into the matter? The question of degree can hardly change right into wrong in any authoritative way, that men with their many varying opinions will agree to accept. We may, and should forever dispute over such movable boundary lines—lines that each man according to his own views and feeling would draw for himself.

If it is right to use unlimited power to take the one-tenth of a man's property, is it also right to take one-half or the whole? If it is not right to take the half, where is the magical undiscoverable point at which right is suddenly converted into wrong? If it is right to restrict a man's faculties (not employed for an act of aggression against his neighbor) in one direction, is it right to restrict them in half a dozen or a dozen different directions? Who shall say? It is a matter of opinion, taste, feeling. Perhaps you answer, we will judge each case on its merits; but then once more you are in the illusory region of words, for, apart from any fixed principle, the merits will be always determined by our varying personal inclinations. It is all slope, ever falling away into slope, with no firm level standing place to be found anywhere.

Nor do I feel quite sure, if we speak the truth, that any of us are much inclined to accept the rule of moderation and good sense in this matter. You and I, who have entered into this great struggle for unlimited power, have made great efforts and sacrifices to obtain it; now that we have won our prize, why should we not reap the full fruits of victory; why should we be sparing and moderate in our use of it? Is not the laborer worthy of his wage; is not the soldier to receive his prize money? If power was worth winning, it must be worth using. If power is a good thing, why should we hold back our hand; why not do all we can with it, and extract from it its full service and usefulness? Our efforts, our sacrifices of time, money and labor, and perhaps of principle—if that is worth counting—were not made for the possession of mere fragmentary pieces of power, but for power to do exactly as we please with our fellow-men. It is rather late in the day, now that we have won the stake, to tell us that we must leave the larger part of it lying on the table; that, having defeated the enemy, we must evacuate his territory, and not even ask for an indemnity to compensate us for our sacrifices. If power, as an instrument, is good in itself, now that we hold it in our hand, why break its point and blunt its edge?

And then what about the great principles, which my friend does not propose exactly to follow, but on which at all events he will be good enough to keep a watchful eye? Where are they? What are they? What great principle remains, when you have sanctioned unlimited power? You can't appeal to any of the great rights—as rights; the rights of self-ownership and self-guidance, the rights of the free exercise of faculties, the rights of thought and conscience, the rights of property, they are no longer the recognized and accepted rules of human actions; they are now reduced to mere expediencies, to which each man will assign such moderate value as he chooses. You are now out in the great wilderness, far away from all landmarks. Around the throne of unlimited power stretches the vast solitude of an empty desert. Nothing can be fixed or authoritative in its presence; by the fact of its existence, by the conditions of its nature, it becomes the one supreme thing, acknowledging— except perhaps occasionally in courtly phrases for soothing purposes—nothing above itself, writing its own ethics, interpreting its own necessities, making of its own safety and continuance the highest law, and contemptuously dismissing all other discrowned rivals from its presence.

Now turn from the discussion of the moral basis of unlimited power to the practical working of our power systems. There is I think one blessed fact that runs through all life—that if a thing is wrong in itself, it won't work. No skill, no ingenuity, no elaborate combinations of machinery, will make it work. No amount of human artifice and contrivance, no alliance with force, no reserves of guns and bayonets, no nation in arms even if almost countless in number, can make it work. So is it with our systems of power. They don't work and they can't work. In no real sense, can you, as the autocrat, govern men; in no real sense, can the people imitate the autocrat and govern each other. The government of men by men is an illusion, an unreality, a mere semblance, that mocks alike the autocrat and the crowd that attempt to imitate him. We think in our amazing insolence that we can deprive our fellow-men of their intelligence, their will, their conscience; we think we can take their soul into our own keeping; but there is no machinery yet discovered by which we can do what seems to us so small and easy a matter. We think that the autocrat governs his slaves, but the autocrat himself is only one slave the more amongst the crowd of other slaves. In the first place he himself is governed by his own vast machinery; helpless he stands—one of the pitiable objects in this world of ours—in the midst of the countless wheels which he can set in motion, but which other forces direct; and then even the wheels have souls of their own, though not perhaps very beautiful ones, and ever likely to go a persistent and obstinate way of their own. But what is of deeper consequence is that his government is silently conditioned by the slaves themselves.

Sunk in their darkness, helpless, inarticulate, they may be; yet for all that they in their turn are slave owners as well as slaves, as always happens wherever you build up these great fabrics of power. While the slaves obey, they also, though they utter no word, in their turn command. If the autocrat disregards that silent voice, disregards the unspoken conditions that they impose upon him, then in its own due time comes the great crash, and his power passes from him, a broken and miserable wreck. You may crush and hold in subjection for a time the external part of men, but you cannot govern and possess their soul. Their soul lies out of your reach, and is in its nature as ungovernable as the wind or the wave. You may trick and deceive it for a time; you may make it the instrument of its own slavery by cleverly arranged systems of conscription, and other governing devices; you may cast it into a deep sleep, but sooner or later it wakes, and rebels, and claims its own inheritance in itself.

In the same way there is no such thing as what is called the self-government of a nation. How can you get self-government by turning one half of a nation into a secondhand copy of a tsar? That, as Mill showed long ago, is not self-government; but government by others. It is true that here, as with the autocrat, a majority can for a season use for its own ends and oppress a minority, can do with it what in its heart it lusts to do, can make it the *corpus vile* of its experiments, can make of it a drawer of water and hewer of wood; but it is only for a short day. Here again that uncompromising thing, the soul, stands in the way, and refuses to be transferred from the rightful to the wrongful owner. The power of the majority wanes, and the power of the minority grows, and the oppressor and the oppressed change places.

But apart from all the deeper reasons that make the subjection of men by men impossible, was there ever such a hopeless, I might say absurd, bit of machinery, only to be compared to a child's attempt to put together a wooden clock out of the chippings left in the wood basket, as the thing which we call a representative system? Invent all the ingenious plans that you like, but by no possibility can you represent a nation for governing purposes. The whole thing is a mere phrase.

Let us see what actually happens. Suppose a nation with 5,000,000 voters—2,000,000 voting on one side, and 3,000,000 on the other. In such a case we start with the astounding, the absurd, the grotesque fact that there is no attempt made to represent the 2,000,000. Even if you had a system of minority representation, it might possibly serve in some small measure to soothe the feelings of the subject race; it would not alter the hard fact of their subjection. But at present the 2,000,000 voters find no place of any kind in our calculations; they are simply swept off the board, not counted. That is the first remarkable feature of the representative system; and that, as you will admit, is not the happiest beginning with which to start. If representation constitutes the moral basis of power, then the fact that out of every five men

two should be left unrepresented, requires a good deal
of explanation; two-fifths of the moral basis at all events
are wholly wanting. We are fond of talking of our
representative system as if it rested on a democratic
foundation; but under which of the three great democratic principles—equality, fraternity, liberty—does the
sweeping off the board of two-fifths of the nation, the
two men out of every five, find its sanction?

Let us, however, for the present leave the 2,000,000
voters to their fate. They are, as we have seen, only a
subject race; and subject races must be duly reasonable,
and not expect too great a share in the privileges of conquering races. Now let us turn to the case of the happy
triumphant 3,000,000 voters, who hold in subjection the
2,000,000 voters. Are they themselves represented in any
true sense? Let us see what happens to them—the majority, who are good enough for a time to take charge of all
of us. Unlimited power means that our lords and masters
of the moment may deal, that they will probably try to
deal, with every, or almost every field of human activity.
If there are, say, ten great state departments, such as
trade, foreign affairs, local government, home government, and the rest; and if we suppose with due moderation
that there are ten great questions connected with each of
these departments, that may at any moment occupy the
attention of our presiding majority, then we have a grand
total of a hundred questions, upon which the opinions of
the 3,000,000 electors will have to be represented. But
alas! for our unfortunate and inconvenient human differences; how can the victorious 3,000,000 be represented
on these hundred questions, when, if they think at all,

they will all think more or less differently from each other? To express fully their many differences, they ought to have nearly 3,000,000 representatives; but we will not ask for perfection; so let us divide the number by a hundred and say 30,000 representatives—an arrangement which, if the representatives met and talked for twenty hours every day in the year, would give, let us say, something over eight seconds of talking time for each representatives during the course of the year as regards each of the hundred questions. When they had each talked their eight or nine seconds, how much real agreement should you expect to find among our 30,000 representatives on their hundred questions?

Place twenty men in a room to discuss one subject; and how many different opinions will you collect at the end, if the twenty men are intelligent, and interested in the subject? Will you not probably find three or four groups of opinions, each group representing a more or less different view? Now bring the 30,000 representatives together, and require them to agree, not on one subject, but on a hundred important and often complicated subjects. Remember they *must* agree—they have no choice— that necessity of agreement overrides everything else, for otherwise they cannot act together. But then comes the question—what is their agreement, forced upon them by the practical necessity of acting together as one man, morally worth? Is it not a mere form, a mere mockery, a mere illusion? They must agree; and they do agree; for the continuance of the party system, the winning of power, the subjecting of their rivals—all this depends on their agreeing; but in what sort of fashion, by what kind of mental legerdemain, is their agreement reached? It can only be reached in one simple way—by a wholesale system of self-effacement. The 30,000 individuals must be content on, say, ninety-five percent of the hundred questions, to have no opinions; or if they have opinions, to swallow ninety-five percent of their opinions at a gulp, and to play the convenient, if somewhat inglorious part of ciphers. Yet under our system it is this larger half of the nation, these 3,000,000 voters, who have undertaken the responsibility of thinking and acting for the nation, of deciding these hundred questions both for themselves and for the rest of us; and the only way of deciding left to them is to efface themselves, and have no opinions—a rather sad anticlimax, I am afraid, to some of our every-day rhetoric on the subject of representative systems.

If we look closely we find that these systems only mean that if we have no personal opinions, we can be represented, so far as it is possible or worthwhile to represent blank sheets of paper; if we have personal opinions, we can't be represented. The question then forces itself upon us, is it a bit of honest work, is it profitable, is it worth the trouble, to construct a huge machinery for the purpose of representing ciphers, who have no opinions; and when we have constructed our illusory, our make-believe machine, to go into the marketplace, and therefrom deliver ourselves of speeches about the excellence of our self-governing system? Is it right and true to set up a moral responsibility on the part of those who profess to govern, that cannot by any possibility be turned into a reality; to ask half the nation to sit in the seat of universal judgment, there to take their part in what is and must be an only half disguised farce? Does it not tell us something of the true nature of power, when we find ourselves obliged to descend to tricks of this kind in order to possess and to use it?

Does it mend matters to say that under our system we choose the best man available, and leave the hundred questions for him to deal with? That is only our old friend, the autocrat, come back once more, with a democratic polish rubbed over his face to disguise and, as far as may be, to beautify his appearance. Our sin consists in the suppression of our own selves and our own opinions; and in one sense we fall lower than the slaves of the autocrat, for they are simply sinned against, but we take an active part in the sin against ourselves.

And now how does this suppression of ourselves come about? There must be some powerful motive acting upon us, to induce us to take our place cheerfully in such a poor sort of comedy. Men don't suppress themselves, except to gain something that they much desire. Let us be frank once more, and confess we are bribed into this self-suppression by our reckless desire for power, and our desire to use the power, when gained, for special interests of our own. The power that we seek to win is a hard taskmaster as regards its conditions, and exacts that humiliating price from us. We take our own bribe for giving up our opinions, and play the part of ciphers, and at the same time bribe those others who are to play their part with us; we ask no questions of our conscience, but go on to the political exchange, and there with a light heart do the necessary selling and buying.

Now follow a little further this process of self-suppression, this process of making the ciphers. When you have once required of men to efface themselves and all the higher part of themselves, in order that they may act together, then follows that bargaining and juggling with the groups, of which I have already spoken. The disinterested opinions—ninety-five percent of them, as we calculated—have vanished, much in the same fashion as the 2,000,000 voters vanished; they are swept off the board, as things for which no place can be found, but which are only very much in the way of the real business in hand; and only a few leading self-interests—three or four perhaps—still remain. Now you may bind unbought men together, in the one and true way, by their opinions; but when they have no opinions, you must find a cement of a coarser and more material kind. Having once turned men into ciphers, nothing remains but to treat them as ciphers. The great trick, the winning of power, requires ciphers, and can't be played in any other fashion. Having once turned men into ciphers, you must appeal to them as good loyal party followers; or you must appeal to them as likely to get more from you than from any other buyer in the market: you can't appeal to them, except in the imaginative moments when you are treading the flowery paths of rhetoric, as men, possessed of conscience, and will, and responsibility, for in that case they might once more regain possession of their suppressed consciences and their higher faculties, and begin to think and judge for themselves—a result that would have very inconvenient consequences; for then they would no longer agree to have one opinion on the hundred subjects; they would divide and scatter themselves in all sorts of direc-

tions; they would be a source of infinite trouble and vexation to the distracted party managers; they would no
longer be of use as fighting material; and the well-disci-
plined army would dissolve into an infinite number of
separate and divergent fragments.

No! As long as party faces party, and the great struggle for power goes on, the rank and file, however intelligent, however well-educated, must be content to think
with the party. They can't think for themselves, for if
they did they would think differently; and if they thought
differently, they could not act together; so they must be
content to be just war material, very like the masses of
conscripts which foreign governments occasionally employ to hurl against each other. If they were anything
else, it would be a very poor fighting show that our political parties would make on their battlefield. The great
struggle for power would die out, would come naturally
to its end, when the suppression of self and the making
of the ciphers had ceased to be.

It is well to notice here that in some other countries
you have not two political parties of the same definite
character as with us, but a large number of groups. The
fact of the groups very slightly affects the situation.
Under every system the vices that go with the seeking
for power return in pretty nearly the same form. The
groups can't form a majority, and obtain power, unless
they amalgamate; which means that each group has its
market price, makes the best bargain that it can for itself,
and for the sake of that bargain consents to act with, and
so to increase the strength and influence of those with
whom it may be in strong disagreement. Of course hope-

less moral confusion arises from this temporary amal-
gamation of the odds and evens, and separate, unlike
pieces, from this making of a common cause by those
who mean different things, and are almost as much opposed to each other as they are to the common enemy,
to whom for the moment they are opposed.

Under no circumstances can we afford to depart from
the great principle that we must never abandon our own
personality, that we must only strive for the ends in which
we ourselves believe, and never consent to enter into
combinations, in which we either are used against our
convictions, or use others against their convictions.
Whenever we descend to "logrolling"—your services to
pay for my services—we are lost in a sea of intrigue and
corruption, and all true guidance disappears. There is no
true guidance for any of us, except in our own best and
highest selves, in our own personal sense of what is true
and right. When that goes, there is little, if anything,
worth the saving.

And now, passing by many incidents in the working
of the great machine, that is so largely indulgent to our
fighting and bargaining propensities, I come to what
seems to me the very heart of Mr. Spencer's social and
political teaching. It is not often given to a man to sum
up in three words a great truth, that is fated sooner or
later to revolutionize the thought and action of all nations; and yet that is, I think, what Mr. Spencer happily
achieved. The three words were, *progress is difference*—
that is, if you or I are to think more clearly, or to act more
efficiently and more rightly than those who have preceded
us, it can only be because at some point we leave the

path which they followed, and enter a new path of our own; in other words, we must have the temper and courage to differ from accepted standards of thought and perception and action. If we are to improve in any direction, we must not be bound up with each other in inseparable bundles, we must have the power in ourselves to find and to take the new path of our own. Is not every improvement of machinery and method, every gain made in science and art, every choosing of the truer road and turning away from the false road that we have hitherto trodden— does it not all arise from those differences of thought and perception which, so long as freedom exists, even in its present imperfect forms, are from time to time born amongst us? Whenever men become merely copies and echoes of each other, when they act and think according to fixed and sealed patterns, is not all growth arrested, all bettering of the world made difficult, if not impossible? What hope of real progress, when difference has almost ceased to exist; when men think in the same fashion as a regiment marches; and no mind feels the life-giving stimulating impulse which the varying competing thoughts of others brings with it?

Do we not see in some parts of the East, when men are bound rigidly together under one system of thought, how difficult, how painful, the next upward step becomes; and when the change comes, how dissolvent and destructive it tends to be? Do we not see the same thing in churches and states nearer home—the more that minds are uniformly subjected to one system, the more difficult becomes the adaptation of the old to the new, the more violent, revolutionary and catastrophic the change when it takes place? Safety only lies in the constant differences which many living minds, looking from their own standpoint, in turn contribute. All unity that exists by means of social or artificial restraint of differences, is slowly but inevitably moving toward its own destruction—a destruction that must finally involve much pain and confusion and disorder, because change and adaptation have been so long resisted.

Now if we accept this simple but most far-reaching truth—*progress is difference*—as I think we must do, let us frankly and loyally accept it with all the great consequences which follow from it. If progress is the child of difference, then it is for us to let our social and political systems favor difference to the fullest extent possible. At no point must we imprison minds under those fighting systems, which always restrain thought and favor mechanical discipline—fighting is one thing and thinking is another; at no point must we stereotype action, preventing its natural and healthy divergence; at no point throw difficulties in the way of effort and experiment; at no point deindividualize men by making them dull repetitions of each other, soulless, automatic ciphers, lost, helpless in their crowd; but everywhere we must allow the natural rewards and inducements and motives to act upon free self-guiding men and women, encouraging them to feel that the work of improvement, the work of world-bettering, the achieving of progress, lies in their own hands, as individuals, and that, if they wish to share in this great common work, they must strive individually to live at their best.

Throughout the whole nation, we must let every man

and woman, instead of looking to their parties and parliaments and governments, feel the full strength of the inspiring inducement to do something in their own individual capacities and to join with others in doing something—the smallest or the greatest thing—better than it has yet been done, and so make their own contribution to the great fund of general good.

Only so can the far-reaching powers which lie in human nature, but which, like the talent, are so often wrapped in the napkin, hidden and unused, find their full scope and development; only so can our aims and ambitions be ennobled and purified; only so can the true respect for the individuality of others soften the strife of opinions, and the intolerant spirit in which we so often look upon all that is opposed to and different from ourselves. As we recognize and respect the individuality both of ourselves and others; as we realize that the bettering of the world depends upon our individual actions and perceptions; that this bettering can only be done by ourselves, acting together in free combination; that it depends upon the efforts of countless individuals, as the raindrops make the streams, and the streams make the rivers, that it cannot be done for us by proxy, cannot be relegated, in our present indolent fashion, to systems of machinery, or handed over to an army of autocratic officials to do for us; and as we realize that we shall have failed in our part, have lived almost in vain, if in some direction, in some department of thought or action, whatever it may be, we have not individually striven to make the better take the place of the good; life will become for all of us a better and nobler thing, with more definite

aims, and greater incentives to useful action. The work
that we do will react on ourselves; and we shall react on
the work. Each victory gained, each new thing well done
will make the men, the fighters for progress; and as the
fighters are raised to a higher capacity, the progress made
will advance with bolder, swifter strides, invading in turn
every highway and byway of life. But this healthy reaction cannot be as long as we live under the depressing
and dispiriting influence of the great machines, that take
the work out of our hands, and encourage in us all a sense
of personal uselessness. The appeal must be straight and
direct to the individuals, to their own self-direction, their
own self-sacrifice, to their own efforts in free unregu-
lated combinations, their own willing gifts and services.

It is in vain that you will ask for the progress, that is
born in the conflict of competing thoughts and perceptions, from the great official departments, into whose
hands you now so complacently resign yourself. They
are incapacitated as instruments of progress by the law
of their own being. Whenever you act and think wholesale, and in authoritative fashion for others, you become
to a certain extent limited and incapacitated in your own
nature. That mental penalty forever dogs the possession
of power. You lose sight of the great and vital ends, and
allow the small things to change places with the all-
important things. You are no more in touch with the living forces that make for progress. Why? Are the reasons
far to seek? The body of officials—however good and
honorable in themselves—from a caste, that administers
the administered, and does not really share in the actual
life of the nation; the chiefs, intent upon the huge ma-

chine, which they direct from behind their office windows; the large body, dutifully following their traditions, and clinging to their precedents. They are cut off from all the great inspirations, for the great inspirations are only likely to come to those who share in the active throbbing life that is not found in any one part, but in the whole, of a free nation, and that exists, as we have seen, as the sum of countless differing contributions.

The best inspirations only readily come to those who live open to all influences, who are not narrowed and limited by that sense of slightly contemptuous superiority, which we all, however excellent we may be, are apt to feel when we are treating others as passive material under our hands. I doubt if you can ever impose your own will by means of force on others, without acquiring in yourself something of this superior scorn. But this scorn is fatal to the great inspirations, for they are only born in us when we are in truest personal sympathy with the upward movement, whatever it may be, when we ourselves are part of it, when we are thinking and feeling freely, and are surrounded by those thinking and feeling like ourselves, for in real free life we are forever giving and receiving, absorbing and radiating. There and there only do you get the true soilbed of progress.

Nor, if our official classes were willing to be helped by the thought of others, is it possible. Under their authoritative systems they have made the people helpless, apathetic, indifferent; and so have to carry the great burden of thinking for a nation on their own shoulders alone. Few people really think or perceive, who can give no practical effect to their thoughts and perceptions; and so it is that we see administered nations grow first indifferent, and then revolutionary. It is thus, in this vicious circle, that bureaucracy ever works. Our bureaucrats, with their universal systems, paralyze and benumb the best thought and energies of the nation; and then themselves are mentally starved in the dead-alive condition of things that they have created. Then again our official classes are not only, like the autocrat, controlled and disabled by their own machinery, but they fall—who could help it?—under the drowsy influence of the ever-revolving wheels. The habit of doing the one thing in the same fixed way depresses the brighter faculties, and the *vis inertiae* becomes the paramount force. The machinery, on which everything depends, takes the first place; its moral and spiritual effect upon the people take the second or third place, or no place at all. Thus it is that every huge administrative system tends to that barren uniformity which is a kind of intellectual death, and from which that essential element of progress—experiment—is necessarily absent. When you have constructed a universal system, embracing the whole nation, you can't experiment. The thousands of wheels must all follow each other in the same track with undeviating uniformity. Even if your official feelings would allow of such an unorthodox proceeding, it is mechanically very difficult to interfere with the regularity and precision that make the working of universal systems possible.

And so it happens that not only is a man with new ideas a real terror inside the walls of a great department, but that there are two phases that succeed each other in turn in the life of these departments. There is the period of somnolence, the mechanical repetition of what had been said and done in past years, the same sending out of the old time-honored forms, the same pigeonholing of the answers, the same holding of inspections, the same administering of the nation by the junior clerks; and with it all, complete insensibility as to what influence the system as a whole is exercising on the soul of the people. The daily thought and care of a good official begins and ends with taking precautions that the system, as a system, is working smoothly and without friction. As to what the system is in itself, it is not his province to think, and he very rarely does think. He did not create it; he is not directly responsible for it—as a rule nobody knows who is responsible for it; his work is simply to make the countless wheels duly follow each other with regularity and precision. That somnolent period, however, only lasts for a time; presently comes the revolutionary period of remorselessly pulling down and then building up in haste—a period in which the department suddenly awakes from its sleep, aroused perhaps by some external impulse, perhaps by the truer perceptions, or perhaps by the wayward fancies of some minister, fresh to office, who longs to inaugurate his own little revolution. Then the sleepers become changed into reformers; and suddenly we are authoritatively assured that we have been following altogether wrong methods, that the old system, under which serious evils have been growing up, must be at once transformed into something of a new and very different order. The nation, dully and dimly aware that things are not as they should be, smiles approvingly, and through its press, faintly applauds; and the plant, perhaps of some twenty years' growth, is straightway torn up by the roots—a fate which after a few years will be again shared by the new thing that now takes its place.

It is not the fault of the officials. If you or I were in their place we should be just as somnolent, and just as revolutionary. The fault lies in the great system itself; and few of us could resist the spell that it exercises. The truth is that you can no more administer a whole nation than you can represent it. You cannot deal with human nature wholesale; you cannot throw it higgledy-piggledy into one common lot, and let half a dozen men, no better or worse than ourselves, take charge of it. No universal system is a living thing: they all tend to become mere machines—machines of a rather perverse kind, that have incurable tricks of going their own way. We are apt to think that our machines dutifully serve and obey us; but in large measure we serve and obey them. They too have souls of their own, and command as well as obey. Unfortunately for us, progress and improvement are not amongst the things that great machines are able to supply at demand. Their soul lies in mechanical repetition, not in difference; while progress requires not only faculties in the highest state of vital activity, but I might almost say continual, mental dissatisfaction with what has been already achieved, and continual preparedness to invade new territory and attempt new victories. Progress depends upon a great number of small changes and adaptations and experiments constantly taking place, each carried out by those who have strong beliefs and clear perceptions of their own in the matter; for the only true experimenter is he who finds and follows his own way, and is free to try his experiment from day to day. But this true experimentation is impossible under universal systems. An experiment can only be tried on a small scale by those who are the clearer-sighted amongst us, and are aiming at some particular end, and when those who are affected by it are willing to take the risk. You can't rightly experiment with a whole nation; and the consequence is that the sin and mistakes of every universal system go on silently accumulating, until the time comes for the next periodical tearing up by the roots of what exists comes due, and once more we start afresh.

And now there are still many other points on which I must not touch today. There is that great subject of excessive public expenditure in all countries, which is like a tide which flows and flows and hardly ever ebbs. A few years ago when some of us began to preach voluntary taxation, as the only effectual means of recovering the gradually disappearing independence of the individual, and of placing governments in their true position of agents, and not, as they are today, of autocrats and masters of the nation, and as the plainest and most direct means of making the recognition of the principle of individual liberty supreme in our national life, I found most of my friends quite content to be used as tax material, even though the sums of money taken from them were employed against their own beliefs and interests. They had lived so long under the system of using others, and then in their turn being used by them, that they were like hypnotized subjects, and looked on this subjecting and using of each other as a part of the necessary and even providential order of things. The great machine had taken possession of their souls; and they only yawned and looked bored, or slightly scornful at any idea of rebelling against it.

In vain we drew the picture of the nobler, happier, safer life of the nation, when men of all conditions voluntarily combined to undertake the great services, class cooperating with class, each bound to the other by new ties of friendship and kindliness, with all its different groups learning to discover their own special wants, to follow their own methods, and make their own experiments. In that way only, as we urged, could we replace the present dangerous and mischief-making strife with blessed fruitful peace, create a happier, better, nobler spirit amongst us all, destroy the old traffic and bargaining of the political market, destroy the fatal belief that one class might rightly prey upon another class, and that all property finally belonged to those who could collect the greater number of votes at the polls. That belief in the omnipotent vote, as we urged, was striking its roots deeper every year—it was the certain, the inevitable result of our party fighting for the possession of power. So long as the vote carried with it the unlimited undefined power of the majority, the giving away of property must always remain as the easiest means of purchasing the owners of the vote; and that belief in the final ownership of property being vested in the voter we could only fight, not by resisting here or there, not by denouncing this or that bit of excessive and wasteful expenditure, but by challenging the rightfulness and good sense of the whole system, by pointing to a truer, nobler, social life, and by resolutely standing on the plain broad principle of individual control over ourselves and our own property. It was in friendly voluntary cooperation, as free men and women, for all public wants and services; in taking each other's hands, in sharing our efforts; it was by destroying the belief in power, the belief in "pooling" property and faculties, the belief in the false right of some men to hold other men in subjection, and to use them as their material; in building up the belief in the true rights, the rights of self-ownership and self-guidance, apart from which everything tends to the confusion and corruption of public life—it was only so that we could ward off the coming danger and the inevitable strife. These great national services, that we had so lightly flung into the hands of our officials, were the true means of creating that higher and better national life, with its friendly interdependence, its need of each other, its respect for each other, which was worth over and over again all the political gifts and compulsions—though you piled them up in a heap as high as Pelion thrown on the top of Ossa. It was only so that the nation would find its true peace and happiness, and that the smoldering dread and hatred of each other could die out.

The years have passed; and I think a change of mood has silently come over many persons. I find that some of those who once clung to compulsion as the saving social bond, as the natural expression of nation life, are willing today to consider whether some better and truer and safer principle may not be found; are willing to consider, as a practical question, if some limit should not be placed on the power to take and to spend in unmeasured quantity the money of others. Our friend the socialist has done, and is doing for us his excellent and instructive work. He stands as a very striking, I might say eloquent landmark, showing us plainly enough where our present path leads, and what is the logical completion of our compulsory interferences, our restrictions of faculties, and our transfer of property by the easy—shall I say the laughable and grotesque?—process of the vote. Into our present system, which so many men accept without thinking of its real meaning, and its further consequences, he introduces an order, a consistency, a completeness of his own. His logic is irresistible. If you can vote away half the yearly value of property under the form of a rate, as we do in some towns at present, then under the same convenient and elastic right you can vote away the nine-tenths or the whole. "*Only* logic," perhaps you lightly answer—but remember, unless you change the direction of the forces, logic always tends to come out victorious in the end.

Let us then take the bolder, the truer, the more manful course. If we believe in property, as a right and just thing; if, as the product of faculties, we believe it to be inseparably connected with the free use of faculties, and therefore inseparably connected with freedom itself; if we believe that it is a mere bit of word mockery to tell us, as our socialist friends do, that they are presenting the world with the newest, the most perfect, the most up-to-date form of liberty, while from their heights of scorn for liberty they calmly deny to all men and women the right to employ their faculties in their own way and for their own advantages, offering us in return a system beyond all words petty and irritating, a system that would provoke rebellion even in the nursery, and which, as a clever French writer wittily remarked, would periodically convulse the state with the ever-recurring insoluble question, might or might not a wife mend the trousers of her husband; if we believe that the socialist, treading in the footsteps of his predecessor, the autocrat, has only discovered one more impossible system of slavery, then let us individually do our best to end the great delusion that has given birth to the socialist, and made him the power that he is today in Europe—that property belongs, not to the property owner, but to those who are good enough to take the trouble to vote.

Don't let us play any longer with these dangerous forces, which, if they win, will for a time wholly change the course of human civilization; and above all don't let us put it in the power of the voter to turn round some future day and say to us, "As long as it served your interests and ambitions, you acknowledged the supremacy of the vote; you acknowledged this right of taking property from each other. You taught us, you sanctioned, through many years, the principle of unlimited power, vested in some men over other men. Is it not now a little late in the day for you suddenly to cry 'halt' in the path along which you have so long led us, because you see new interests and ambitions taking their place by the side of your own discredited interests and ambitions, which are no longer able to satisfy the heart of the nation? If the old game was good enough and right enough in your hands, when you were our leaders, so is the new game right and good enough in our hands, now that it is our turn to lead."

What true, what sufficient answer would there remain

for us to make? Were it not better to repent of our past sins today, while there is yet time and opportunity to do something to repair them? If we are only to begin to quarrel with power and its consequences when we find that it has already slipped away from our hands, shall we not be to much like the gray-haired sinner who turns saint in that sad period when the pleasures of life have already ceased to exist for him? Better to repent while there is still something to sacrifice and renounce; and we can still give some proof that our repentance is the child of real conviction.

Let us try to clear our thoughts, and know our own minds in this great matter. Do we or do we not mean to consent to that final act in the long drama which is euphemistically called "the nationalizing of property"? If we do not mean to consent to that last crowning act of the process of voting away the property of each other, then it is not only an unworthy weakness on our part, but a cruel wrong to encourage by our words and actions in the mass of the people a belief, which someday, when it grows to its full strength and height, we shall scornfully, whatever our scorn may then avail, disown and reject, forgetting with our changed attitude how we once planted that belief in their hearts, used it, and played with it for the sake of our ambition and our desire to possess power. When the great bitter strife comes—as it must come—shall we not be constrained with shame to accuse ourselves, and to acknowledge our misleading of the people, our responsibility in the past for the infinite calamities we have brought both upon them and upon ourselves. Do not let us wait for that future so fraught with evil, which our own carelessness of thought, our disregard of the great principles, our love of the wildly exciting political game, and our subservience to party interests are preparing for us.

The hours of the day are not yet spent. The temper of our people is a noble generous temper, if you appeal to it in the true way, appealing for right's sake, for principle's sake, not merely for the sake of class or party or personal interests, not merely for the sake of the many pleasant things that belong to the possession of property. Let us make some sacrifice of our political ambitions, and take our stand on the truest, highest ground.

Our task is to make it clear to the whole nation that a great principle, that which involves the free use of faculties, the independence of every life, the self-guidance and self-ownership, the very manhood of all of us, that commands and constrains us to preserve the inviolability of property for all its owners, whoever they may be. The inviolability of property is not simply the material interest of one class that happens today to possess it; it is the supreme interest of all classes. True material prosperity can only be won by the great body of the nation through the widest measure of liberty—not the half and half, not the mock system, that exists at present. Create the largest and most generous system of liberty, create—as you will do with it—the vital energizing spirit of liberty, and in a few short years the working classes could cease to be the propertyless class; would become with their great natural qualities the largest property owners in the country.

But this can only be, as they set themselves in earnest

to *make* property instead of *taking* it, and to put the irresistible pence and shillings together for the carrying out of all the great services. This in truth was the splendid campaign on which he had entered, when the politician, sometimes hungering to play the important part, and to exalt his small restless self, sometimes misled by nobler dreams, drew his deluding herring across the path, and pointed to the easier downhill way of the common fund and the all-powerful vote. It is the politician with his cheap liberality and his giving away of what does not belong to him, who perpetuates the depressed and unprogressive condition of a large part of the people; he is only too much like those who nurse poverty by their careless and misplaced charity. He stands in the way of the true efforts of the people, of their friendly cooperation, their discovery of all that they could achieve for their own happiness and prosperity, if they acted together in their free self-helping groups.

Let us never forget the power of the accumulated pence. If we could persuade a million men and women to lay aside one halfpenny a week, at the end of a year they would have over £100,000 to invest in farms, houses, recreation grounds, in all that they felt they most needed. With the acquisition of property would come many of the helpful and useful qualities—the self-confidence, the faculty of working together, and of managing property, and the proud inspiring ambition to remake in peaceful ways, unstained by any kind of violence, and therefore challenging and encountering no opposing forces, the whole condition of society, as it exists today. Such is the goal to which we, who disbelieve in force, must ever point the way. It is for us to show that everything can be gained by voluntary effort and combination, and nothing can be permanently and securely gained by force. In every form, where men hold men in subjection to themselves, force is always organized against itself, is always tending sooner or later to destroy itself. Autocrat, restless politician, or socialist, they are all only laborers in vain. There is a moral gravitation that in its own time drags all their work remorsely to the ground. Everywhere, across that work, failure is written large. There are many reasons. In the first place, force begets force, and dies by the hand of its own offspring; then those who use force never act long together, for the force temper leads them to turn their hand against each other; then the continued use of force, as is natural, develops a superhuman stupidity, a failure to see the real meaning and drift of things, in those who use it; but greatest of all reasons, the soul of man is made for freedom, and only in freedom finds its true life and development. So long as we suppress that true life of the soul, so long as we deny to it the full measure of its freedom, we shall continue to strive and to quarrel and to hate, and to waste our efforts, as we have done through so many countless years, and shall never enter the fruitful path of peace and friendship that waits for us. Once show the people, make it clear to their heart and understanding, that it is liberty alone that can lead us into this blessed path of peace and friendship; that it alone can still the strife and the hatreds; that it alone is the instrument of progress of every kind; that it alone in any true sense can make and hold together and preserve a nation—which, if it rejects liberty, must in the end tear itself to pieces in the great hopeless aimless strife —once show them this supreme truth, feeling it yourself in the very depths of your heart, and so speak to them— and then you will find, as you touch the nobler, more generous part of their nature, that gradually, under the influence of the truer teaching, they will learn to throw aside the false bribes and mischievous attractions of powers, and to turn away in disgust from that mad destructive game in which they and we alike have allowed ourselves for a time to be entangled.

It is not the socialist party, it is not any of the labor parties who have done the most to lead astray the people, and to teach them to believe that political power is the rightful instrument for securing all that their heart desires. These extreme parties have simply trodden more boldly the path in which we went before them. They have only been the pupils—the too apt pupils—in our school, who have bettered our own teaching. It is we, the richer classes, who in our love of power, our desire to win the great game, have done the great wrong, have misled and corrupted the people; and the fault and the blame and the shame will rest in the largest measure with us, when the evil fruit grows from the seed that we so recklessly planted. When the chickens come home to roost, we shall only have to say, as so many have said before us—*tu l'as voulu, Georges Dandin.* Let us then, who have made the great mistake, let us try to redeem it; let us show the people that there is a nobler, happier form of life than to live as two scrambling, quarreling crowds, mad for their own immediate interests, void of all scruple or restraint. Let us shake ourselves free from this miserable party fighting; let us speak only in the name of the great rights, the great all-guiding, ever-enduring principles; let us oppose the power of some men over other men, as a thing that is in itself morally untrue, untrue from every higher point of view, that is *lèse-majesté* as regards all the best and noblest conceptions of what we are—beings gifted with free responsible souls—as the source of hopeless confusion and scramble and injustice; and let us steadfastly set our faces toward the one great ideal of making a nation, in which all men and women will love their own liberty—without which life is as salt that has lost its savor, and is only fit to be cast away—as deeply as they respect and seek to preserve the liberty of others.

A few words to prevent a possible misunderstanding. I have not been preaching any form of anarchy, which seems to me—even in its most peaceful and reasonable forms, quite apart from the detestable bomb—merely one more creed of force. (I am not referring here to such a form of anarchy—passive resistance under all circumstances, as Tolstoy preaches—into the consideration of which I cannot enter today.) Anarchy is a creed, which, as I believe, we can never rightly class among the creeds of liberty. Only in condemning anarchy we shall do well to remember that, like socialism, it is the direct product, the true child of those systems of government that have taught men to believe that they may rightly found their relations to each other on the employment of force. Both the anarchist and the socialist find some measure of justification in the practice and teaching of all our modern governments, for if force is a right thing in itself, then it becomes merely a secondary question, on which we may all differ, as to the quantity and quality of it to be employed, the purposes for which we may use it, or in what hands the employment of it should be placed. There is, there can be, nothing sacred in the division of ourselves into majorities and minorities. You may think right to take only half a man's property from him by force; I may prefer to take the whole. You may think right to entrust the use of force to every three men out of five; I may prefer to entrust it, as the anarchist does, to each one of the five separately; or as some Russians and some Germans do, to the autocrat or half-autocrat, and his all-embracing bureaucracy. Who shall decide between us? There is no moral tribunal before which you can summon unlimited power, for it acknowledges, as we have seen, nothing higher than itself; if it did acknowledge any moral law above itself, its wings would be clipped, and its nature changed, and it would no longer be unlimited.

Now glance for a moment at the true character of anarchy, and see why we must refuse to class it among the creeds of liberty, though many of the reasonable anarchists are inspired, as I believe, by a real love of liberty. Under anarchy, if there were 5,000,000 men and women in a country, there would be 5,000,000 little governments, each acting in its own case as council, witness, judge, and executioner. That would be simply a carnival, a pandemonium of force; and hardly an improvement even upon our power-loving, force-using governments. Force, as I believe, with Mr. Spencer, must rest, not in the hands of the individual, but in the hands of a government—not to be, as at present, an instrument of subjecting the two men to the three men, not to be exalted into the supreme thing, lifted up above the will and conscience of the individual, judging all things in the light of its own interests, but strictly as the agent, the humble servant of universal liberty, with its simple duties plainly, definitely, distinctly marked out for it. Our great purpose is to get rid of force, to banish it wholly from our dealings with each other, to give it notice to quit from this changed world of ours; but as long as some men, like Bill Sykes and all his tribe, are willing to make use of it for their own ends; or to make use of fraud, which is only force in disguise, wearing a mask, and evading our consent, just as force with violence openly disregards it; so long we must use *force to restrain force.* That is the one and only one rightful employment of force—force in the defense of the plain simple rights of liberty, of the exercise of faculties, and therefore of the rights of property, public or private, in a word of all the rights of self-ownership; force used defensively against force used aggressively. The only true use of force is for the destruction, the annihilation of itself, to rid the world of its own mischief-making existence. Even when used defensively, it still remains an evil, only to be tolerated in order to get rid of the greater evil. It is the one thing in the world to be bound down with chains, to be treated as a slave, and only as a slave, that must always act under command of something better and higher than itself. Wherever and whenever we use it, we must surround it with the most stringent limits, looking on it, as we should look on a wild and dangerous beast, to which we deny all will and free movement of its own. It is one of the few things in our world to which liberty must be forever denied. Within those limits the force, that keeps a clear and open field for every effort and enterprise of human activity—that are in themselves untainted by force and fraud—such force is in our present world a necessary and useful servant, like the fire which burns in the fireplaces of our rooms and the ranges of our kitchens; force, which once it passes beyond that purely defensive office, becomes our worst, our most dangerous enemy, like the fire which escapes from our fireplaces and takes its own wild course. If then we are wise and clear-seeing, we shall keep the fire in the fireplace, and never allow it to pass away from our control.

ESSAY NINE

A PLEA FOR VOLUNTARYISM

This essay was published in The Voluntaryist Creed *(Oxford University Press, 1908). It was completed shortly before Herbert's death as a series of lectures for the British Constitution Association and never circulated for supporting signatures, as originally intended.*

We, who call ourselves voluntaryists, appeal to you to free yourselves from these many systems of state force, which are rendering imposible the true and happy life of the nations of today. This ceaseless effort to compel each other, in turn for each new object that is clamored for by this or that set of politicians, this ceaseless effort to bind chains round the hands of each other, is preventing progress of the real kind, is preventing peace and friendship and brotherhood, and is turning the men of the same nation, who ought to labor happily together for common ends, in their own groups, in their own free unfettered fashion, into enemies, who live conspiring against and dreading, often hating each other.

Look at the picture that you may see today in every country of Europe. Nations divided into two or three parties, which are again divided into several groups, facing each other like hostile armies, each party intent on humbling and conquering its rivals, on treading them under their feet, as a conquering nation crushes and tramples on the nation it has conquered. What good, what happiness, what permanent progress of the true kind can come out of that unnatural, denationalizing, miserable warfare? Why should you desire to compel others; why should you seek to have power— that evil, bitter, mocking thing, which has been from of old, as it is today, the sorrow and curse of the world—over your fellow-men and fellow-women? Why should you desire to take from any man or woman their own will and intelligence, their free choice, their own self-guidance, their inalienable rights over themselves; why should you desire to make of them mere tools and instruments for your own advantage and interest; why should you desire to compel them to serve and follow your opinions instead of their own; why should you deny in them the soul— that suffers so deeply from all constraint—and treat them as a sheet of blank paper upon which you may write your own will and desires, of whatever kind they may happen to be? Who gave you the right, from where do you pretend to have received it, to degrade other men and women from their own true rank as human beings, taking from them their will, their conscience, and intelligence—in a word, all the best and highest part of their nature— turning them into mere empty worthless shells, mere shadows of the true man and women, mere counters in the game you are mad enough to play, and just because you are more numerous or stronger than they, to treat them as if they belonged not to themselves, but to you? Can you believe that good will ever come by morally and spiritually degrading your fellow-men? What happy and safe and permanent form of society can you hope to build on this pitiful plan of subjecting others, or being yourselves subjected by them?

We show you the better way. We ask you to renounce this old, weary, hopeless way of force, ever tearstained and bloodstained, which has gone on so long under emperors and autocrats and governing classes, and still goes on today amongst those who, while they condemn emperors and autocrats, continue to walk in their footsteps, and understand and love liberty very little more than those old rulers of an old world. We bid you ask yourselves—What is all our boasted civilization and gain in knowledge worth to us, if we are still, like those who had not attained to our civilization and knowledge, to hunger for power, still to cling to the ways of strife and bitterness and hatred, still to oppress each other as in the days of the old rulers? Don't be deceived by mere words and phrases. Don't think that everything was gained when you got rid of autocrat and emperor. Don't think that a change in the mere form—without change in the spirit of men—can really alter anything, or make a new world. A voting majority, that still believes in force, that still believes in crushing and ruling a minority, can be just as tyrannous, as selfish and blind, as any of the old rulers. Happy the nation that escapes from autocrat, from emperor, and from its bureaucratic tyrants; but that is only the beginning of the new good life; that counts only for the first steps in the true path. When that is done, the true goal has still to be won, the great lesson still remains to be learned. The old curse, the old sorrow, did not simply lie in the heart of autocrat and emperor; it lay in the common desire of men to rule and possess for their own advantage the minds and bodies of each other. It is that fatal, deluding desire which even yet today prevents our realizing the true and happy life. As a writer has well said —many nations have been powerful, but has any one of them found the true life—as yet? It is this vainest of all vain desires that we have to renounce, trample upon, cast clean out of our hearts, if we are to win the better things. We have to learn that our systems of force destroy all the great human hopes and possibilities; that as long as we believe in force there can be no abiding peace or friendship between us all; that a half-disguised civil war will forever smolder in our midst; that each half of the nation must live, as it were, sword in hand, ever watching the other half, and given up, as we said, to suspicion and dread and hatred, knowing that, if once defeated in the great contest, its own deepest belief and interests will be roughly set aside and trampled on; that it must accept the hard lot of the conquered, kneeling down in the dust and submitting to whatever its opponents choose to decree for it; that it will have no rights of its own; no rights over its own life, over its own actions and property; no share in the common country, no share in the guidance of its fortunes; no voice in the laws passed; it will be a mere helpless crowd, defranchised, and decitizenized, a degraded and subject race, bound to do the hard bidding of its conquerors. Can you for a single moment believe that the subjecting of others in this conqueror's and conquered fashion is the true end of our existence here, the true fulfilling of man's nature, with all its great gifts and hopes and aspirations?

And are the conquerors in the great conflict better off

—if we try to see clearly—than the conquered? We can only answer no; for power is one of the worst, the most fatal and demoralizing of all gifts you can place in the hands of men. He who has power—power only limited by his own desires—misunderstands both himself and the world in which he lives; he sees through a glass darkly, which dims and perverts his whole vision; he magnifies and exalts his own little self; he fondly imagines he may follow the lusts of his heart wherever they lead him; and disowns the control of the great principles, that stand forever above us all, and refuses, alike to the autocrat and the voting majority, the rule and the subjecting of the lives of others. If we feel shame and sorrow for those who are subjected, we may feel yet more shame and sorrow for the blind, self-deceiving instruments of their subjection. They in their pride sink to a lower depth than those whom they subject. Better it were to be amongst those who wear the chain than amongst those who bind it on the hands of other men. For those who suffer in subjection there is some hope, some glimmering of light, some teachings that come from the passionate desire for the liberty denied to them; but for those who cling to and believe in possessing power there is only darkness of soul, where no light enters, until at last, through a long bitter experience, they learn how that for which they sacrificed so much has only turned to their own deepest injury. See how power hardens and brutalizes all of us. It not only makes us selfish, unscrupulous, and intriguing, scornful and intolerant, corrupt in our motives, but it veils our eyes and takes from us the gift of seeing and understanding. Power and stupidity are forever wedded together. Cunning there may be; but it is a cunning that in the end tricks and deceives itself. Power forever tends not only to develop in us the knave, but also to develop the fool. If you wish to know how power spoils character and narrows intelligence, look at the great military empires; their steady perseverance in the roads that lead to ruin; their dread of free thought and of liberty in all its forms; look at the sharp repressions, the excessive punishments, the love of secrecy, the attempt to drill a whole nation into obedience, and to use the drilled and subject thing for every passing vanity and aggrandizement of those who govern. Look also at the great administrative systems. See how men become under them helpless and dispirited, incapable of free effort and self-protection, at one moment sunk in apathy, at another moment ready for revolution. Do you wonder that it is so? Is it wonderful that when you replace the will and intelligence and self-guidance of the individual by systems of vast machinery, that men should gradually lose all the better and higher parts of their nature—for of what use to them is that better and higher part, when they may not exercise it? Ought we to feel surprise, when we see them become like overrestrained children, peevish, discontented and quarrelsome, unable to control and direct themselves, and ever loud in their complaints that enough cake and jam do not fall to their share?

Endless are the evils that power brings with it, both to those who rule and are ruled. If you hold power, your first aim and end are necessarily to preserve that power. With power, as you fondly imagine, you possess all that the world has to offer; without power you seem to yourself only portionless, abject, humiliated—the gate flung in your face, that leads to the palace of all the desirable things. When you once play for so vast a stake, what influence can mere right or wrong have in your counsels? The course that lies before you may be right or wrong, tolerant or intolerant, wise or foolish, but the fatal gift of power, that you have been mad enough to desire and to grasp at, gives you no choice. If you mean to have and to hold power, you must do whatever is necessary for the having and holding of it. You may have doubts and hesitations and scruples, but power is the hardest of all taskmasters, and you must either lay these aside, when you once stand on that dangerous, dizzy height, or yield your place to others, and renounce your part in the great conflict. And when power is won, don't suppose that you are a free man, able to choose your path and do as you like. From the moment you possess power, you are but its slave, fast bound by its many tyrant necessities. The slave owner has no freedom; he can never be anything but a slave himself, and share in the slavery that he makes for others. It is, I think, plain it must be so. Power once gained, you must anxiously day by day watch over its security, whatever its security costs, to prevent the slippery thing escaping from your hands. You tremble at every shadow that threatens its existence. You are haunted by a thousand dreads and suspicions. It becomes, whether you wish it or not, your first, your highest law, and all other things fall into the second and third place. Once you plunge into this all-absorbing game of striving for power, you must go where the strong tide carries you; you must put away conscience and sense of right, and

play the whole game relentlessly out, with the unflinch-
ing determination to win what you are striving for. In
that great game there is no room left for inconvenient and
embarrassing scruples. You can't afford to let your opponents defeat you and wrest the power that you hold
from your hands. You can't afford to let them become
your masters and trample, as conquerors, upon all the
rights and beliefs that are sacred to you. Whatever the
price to pay, whatever sacrifice it demands of what is
just and upright and honorable, you must harden your
heart, and go on to the bitter end. And thus it is that
seeking for power not only means strife and hatred, the
splitting of a nation into hostile factions, but forever
breeds trick and intrigue and falsehood, results in the
wholesale buying of men, the offering of this or that
unworthy bribe, the playing with passions, the poor
unworthy trade of the bitter unscrupulous tongue, that
heaps every kind of abuse, deserved or not deserved,
upon those who are opposed to you, that exaggerates
their every fault, mistake, and weakness, that caricatures,
perverts their words and actions, and claims in childish
and absurd fashion that what is good is only to be found
in your half of the nation, and what is evil is only to be
found in the other half.

Such are the fruits of the strife for power. Evil they
must be, because power is evil in itself. How can the
taking away from a man his intelligence, his will, his
self-guidance be anything but evil? If it were not evil in
itself, there would be no meaning in the higher part of
nature, there would be no guidance in the great principles
—for power, if we once acknowledge it, must stand above

everything else, and cannot admit of any rivals. If the power of some and the subjection of others are right, then men would exist merely as the dust to be trodden under the feet of each other; the autocrats, the emperors, the military empires, the socialist, perhaps even the anarchist with his detestable bomb, would each and all be in their own right, and find their own justification; and we should live in a world of perpetual warfare, that some devil, as we might reasonably believe, must have planned for us. To those of us who believe in the soul—and on that great matter we who sign hold different opinions— the freedom of the individual is not simply a question of politics, but it is a religious question of the deepest meaning. The soul to us is by its own nature a free thing, living its life here in order that it may learn to distinguish and choose between the good and the evil, to find its own way—whatever stages of existence may have to be passed through—toward the perfecting of itself. You may not then, either for the sake of advancing your own interests, or for the sake of helping any cause, however great and desirable in itself, in which you believe, place bonds on the souls of other men and women, and take from them any part of their freedom. You may not take away the free life, putting in its place the bound life. Religion that is not based on freedom, that allows any form of servitude of men to men, is to us only an empty and mocking word, for religion means following our own personal sense of right and fulfilling the commands of duty, as we each can most truly read it, not with the hands tied and the eyes blinded, but with the free, unconstrained heart that chooses for itself. And see clearly that you cannot divide men up into separate parts—into social, political and religious beings. It is all one. All parts of our nature are joined in one great unity; and you cannot therefore make men politically subject without injuring their souls. Those who strive to increase the power of men over men, and who thus create the habit of mechanical obedience, turning men into mere state creatures, over whose heads laws of all kinds are passed, are striking at the very roots of religion, which becomes but a lifeless, meaningless thing, sinking gradually into a matter of forms and ceremonies, whenever the soul loses its freedom. Many men recognize this truth, if not in words, yet in their hearts, for all religions of the higher kind tend to become intensely personal, resting upon that free spiritual relation with the great Oversoul—a relation that each must interpret for himself. And remember you can't have two opposed powers of equal authority; you can't serve two masters. Either the religious conscience and sense of right must stand in the first place, and the commands of all governing authorities in the second place; or the state machine must stand first, and the religious and moral conscience of men must follow after in humble subjection, and do what the state orders. If you make the state supreme, why should it pay heed to the rule of conscience, or the individual sense of right; why should the master listen to the servant? If it is supreme, let it plainly say so, take its own way, and pay no heed, as so many rulers before them have refused to do, to the conscience of those they rule.

And here we ought to say that amongst those who sign this appeal are some who, like the late Mr. Bradlaugh—

a devoted fighter for liberty—reject the doctrine of soul and would not, therefore, base their resistance to state power on any religious ground. But apart from this great difference that may exist between us, we, who sign, are united by the same detestation of state power, and by the same perception of the evils that flow from it. We both see alike that placing unlimited power—as we do now— in the hands of the state means degrading men from their true rank, the narrowing of their intelligence, the encouragement of intolerance and contempt for each other, and therefore the encouragement of sullen, bitter strife, the tricks of the clever tongue, practiced on both the poor and rich crowd, and the evil arts of flattery and self-abasement in order to conciliate votes and possess power, the excessive and dangerous power of a very able press, which keeps parties together, and too often thinks for most of us, the repression of all those healthy individual differences that make the life and vigor of a nation, the blind following of blind leaders, the reckless rushing into national follies, like the unnecessary Boer War—that might have been avoided, as many of us believe, with a moderate amount of prudence, patience, and good temper—just because the individuals of the nation have lost the habit of thinking and acting for themselves, have lost control over their own actions, and are bound together by party ties into two great childlike crowds; means also the piling up of intolerable burdens of debt and taxation, the constant and rather mean endeavor to place the heaviest of these burdens on others—whoever the others may be, the carelessness, the high-handedness, the insolence of those who spend money compulsorily taken, the flocking together of the evil vultures of many kinds where the feast is spread, the deep poisonous corruption, such as is written in broad characters over the government of some of the large towns in the United States—a country bound to us by so many ties of friendship and affection, and in which there is so much to admire—a corruption, that in a lesser degree has soiled the reputation of some of the large cities of the Continent, and is already to be found here and there sporadically existing amongst us in our own country; and which only too surely means at the end of it all the setting up of some absolute form of government, to which men fly in their despair, as a refuge from the intolerable evils they have brought upon themselves—a refuge that after a short while is found to be wholly useless and impotent, and is then violently broken up, perhaps amidst storm and bloodshed, to be once more succeeded by the long train of returning evils, from which men had sought to escape in the vain hope that more power would heal the evils that power had brought upon them.

Such are the fruits of power and the strife for power. It must be so. Set men up to rule their fellow-men, to treat them as mere soulless material with which they may deal as they please, and the consequence is that you sweep away every moral landmark and turn this world into a place of selfish striving, hopeless confusion, trickery and violence, a mere scrambling ground for the strongest or the most cunning or the most numerous. Once more we repeat—don't be deluded by the careless everyday talk about majorities. The vote of a majority is a far lesser evil than the edict of an autocrat, for you can appeal to a majority to repent of its sins and to undo its mistakes, but numbers—though they were as the grains of sand on the seashore—cannot take away the rights of a single individual, cannot turn man or woman into stuff for the politician to play with, or overrule the great principles which mark out our relations to each other. These principles are rooted in the very nature of our being, and have nothing to do with minorities and majorities. Arithmetic is a very excellent thing in its place, but it can neither give nor take away rights. Because you can collect three men on one side, and only two on the other side, that can offer no reason—no shadow of a reason—why the three men should dispose of the lives and property of the two men, should settle for them what they are to do, and what they are to be: that mere rule of numbers can never justify the turning of the two men into slaves, and the three men into slave owners. There is one and only one principle, on which you can build a true, rightful, enduring and progressive civilization, which can give peace and friendliness and contentment to all differing groups and sects into which we are divided—and that principle is that every man and woman should be held by us all sacredly and religiously to be the one true owner of his or her faculties, of his or her body and mind, and of all property, inherited or—honestly acquired. There is no other possible foundation—see it wherever you will—on which you can build, if you honestly mean to make this world a place of peace and friendship, where progress of every kind, like a full river fed by its many streams, may flow on its happy fertilizing course, with ever broadening and deepening volume. Deny that principle, and we become at once like travelers who leave the one sure and beaten path and wander hopelessly in a trackless desert. Deny that self-ownership, that self-guidance of the individual, and however fine our professed motives may be, we must sooner or later, in a world without rights, become like animals, that prey on each other. Deny human rights, and however little you may wish to do so, you will find yourself adjectly kneeling at the feet of that Old World god Force—that grimmest and ugliest of gods that men have ever carved for themselves out of the lusts of their hearts; you will find yourselves hating and dreading all other men who differ from you; you will find yourselves obliged by the law of the conflict into which you have plunged, to use every means in your power to crush them before they are able to crush you; you will find yourselves day by day growing more unscrupulous and intolerant, more and more compelled by the fear of those opposed to you, to commit harsh and violent actions, of which you would once have said, Is thy servant a dog that she should do these things? You will find yourselves clinging to and welcoming Force, as the one and only form of protection left to you, when you have once destroyed the rule of the great principles. When once you have plunged into the strife for power, it is the fear of those who are seeking for power over you that so easily persuades to all the great crimes. Who shall count up the evil brood that is born from power—the pitiful fear, the madness, the despair, the overpowering craving for revenge, the treachery, the unmeasured cruelty? It is liberty alone, broad as the sky above our heads, and planted deep and strong as the great mountains, that allows the better and higher part of our nature to rule in us, and subdues those passions that we share with the animals.

We ask you then to limit and restrain power, as you would restrain a wild and dangerous beast. Make everything subservient to liberty; use state force only for one purpose—to prevent and restrain the use of force amongst ourselves, and that which may be described as the twin brother of force, wearing a mask over its features, the fraud, which by cunning sets aside the consent of the individual, as force sets it aside openly and violently. Restrain by simple and efficient machinery the force and fraud that some men are always ready to employ against other men, for whether it is the state that employs force against a part of the citizens, or one citizen who employs force or fraud against another citizen, in both cases it is equally an aggression upon the rights, upon the self-ownership of the individual; it is equally in both cases the act of the stronger who in virtue of his strength preys upon the weaker. Safeguard therefore the lives and the property of every citizen against the force or the cunning of Bill Sykes and all his tribe. Make of our world a fair open field where we may all act, according to our own choice, individually, or in cooperation, for every unaggressive purpose, and where good of every kind will fight its own open unrestrained fight with evil of every kind. Don't believe in suppressing by force any form of evil—always excepting the direct attacks upon person and property. An evil suppressed by force is only driven out of sight under the surface—there to fester in safety and to take new and more dangerous forms. Remember that striking story of the German liberals, when Bismarck had directed his foolish and useless weapon of repressive laws against the socialists. "You have driven the socialists into silence"—they said—"you have forbidden their meetings and confiscated their papers; yet for all that the movement goes on more actively than ever underground and hidden from sight. And we who are opposed to socialism are also silenced. We have now no enemy to attack. The enemy has vanished out of our sight and out of our reach. How can we answer or reason with those who speak and write no word in public, and only teach and make new recruits in secret and in the dark?"

So it is always. You strike blindly, like a child in its passion, with your weapons of force, at some vice, at some social habit, at some teaching you consider dangerous, and you disarm your own friends who would fight your battle for you—were they allowed to do so—in the one true way of discussion and persuasion and example. You prevent discussion, and the expression of all healthier opinion, you disarm the reformers and paralyze their energies—the reformers who, if left to themselves, would strive to move the minds of men, and to win their hearts, but who now resign themselves to sleep and to indifference, fondly believing that you with your force have fought and won their battle for them, and that nothing now remains for them to do. But in truth you have done nothing; you have helped the enemy. You may have made the outside of things more respectable to the careless eye, you may have taught men to believe in the things that seem, and in reality are not; but you have left the poisonous sore underneath to work its own evil undisturbed, in its own way and measure. The evil, whatever it was, was the result of perverted intelligence or perverted nature; and your systems of force have left that intelligence and that nature unchanged; and you have done that most dangerous of all things—you have strengthened the general belief in the rightfulness and usefulness of employing force. Do you not see that of all weapons that men can take into their hands force is the vainest, the weakest? In the long dark history of the world, what real, what permanent good has ever come from the force which men have never hesitated to use against each other? By force the great empires have been built up, only in due time to be broken into pieces, and to leave mere ruins of stones to tell their story. By force the rulers have compelled nations to accept a religion—only in the end to provoke that revolt of men's minds which always in its own time sweeps away the work of the sword, of the hangman and the torture table. What persecution has in the end altered the course of human belief? What army, used for ambitious and aggressive purposes, has not at last become as a broken tool? What claim of a church to exercise authority and to own the souls of men has not destroyed its own influence and brought certain decay on itself? Is it not the same today, as it has been in all the centuries of the past? Has not the real prosperity, the happiness, the peace of a nation increased just in proportion as it has broken all the bonds and disabilities that impeded its life, just in proportion as it has let liberty replace force; just in proportion as it has chosen and established for itself all rights of opinion, of meeting, of discussion, rights of free trade, rights of the free use of faculties, rights of self-ownership as against the wrongs of subjection? And do

you think that these new bonds and restrictions in which
the nations of today have allowed themselves to be
entangled—the conscription which sends men out to
fight, consenting or not consenting, which treats them as
any other war material, as the guns and the rifles dis-
patched in batches to do their work; or the great systems
of taxation, which make of the individual mere tax material, as conscription makes of him mere war material; or
the great systems of compulsory education, under which
the state on its own unavowed interest tries to exert more
and more of its own influence and authority over the
minds of the childern, tries—as we see especially in other
countries—to mold and to shape those young minds for
its own ends—"Something of religion will be useful—
school-made patriotism will be useful—drilling will be
useful"—so preparing from the start docile and obedient
state material, ready-made for taxation, ready-made for
conscription—ready-made for the ambitious aims and
ends of the rulers—do you think that any of these modern systems, though they are more veiled, more subtle,
less frank and brutal than the systems of the older governments, though the poison in them is more thickly
smeared with the coating of sugar, will bear different
fruit, will work less evil amongst us all, will endure longer
than those other broken and discredited attempts, which
men again and again in their madness and presumption
have made to possess themselves of and to rule the bodies
and minds of others? No! one and all they belong to the
same evil family; they are all part of the same conspiracy
against the true greatness of human nature; they are all
marked broad across the forehead with the same old

curse; and they will all end in the same shameful and sorrowful ending. Over us all is the great unchanging law, ever the same, unchanged and unchanging, regardless of all our follies and delusions, that come and go, that we are not to take possession of and rule the body and mind of others; that we are not to take away from our fellow beings their own intelligence, their own choice, their own conscience and free will; that we are not to allow any ruler, be it autocrat, emperor, parliament, or voting crowd, to take from any human being his own true rank, making of him the degraded state material that others use for their own purposes.

"But"—some of your friends may say—"look well at the advantages of this state force. See how many good things come to you by taking money out of the pockets of others. Would the rich man continue to serve your needs, if you had not got your hands upon him, and held him powerless under your taxation system? No! He would be only too glad to find an escape from it. Keep then your close grips upon him, now that you once hold him in it; and by more and more skillful and searching measures relieve him of what you want so much, and what is merely superfluous to him. Why spare your beast of burden? What is the use of your numbers, of your organizations, of the all-powerful vote, that can alone equalize conditions, making the poor man rich, and the rich man poor, if you are tempted to lay the useful weapon of force aside? Force in the old days was used against you; it is your turn now to use force, and spare not. Think well of what the vote can do for you. There lies the true magician's wand. You want pensions, provision for old age and sickness, land, houses, a minimum wage, lots and lots of education, breakfast and dinner for the children who go to school, scholarships for the clever pupils, libraries, museums, public halls, national operas, amusements and recreations of all kinds, and many another good thing which you will easily enough discover when you once begin to help yourselves—for, as the French say, the appetite comes with the eating; and there stand the richer classes with their laden pockets, only encumbered with the wealth that, if they knew it, they would be better without, defenseless, comparatively few and weak, with no power to stand against the resistless vote, if you once turn your strength to good account and learn how to organize your numbers for the great victory. Of course they will give you excellent reasons why you should keep your hands off them, and let them go free. Don't be fooled any longer by mere words. Force rules everything in this world; and today it is at last your turn to use force, and enter into possession of all that the world has to offer."

We answer—that all such language is the language of passionate unthinking children, who, regardless of right or wrong, with no questions of conscience, no perception of consequences, snatch at the first glittering thing that they see before them; that those who once listen to these counsels of violence would be changed in their nature from the reasonable man to the unreasonable beast; that all such counsels mean revolt against the great principles, against the honest and true methods that alone can redeem this world of ours, that, if faithfully followed, will in the end make a society happy, prosperous and progressive in its every part, ever leveling up, ever peacefully redistributing wealth, ever turning the waste places of life into the fruitful garden. But in violence and force there is no redemption. Force—whether disguised or not under the forms of voting—has but one meaning. It means universal confusion and strife; it means flinging the sword—that has never yet helped any of us—into the scale and preparing the way for the utterly wasted and useless shedding of much blood. Even if these good things, and many more of the same kind, lay within your grasp, waiting for your hand to close upon them, you have no right to take them by force, no right to make war upon any part of your fellow citizens, and to treat them as mere material to serve your interests. The rich man may no more be the beast of burden of the poor man, than the poor may be the beast of burden of the rich. Force rests on no moral foundations; you cannot justify it; it rests on no moral basis; you cannot reconcile it with reason and conscience and the higher nature of men. It lies apart in its own evil sphere, separated by the deepest gulf from all that makes for the real good of life— a mere devil's instrument. Even if force tomorrow could lay at your feet all the material gifts which you rightly desire, you may not, you dare not, for the sake of the greater good, for the sake of the higher nature that is in all of us, for the sake of the great purposes and the nobler meanings of life, accept what it offers. Our work is to make this life of ours prosperous, happy and beautiful for all who share in it, working with the instruments of liberty, of peace, and of friendship—these and these only are the instruments which we may take in our hands, these are the only instruments that can do our work for us.

Those who bid you use force are merely using language of the same kind as every bloodstained ruler has used in the past, the language of those who paid their troops by pillage, the language of the war-loving German general, who in old days looked down from the heights surrounding Paris, and whispered with a gentle sigh—"What a city to sack!" It is the language of those who through all the past history of the world have believed in the right of conquering, in the right of making slaves, who have set up force as their god, who have tried to do so by the violent hand whatever smiled to their own desires, and who only brought curses upon themselves, and a deluge of blood and tears upon the world. Force—whatever forms it takes—can do nothing for you. It can redeem nothing; it can give you nothing that is worth the having, nothing that will endure; it cannot even give you material prosperity. There is no salvation for you or for any living man to be won by the force that narrows rights, and always leaves men lower and more brutal in character than it found them. It is, and ever has been the evil genius of our race. It calls out the reckless, violent, cruel part of our nature, it wastes precious human effort in setting men to strive one against the other; it turns us into mere fighting animals; and ends, when men at last become sick of the useless strife and universal confusion, in "the man on the black horse" who calls himself and is greeted as "the savior of society." Make the truer, the nobler choice. Resist the blind and sordid appeal to your interests of

the moment, and take your place once and for good on
the side of the true liberty, that calls out all the better and
higher part of our nature, and knows no difference between rulers and ruled, majorities and minorities, rich
and poor. Declare once and for good that all men and
women are the only true owners of their faculties, of
their mind and body, of the property that belongs to
them; that you will only build the new society on the
one true foundation of self-ownership, self-rule, and
self-guidance; that you turn away from and renounce
utterly all this mischievous, foolish and corrupt business
of compelling each other, of placing burdens upon each
other, of making force, and the hateful trickery that
always goes with it, into our guiding principles, of treating first one set of men and then another set of men as
beasts of burden, whose lot in life it is to serve the purposes of others. True it is that there are many and many
things good in themselves which you do not yet possess,
and which you rightly desire, things which the believers
in force are generous enough to offer you in any profu-
sion at the expense of others; but they are merely cheat-
ing you with vain hopes, dangling before your eyes the
mocking shows of things that can never be. Force never
yet made a nation prosperous. It has destroyed nation
after nation, but never yet built up an enduring prosperity. It is through your own free efforts, not through the
gifts of those who have no right to give them, that all
these good things can come to you; for great is the essential difference between the gift—whether rightly or
wrongly given—and the thing won by free effort. That
which you have won has made you stronger in your-

selves, has taught you to know your own power and resources, has prepared you to win more and more victories. The gift flung to you has left you dependent upon others, distrustful and dispirited in yourselves. Why turn to your governments as if you were helpless in yourselves? What power lies in a government, that does not lie also in you? They are only men like you—men, in many ways disadvantaged, overweighted by the excessive burdens they have taken on themselves, seldom able to give concentrated attention to any one subject, however important; necessarily much under the influence of subordinates, from whom they must gather the information on which they have to act; often turned from their own course by the dissensions and differences of their followers; always obliged to plan and maneuver in order to keep their party together, and then losing their own guiding purpose, and tempted into misleading and unworthy courses; often deciding the weightiest matters in a hurry, as in the case of the famous Ten Minutes Reform Bill; and physically leading a life which overtaxes health and endurance with the call made upon it, by the care of their own office, their attendance far into the night at the House, their social occupations, the necessity to follow carefully all that is passing in the great theater of European politics, and of studying the questions which each week brings with it. Think carefully, and you will feel that all these rash attempts of the handful of men, that we call a government, to nurse a nation are a mere delusion. You can't throw the cares and the wants and the hopes of a whole people on some sixteen or eighteen overburdened workers. You might as well try to put the sea into a quart pot. A handful of men can't either think or act for you. Their task is impossible. If they try to do so, they can only be as blind guides who lead blind followers into the ditch. It all ends in scramble and confusion, in something being done in order to have something to show, in great expectations and woeful disappointments, in rash action and grievous mistakes, resulting from hurry and overpressure and insufficient knowledge, which lead the nation in wrong directions, and bring their long train of evil consequences. Why place your fortunes, all that you have, and all that you are, in other hands? You have in yourselves the great qualities— though still undeveloped—for supplying in your own free groups the growing wants of your lives. You are the children of the men who did so much for themselves, the men who broke the absolute power; who planted the colonies of our race in distant lands, who created our manufacturers, and carried our trade to every part of the world; who established your cooperative and benefit societies, your trade unions, who built and supported your Nonconformist churches. In you is the same stuff, the same power to do, as there was in them; and if only you let their spirit breathe again in you, and tread in their footsteps, you may add to their triumphs and successes tenfold and a hundredfold. As the French well say: "Ou les pères ont passé, passeront bientôt les enfants" (Where the fathers passed, there soon shall the children pass). To this point—the work to be undertaken in your own free groups, without any compulsion and subjection of others —we will return later.

But nothing can be well and rightly done, nothing can

bear the true fruit, until you become deeply and devotedly in love with personal liberty, consecrating in your hearts the great and sacred principle of self-ownership and self-direction. That great principle must be our guiding star through the whole of this life's pilgrimage. Away from its guiding we shall only continue to wander, as of old, hopelessly in the wilderness. For its sake we must be ready to make any and every sacrifice. It is worth them all—many times worth them all. For its sake you must steadily refuse all the glittering gifts and bribes which many politicians of both parties eagerly press upon you, if you will but accept them as your leaders, and lend them the power which your numbers can give. Enter into none of these corrupt and fatal compacts. All such leaders are but playing with you, fooling you for their own ends. In the pride and vanity of their hearts they wish to bind you to them, to make you dependent upon them. You are to fight their battles, and you will be paid in return much in the same manner as the old leaders paid their soldiers by giving them a conquered city to sack. Can any real good come to you by following that unworthy and mercenary path? When once you have become a mere pillaging horde, when once you have lost all guidance and control and purpose of your own, bound to your leaders, and dependent on them for the sake of the spoils that they fling to you, do you think that any of the greater and nobler things of life will still be possible to you? The great things are only possible for those who keep their hearts pure and exalted, and their hands clean, who are true to themselves, who follow and serve the fixed principles that are above us all, and are our only true guides, who never sell themselves into the hands of others. Your very leaders, who have cheated you, and used you, will despise you; and in your own hearts, if you dare honestly to search into them, you will despise yourselves. But your self-contempt will hardly help you. You will have lost the great qualities of your nature; the old corrupt contract, into which you have entered, will still bind you; you may in your wild discontent revolt against your leaders; but as in the legends of the evil controlling spirit, that both serves and enslaves, you will each be a fatal necessity to the other. You have linked your fortunes together, and it will be hard to dissolve the partnership. Remember ever the old words—as true today as when they were first spoken—"What shall it profit a man if he gain the whole world, and lose his own soul?" If you lose all respect for the rights of others, and with it your own self-respect; if you lose your own sense of right and fairness, if you lose your belief in liberty, and with it the sense of your own worth and true rank; if you lose your own will and self-guidance and control over your own lives and actions, what can all the buying and trafficking, what can all the gifts of politicians give you in return? Why let the true diamond be taken from you in exchange for the worthless bit of glass? Is not the ruling of your own selves worth a hundred times this mad attempt to rule over others? If your house were filled with silver and gold, would you be happy if your own self no more belonged to you? Have you ever carefully thought out what life would be like under the schemes of the socialist party, who offer us the final, the logical completion of all systems of force? Try to picture the huge overweighted groaning machine of government; the men who direct it vainly, miserably struggling with their impossible task of managing everything, driven for the sake of their universal system to extinguish all differences of thought and action, allowing no man to possess his own faculties, or to enjoy the fruit that he has won by their exercise, to call land or house or home his own, allowing no man to do a day's work for another, or to sell and buy on his own account, denying to all men the ownership and possession of either body or mind, necessarily intolerant, as the tsar's government is intolerant, of every form of free thought and free enterprise, trembling at the very shadow of liberty, haunted by the perpetual terror that the old love of self-guidance and free action might some day again awake in the breast of men, obliged to exercise a discipline, like that which exists in the German army, from fear that the first beginning of revolt might prove the destruction of the huge trembling ill-balanced structure, with no sense of right— right a mere word that would be lost to their language— but only the ever-present, ever-urgent necessities of maintaining their unstable power, which was always out of equilibrium, always in danger, because opposed to the essential nature of men—that unconquerable nature, which has always broken and will always break in its own time these systems of bondage. Picture also the horde of countless officials, who would form a bureaucratic, all-powerful army, vast as that which exists in Russia, and probably as corrupt—for the same reason— because only able to fulfill their task, if allowed to have supreme unquestioned power; always engaged in spying, restraining, and repressing, forever monotonously repeating, as if they governed a nursery—"Don't, you mustn't"; and then picture imprisoned under the bureaucratic caste a nation of dispirited ciphers—ciphers, who would be as peevish, discontented and quarrelsome as shut-up children, because shut off by an iron fence from all the stimulating influences of free life, and forbidden, as if it were a crime, to exercise their faculties according to their own interests and inclinations; picture also the intense, the ludicrous pettiness that would run through the whole thing. As a French writer (Leroy Beaulieu) wittily said—it would be a great state question, ever recurring to trouble the safety of the trembling quavering system, whether or no a wife should be allowed to mend the trousers of her husband. Who could exorcise and lay to rest that insoluble problem, for if the wife were once allowed to perform this bit of useful household duty, might not the whole wicked unsocialistic trade of working for others, in return for their sixpences and shillings, come flowing back with irresistible force? Such is the small game that you are obliged to hunt, such are the minute pitiful necessities to which you are obliged to stoop, when once you construct these great state machineries, and take upon yourself, in your amazing and ignorant presumption, to interfere with the natural activities of human existence.

See also another truth. There are few greater injuries that can be inflicted on you than taking out of your hands the great services that supply your wants. Why? Because the healing virtue that belongs to all these great services —education, religion, the winning of land and houses, the securing of greater comfort and refinement and amusement in your lives—lies in the winning of these things for yourselves by your own exertions, through your own skill, your own courage, your friendly cooperation one with another, your integrity in your common dealings, your unconquerable self-reliance and confidence in your own powers of doing. This winning, these efforts, are the great lessons in lifelong education; that lasts from childhood to the grave; and when learned, they are learned not for yourselves alone, but for your children, and your children's children. They are the steps and the only steps up to the higher levels. You can't be carried to those higher levels on the shoulders of others. The politician is like those who boasted to have the keys of earth and heaven in their pocket. Vainest of vain pretenses! The keys both of heaven and earth lie in your own pocket; it is only you—you, the free individuals—who can unlock the great door. All these great wants and services are the means by which we acquire the great qualities which spell victory; they are the means by which we become raised and changed in ourselves, and by which, as we are changed, we change and remake all the circumstances of our lives. Each victory so gained prepares the way for the next victory, and makes that next victory the easier, for we not only have the sense of success in our hearts, but we have begun to acquire the qualities on which it depends. On the other hand the more of his ready-made institutions the politician thrusts upon you, the weaker, the more incapable you become, just because the great qualities are not called out and exercised. Why should they be called out? There is no need for them; their practice ground is taken away; and they simply lie idle,

rusting, and at last ceasing to be. Tie up your right hand
for three months and what happens? The muscles will
have wasted, and your hand will have lost its cunning and
its force. So it is with all mental and moral qualities.
Given time enough, and a politician with his restless
scheming brain and his clumsy hands would enfeeble
and spoil a nation of the best and truest workers. He is
powerless to help you; he can only stand in your way, and
prevent your doing.

Refuse then to put your faith in mere machinery, in
party organizations, in acts of Parliament, in great un-
wieldy systems, which treat good and bad, the careful
and the careless, the striving and the indifferent, on the
same plan, and which on account of their vast and cum-
brous size, their complexity, their official central management, pass entirely out of your control. Refuse to be
spoon-fed, drugged and dosed, by the politicians. They
are not leading you toward the promised land, but further
and further away from it. If the world could be saved by
the men of words and the machine makers, it would have
been saved long ago. Nothing is easier than to make
machinery; you may have any quantity of it on order in
a few months. Nothing is easier than to appoint any
number of officials. Unluckily the true fight is of another
and much sterner kind; and the victory comes of our own
climbing of the hills, not by sitting in the plain, with
folded hands, watching those others who profess to do
our business for us. Do you think it likely or reasonable,
do you think it fits in with and agrees with your daily
experience of this fighting, working world of ours, that
you could take your chair in the politician's shop, and

order across his counter so much prosperity and progress and happiness, just as you might order cotton goods by the piece or wheat by the quarter? Be brave and clear-sighted, and face the stern but wholesome truth, that it is only you, you with your own hands, you with your unconquerable resolve, without any dependence on others, without any of these childish and mischievous party struggles, which are perhaps a little more exciting than cricket, or football, or even "bridge" to some of us, but a good deal more profitless to the nation than digging holes in the earth and then filling them up again, without any use of force, without any oppression of each other, without any of these blind reckless attempts to humiliate and defeat those who hold different beliefs from ourselves, and who desire to follow different methods from those which we follow, without any division of the nation into two, three or more hostile camps, ever inspired with dread and hatred of each other—it is only you yourselves, fighting with the good, pure, honest weapons of persuasion and example, of sympathy and friendly cooperation—it is only you, calling out in yourselves the great qualities, and flinging away all the meaner things, the strifes, the hates, the jealousies, the mere love of fighting and conquering—it is only you, treading in the blessed path of peace and freedom, who can bring about the true regeneration of society, and with it the true happiness of your own lives.

And through it all avoid that favorite, that much loved snare of the politician, by which he ever seeks to rivet his hold upon you, refuse to attack and weaken in any manner the full rights of property. You, who are workers, could not inflict on your own selves a more fatal injury. Property is the great and good inducement that will call out your efforts and energies for the remaking of the present form of society. Deprive property of its full value and attractiveness, and we shall all become stuff only fit to make the helpless incapable crowd that the socialist so deeply admires, and hopes so easily to control. But it is not only for the sake of the "magic of property," its power to call out the qualities of industry and saving; it is above all because you cannot weaken the rights of property without diminishing, without injuring that first and greatest of all possessions—human liberty; it is for that supreme reason that we must resist every attempt of the politician to buy votes by generously giving away the property that does not belong to him. The control of his own property by the individual, and the liberty of the individual can never be separated from each other. They must stand, or fall, together. Property, when earned, is the product of faculties, and results from their free exercise; and, when inherited, represents the full right of a man, free from all imaginary and usurped control of others, to deal as he likes with his own. Destroy the rights of property, and you will also destroy both the material and the moral foundations of liberty. To all men and women, rich or poor, belong their own faculties, and as a consequence, equally belongs to them all that they can honestly gain in free and open competition, through the exercise of those faculties.

It is idle to talk of freedom, and, while the word is on one's lips, to attack property. He who attacks property, joins the camp of those who wish to keep some men in subjection to the will of others. You cannot break down any of the defenses of liberty, you cannot weaken liberty at any one point, without weakening it at all points. Liberty means refusing to allow some men to use the state to compel other men to serve their interests or their opinions; and at whatever point we allow this servitude to exist, we weaken or destroy in men's minds the sacredness of the principle, which must be, as regards all actions, all relations, our universal bond. But it is not only for the sake of liberty—though that is far the greater and higher reason—it is also for the sake of your own material progress—that you, the workers, must resolutely reject all interference with, all mutilations of the rights of property.

For the moment the larger part of existing property belongs to the richer classes; but it will not be so, as soon as ever you, the workers, take out of the hands of the politicians, and into your own hands, the task of carving out your own fortunes. The working body of the people must no longer be content—not for a single day—to be the propertyless class. In every city and town and village they must form their associations for the gaining of property; they must put their irresistible pence and shillings together, so that, step by step, effort upon effort, they may become the owners of land, of farms, of houses, of shops, of mills, and trading ships; they must take shares in the great well-managed trading companies and railways, until the time comes, as their capital increases, when they will be able to become the owners at first of small trading concerns, established by themselves, and then later of larger and more important concerns. They must—for all reasons, the best and the second best—become the owners of property. Without property no class can take its true place in the nation. They must devote much of their resolution and self-denial to the steady persistent heaping together of the pence and shillings for this purpose. As they become possessed of property, they will see a definite goal lying before themselves—one good and useful ambition ever succeeding to another. The old dreary hopelessness will disappear, they will gain in power and influence; the difference between classes will disappear; they will break the enfeebling and corrupting influence of the politicians—what influence would remain to the man of words if he could no longer offer gratis—in return for nothing but votes—the property of others, without any greater exertion on the part of the people than marking their voting papers in his favor? And with the acquiring of property, the workers will also acquire the qualities that the management of property brings with it; while they add a new interest, a new meaning to their lives. We appeal to the many thousands of strong, capable, self-denying men that are to be found among us. Is the gaining of property only a dream; is the thing so very difficult, so far out of your reach? Say that a million men and women begin tomorrow to subscribe one halfpenny a week—who would miss that magical halfpenny, which is to transform so many things?—at the end of the year you will have a fund of over £100,000 to start with—not we think, a bad beginning for the great campaign. In many cases the property, such as land and houses, that you would so acquire, you would probably rent or redistribute on remunerative but easy terms to your own members; in the case of workers in towns, you would be able to allow those of your members who desired rest and change, to work for a time on your farms, and you would also be able to make a holiday ground and common meeting place of some farm that belonged to you, and that could be easily reached by that true instrument of social progress for men and women, the bicycle. Many will be the new forms of health and comfort and amusement that will become possible to you, when once you steadily determine to pile the pence and the shillings together for becoming owners of property; and when once you have put your hand to this good work, you must not relax your efforts until you have become, as you will become before many years have passed, the greatest of property holders in the nation. All is possible to you if you resolutely fling away from you the incitements to strife, the tamperings with liberty and individual property, and pile up the pence and the shillings for the acquiring of your own property. Resist, therefore, all reckless, unthinking appeals made to you to deprive the great prize of any part of its attractions. If you surround property with state restrictions, interfere with free trade and any part of the open market, interfere with free contract, make compulsory arrangements for tenant and landowner, allow the present burdens of rate and tax to discourage ownership and penalize improvements, you will weaken the motives for acquiring property, and blunt the edge of the most powerful material instrument that exists for your own advancement. Only remember—as we have said—that great as is your material interest in safeguarding the rights of individual property, yet higher and greater are and ever will be the moral reasons that forbid our sanctioning any attack upon it, or our suffering state burdens and restrictions and impediments to grow round it. True liberty—as we said—cannot exist apart from the full rights of property; for property is—so to speak—only the crystallized form of free faculties. They take the name of liberty in vain, they do not understand its nature, who would allow the state—or what goes by the name of the state—the worthy eighteen or twenty men who govern us —to play with property. Everything that is surrounded with state restrictions, everything that is state-mutilated, everything taxed and burdened, loses its best value, and can no longer call out our energies and efforts in their full force. Preserve, then, at its best and strongest the magic of property; leave to it all its stimulating and transforming virtues. It is one of the great master keys that open the door to all that in a material sense you rightly and proudly wish to do and to be.

Many other points remain; we can only touch here on a few of them. Keep clear of both political parties, until one of them seriously, earnestly, with deep conviction, pledges itself to the cause of personal liberty. At present they are both of them opportunist, seeking power, rejecting fixed principles. It is true that we owe great debts to the Liberal Party in the past, but at present it is deserting its own best traditions, ceasing to guide and inspire the people, fighting the downhill not the uphill battles, and intent on playing the great game. Someday, as we may hope, it may refind its better self and breathe again the spirit of true exalted leadership, and regardless of its own

fortunes for the hours place itself openly on the side of
Mr. Spencer's "widest possible liberty." But today both
parties mean anything or nothing; they represent only
too often mere scrambling, mere lust for power. It is true
that one or other of the two parties may mean to you
some of the things that you yourselves mean, but it will
also mean a great many things that you do not mean.
They both believe in subjecting some men to the will of
other men, in using the state as the instrument of universal force, and you cannot rightly take your place in
their ranks, or fight with them. Have nothing to do with
the scramble for power. Hold on your own course and
stand "foursquare to all the winds." Pick out your boldest
and most resolute men, and fight every by-election. Don't
fight to win, but fight to teach and inspire. The more
resolutely you stand on your own ground, the more men
of both parties, who begin to see the worthlessness and
the mischief of these party conflicts, and the growing
danger of using force, will come to you and join your
small army. Few as you are today, you are stronger than
the huge ill-assorted crowds—representing many conflicting opinions—that stand opposed to you, for no one can
measure the strength that a great and true cause, devotedly followed, gives to those who consistently serve
it. Fight the battle of liberty at every point. Give your
best help to those who are resisting municipal trading, or
resisting interference with home work, or resisting the
placing of power in the hands of the medical or any other
profession. You must not confer any form of authority
or monopoly on any profession; you must not give to any
of them the power to force their services upon us. Let

every profession that will, organize itself and make rules for its own members; but we, the public, must remain free in every respect to take or to leave what they offer to us. The monopolies that they all so dearly love are fatal to their own efficiency, and to their own higher qualities, as well as full of danger to the public. We all lose our best perceptions, we all become intellectually hidebound, we all begin to believe that the public exist for us, exist for our professional purposes, whenever we are protected by a monopoly. In the same way never hand over any question to be decided but those who are called experts. The knowledge of the experts is very useful and valuable, but wisdom and discernment and well-balanced judgment are different things from knowledge, and they do not always keep company. Knowledge is great, someone has written, but prejudice is greater. The experts are excellent as advisers, but never as authoritative judges, allowed to stand between the public and the questions that affect its interest. The real service that the experts can perform for us is to place their knowledge in the clearest and simplest form before us all, and to explain their reasons for advising a certain course. There is no limit to the mistakes that the most learned men may make when they are allowed to deliver judgment behind closed doors, when they are not called upon to submit their reasons to open discussion, and to justify publicly the counsels that they offer.

Strive also to make this great empire of ours an instrument of help and usefulness and friendliness for the whole world. It is a great world trust placed in our hands, that we must interpret in no selfish and narrow, in no boastful and vainglorious spirit. Cast away all the tawdry and sordid dreams of an empire stronger than all other nations; but let it rest on the one true foundation of peace and friendship, and as far as lies with you of free intercourse between all nations—an empire of equal generous rights, with no privileges reserved for any of us. So, and only so, shall this great empire endure, saved from the fate that has so justly swept away all the other great empires, that were founded on meaner and more selfish conceptions. Have nothing to do with this pitiful cowardly un-English war against the aliens. Even if your interests should seem to suffer for a while—which there is strong reason for believing would not be the case—we ask you to make this sacrifice for the sake of the liberty of all, even the poorest, and for the sake of the proud traditions of our race. Unswerving, disinterested devotion to the principle of universal liberty, and to those noble traditions that have always opened the gates of this country to the suffering and oppressed, will far, far outbalance any hurt that may for a time result from the presence with us of the suffering and oppressed. Plead always that there should be no unworthy exceptions; all such exceptions are bad in themselves, and have the bad habit of becoming the rule. The temper of timorous selfishness that would exclude any aliens, that would treat any natives as different from our own flesh and blood, is our real danger—the danger that threatens our true greatness. Indulge that temper in any one direction, and you will presently encourage it to become the evil genius of the nation.

Last, let us all work together, to soften and improve the relations of capital and labor. War between capital and labor is only too like the unreasonable and disastrous war between nations, or between parties in a nation. All war is a crime, and, as all crimes are, a mischievous folly—in almost all cases a mere outburst of childishness. Everywhere we have to learn the wise art of pulling in friendly forbearing fashion with each other, and not against each other; everywhere we have to learn to abandon the useless wasteful brutal methods of war, and to enter the blessed and fruitful paths of peace. Is there any war of any kind, that might not have been avoided by better temper, more patience, and a stronger love of peace? Is there any war, excepting on very rare occasions the wars to repel invasion or the attacking of great human rights, that in the end has not brought disappointment and sorrow, and bitter fruits of its own, as much or even more to the nation that was successful, as to the nation that was unsuccessful? And who profits from these great labor contests, and the stirring of hurtful passions, that goes with them? Friendship, friendly cooperation, the making of common cause for common ends, are the true ends to be aimed at between labor and capital; and each contest makes the good day of reconciliation more difficult, puts it further and further from us. We cannot choose in this great matter. There is only one way. We *must* be friends. Nothing less than honest heartfelt friendship will mend the old evils, and make the happier future. As we asked, who profits by these contests? If you—the workers—win today, the capitalists organize themselves tomorrow more strongly than before; if the capitalists win, the workers in the same way strengthen their fighting forces. And so —just as between nations—runs forever the vicious circle. And as with the nations, so our labor strife is not only lost and wasted, but it fatally injures both sides alike —both the conquerors and the conquered. Let us then love and honor peace, cling to her, open our hearts to her, make sacrifices for her, bear and forbear for her sake, place her great ends before everything else, and resolve that, as far as lies with us, her happy reign shall at last be established over the whole land. Peace—always hand in hand with her great sister liberty—not only represents the higher meaning of our moral life, but also like liberty represents the greatest material interest that the workers have; their industry and skill will never bear their full fruits as long as we cling to war, and the destructive methods of force. Capital and labor, like the rest of us, must obey the great moral law and tread in the path of peace and friendship. It is their duty, as it is the duty of all of us in the other relations of life—worthy of every effort, of all patience and sacrifice on our part. Only with peace can the true prosperity come. With peace and friendship, trade and enterprise would develop a much more vigorous life, and find for themselves many new directions. Nothing limits enterprise so fatally, and with it the employment of the workers, as the dissensions and quarrels between capital and labor. With peace and friendship not only does more and more capital flow into trade and production; but new enterprises are confidently undertaken in every direction; and then, as the consequence, wages rise in the one true healthy manner—with the security that peace brings, capital bidding against capital, and the capitalist accepting lower profits. All insecurity, all disturbance of trade relations, must be paid for, and they are paid for by the worker; for insecurity and uncertainty mean that a higher rate of profit is necessary to tempt the investment of capital lying idle, and therefore necessarily results in lower wages.

Reorganize then your trade societies on a peace basis, or establish new unions on that basis. Preserve your independence; but do all in your power to enter into friendly alliances with capital. Remember that friendship is the triumph of good sense and wise temper; strife is the indulgence of the undisciplined, the childish part of our nature. Form associations in which both the workers and the capitalists would be represented; where they would meet and take common action, as friends, working together to make the conditions of labor better, more comfortable, more sanitary, and using every peace expedient to remove difficulties as they arise. If times of depression come, and wages fall low, use the common fund to draft away some of the workers, find temporary employment for them on the farms and lands that you will acquire as your own, start workshops of your own, which in some cases might provide articles of home use and comfort for your members; and let your unemployed members in turn receive a grant to enable them to spend their unoccupied time usefully in study and education. At present an unoccupied workman wastes time and temper during a slack time. Like his own tools he rusts and deteriorates with them. Why should that be so? Have your own classes and day schools, and let the unoccupied men turn the time to golden use. But through it all, even if you strike, refuse as a matter of principle, as faithful followers of liberty in everything, to use any of the old bad methods of force. If, after every effort, after attempting mediation and arbitration, you cannot agree about wages with the employers, and if you think it wise and right and necessary to do so, throw up your work; but if there are those who will take the wage that you are unwilling to take— let them do so, without let or hindrance. It is their right; and we must never deny or fight against a human right for the sake of what seems to be our interest of the moment. We say what "seems" to be; for in the end you will gain far more by clinging faithfully to the methods of peace and respect for the rights of others than by allowing yourselves to use the force that always calls out force in reply, always brings its own far-reaching hurtful consequences, for the sake of the advantage or victory of the moment. Once be tempted to use force, and force will become your master, your tyrant, tempting you again and again to seek its aid and to enter its service. No man employs force today without being easily persuaded to use it once more tomorrow, and then again the next day. There are in all that we do only two ways—the way of peace and cooperation, the way of force and strife. Can you hesitate between them? Do not good sense and right sense plead for the one and against he other? Set yourselves then to discover and practice every conciliatory method; wherever practicable, become shareowners and partners in the concerns where you labor, and make it your pride to join hands frankly with the employers, wiping out forever the old disastrous war feeling, that has brought so much useless suffering and loss with it.

Remember, also, as another great and vital interest, to keep a free and open market in everything. Only so again

can you get the fullest return of your labor. High wages
are of little profit, when prices rule high, and production
becomes a dull monopoly, benumbing the best energies
of the producers. Under a monopoly we all grow stupid,
unperceiving, apathetic, given up to routine. Leave all
traders free to bring to your door the best articles that
the world produces at the lowest cost. If they are better
and cheaper than what you produce, they will be the
truest incentive for greater exertions both on your part
and on the capitalist's part. It is only the coward's policy
to kneel down in the dust, and wail, and confess inferior-
ity, as regards the producers of other nations. Take up
the challenge bravely, from whatever quarter it comes;
improve method and process and machinery—above all
improve the relations between capital and labor; on that,
more perhaps than on anything else, industrial victory
depends. Be willing to learn from all, of any country, who
have anything useful to teach. Never be tempted to build
Chinese walls for your protection, and to go indolently
to sleep behind them. Your system of free trade is another great world trust placed in your hands. You stand
before all nations holding a bright and shining light, that
if you are true to the great destiny of our country you will
never allow to be dimmed or extinguished. Mr. Cobden
spoke the truth when he said that you would convert the
other nations to your own brave way of competition; only
he did not allow enough for all the reactionary influences,
the narrow unenlightened so-called patriotism, the timidities of some traders and their desire to take their ease
comfortably, and not to overexert themselves, so long as
they could compel the public to buy at their own price,

and to accept their own standard of good workmanship, the warlike emperors, the chauvinists of all countries, the extravagant spendings with the resulting difficulties of getting blood from a stone, and the temptation of scraping revenue together in any mischievous fashion that offered itself, the party intrigues, the effort to discover something that would serve as an attractive policy, the unavowed purpose of some politicians, living for party, and keen for power, to bind a large part of the people by the worst of bonds to their side by means of a huge and corrupt money interest. But the consequences of protection are fighting their battle everywhere on the side of free trade—as the consequences of folly and blindness always fight on the side of the better things; and if we remain faithful to our great trust will in their due time fulfill Mr. Cobden's words. The high prices and dear living, the harassing interferences with trade, the rings and corners, the trickeries and corruption, that all tread so close on the heels of protection, the wild extravagance, the domineering insolent attitude of the state-made monopolists, the ever-growing power of the governments to go their own way, where they can gather vast sums of money so easily through their unseen tax collectors, the ever-spreading socialism, that is only protection made universal—all these things are preaching their eloquent lesson, and slowly preparing the way in other countries for free trade. Sooner or later the world after years of bitter experience learns to unmask all the impostor systems that have traded in its hopes and passions and fears. The thin coating wears off, and the baser metal betrays itself underneath. So it will fare with the protection, that asks you to be credulous enough to tie up your left hand in order that your right hand may work more profitably. It is true that in protected countries the wages of the workers may be pushed up higher than in the case of free trade countries, but life will remain harder and more difficult. Why? Because, as we have said, prices rule so high; corners and combinations flourish; trickery and corruption find their opportunity; more vultures of every kind flock to the feast; and with the feast of the vultures the burden of rates and taxes becomes intolerable. The whole thing hangs together. Establish freedom and open competition in everything, and all forms of trade and enterprise, all relations of men to each other, tend to become healthy and vigorous, pure and clean. The better and more efficient forms—as they do throughout nature's world—slowly displacing the inefficient forms. It must be so; for in the fair open fight the good always tend to win over the bad, if only you restrain all interferences of force. It is so with freedom everywhere and in all things. Freedom begets the conflict; the conflict begets the good and helpful qualities; and the good and helpful qualities win their own victory. They must do so; for they are in themselves stronger, more energetic, more efficient, than the forces—the trickeries, the corruptions, the timidities, the selfishness—to which they are opposed. The same truth rules our good and bad habits. Only keep the field open and allow the fair fight, and the bad at last must yield to the good. Sooner or later the time comes when the clearer sighted, the more rightly judging few denounce some evil habit that exists; gradually their influence and example act on others in ever-widening circles, until many men grow ashamed of what they have so long done, and the habit is abandoned. Such is the universal law of progress, which prevails in everything, so long as we allow the free open fight between all good and evil. But in order that the good may prevail there must be life and vigor in the people, and this can only be where freedom exists. If freedom does not exist, if life and vigor have died, then protection—whatever its form—cannot prevent, it can only put off for a short time the inevitable ruin and disaster. Nations only continue to exist as long as they keep in themselves the great simple virtues. As we have seen again and again, they go to pieces, and yield their places to others when once the fatal corruption takes root in their character; corruption can only be fought by liberty with its strengthening, raising, purifying influences. Protection, that is artificial in its nature, protection that rests on force, always means, if long enough continued, failure and death in the end; for it prevents our developing the qualities which can alone enable us to keep our place in a world that never stands still. As Mr. Darwin pointed out so clearly, those races of plants and animals, which for a time were protected by mountains or desert or an arm of the sea, were doomed to fail when at last they came into competition with the unprotected forms. So is it with us men. If you wish to understand the deadly influences of protection, if you wish for a practical example, look carefully at all the distorted and perverted growths of trade enterprise that exist in some protected countries, the unwholesome combinations, the universal selfish scramble, the poisonous mixture of politics and trade influences, the use of the state power to watch over and favor great moneyed monopolies, the long endurance of the public that tolerates the vilest things at the hands of its politicians, and you will realize how deadly is every form of protection, that resting on force sends us to sleep, and how vital is the liberty that forever fights the evil by opposing it to the good, that never sleeps, that is always stirring us into new forms of doing and resisting, and forever tends to make the better take the place of the good. There is only one true form of protection, and that is universal liberty with its ceaseless striving and effort.

Strongly as we are opposed to the protectionists, who whitewash their creed under the name of tariff reform, it is fair to remember one plea on their behalf. They have one true grievance. As long as the present extravagant spending goes on in its compulsory fashion they may fairly complain that the income tax payers are likely to be unjustly treated. The remedy does not lie in extending our compulsory system of taking from the public but in limiting it, and presently transforming it into voluntary giving. Under our compulsory system free trade will never be a safe possession. It is with us today, it will be tomorrow. If we were pushed again to a war, as we were pushed headlong into the Boer War, just because one statesman got into a temper, shut his eyes and put his head down, and another statesman looked sorrowfully on, like the gods of Olympus, smiling at the follies of the human race, we should at once hear the double cry ringing in our ears for conscription and protection—conscription to force us to fight with our conscience or against our conscience; protection to force us to pay for what we might look on as a crime and a folly. You may be sure that free trade will sooner or later be swept away, unless we go boldly forward in its own spirit and in its own direction and destroy the compulsory character of taxation. There lies the stronghold of all war and strife and oppression of each other. As long as compulsory taxation lasts—in other words giving power to some men to use other men against their beliefs and their interests—liberty will be but a mocking phrase. Between liberty and compulsory taxation there is no possible reconciliation. It is a struggle of life and death between the two. That which is free and that which is bound can never long keep company. Sooner or later one of the two must prevail over the other. If a war came, Conservative ministers would see their great opportunity, and with rapture of heart would fasten round us the two chains that they dearly love, conscription and protection. Liberal ministers would sorrowfully shake their heads, wring their hands, utter a last pathetic tribute to liberty and free trade, and with handkerchiefs to their eyes would take the same course. If you mean to secure the great victory just gained for free trade you must go boldly and resolutely on in the same good path. Dangers lie strewn around you on every side. There is no security for what you have gained, but in pressing forward. There is one and only one way of permanently saving free trade, and that is to sweep away all the compulsory system in which we are entangled.

And now place before yourselves the picture of the nation that not simply out of self-interest but for rights' sake and conscience's sake took to its heart the great cause of true liberty, and was determined that all men and women should be left free to guide themselves and take charge of their own lives; that was determined to oppress and persecute and restrain the actions of no single person in order to serve any interest or any opinion or any class advantage; that flung out of its hands the bad instrument of force—using force only for its one clear, simple and rightful purpose of restraining all acts of force and fraud, committed by one citizen against another, of safeguarding the lives, the actions, the property of all, and thus making a fair open field for all honest effort; think, under the influences of liberty and her twin sister peace—for they are inseparably bound together—neither existing without the other—how our character as a people would grow nobler and at the same time softer and more generous— think how the old useless enmities and jealousies and strivings would die out; how the unscrupulous politician would become a reformed character, hardly recognizing his old self in his new and better self; how men of all classes would learn to cooperate together for every kind of good and useful purpose; how, as the results of this free cooperation, innumerable ties of friendship and kind- liness would spring up amongst us all of every class and condition, when we no longer sought to humble and crush each other, but invited all who were willing to work freely with us; how much truer and more real would be the campaign against the besetting vices and weakness of our nature, when we sought to change that nature, not simply to tie men's hands and restrain external action, no longer setting up and establishing in all parts of life that poor weak motive—the fear of punishment—those clumsy useless penalties, evaded and laughed at by the cunning, that have never yet turned sinner into saint;

how we should rediscover in ourselves the good vigorous stuff that lies hidden there, the power to plan, to dare and to do; how we should see in clearer light our duty toward other nations, and fulfill more faithfully our great world trust; how we should cease to be a people divided into three or four quarrelsome unscrupulous factions—ready to sacrifice all the great things to their intense desire for power—and grow into a people really one in heart and mind, because we frankly recognized the right to differ, the right of each one to choose his own path because we respected and cherished the will, the intelligence, the free choice of others, as much as we respect and cherish these things in ourselves, and were resolved never to trample, for the sake of any plea, for any motive, on the higher parts of human nature, resolved that—come storm or sunshine—we would not falter in our allegiance to liberty and her sister peace, that we would do all, dare all, and suffer all, if need be, for their sake, then at last the regeneration of society would begin, the real promised land, not the imaginary land of vain and mocking desires, would be in sight.

And now for the practical measures that we must set before ourselves:

1.   So far as force is concerned, we must use state force only to protect ourselves against those who would employ force or fraud; using it to safeguard all public and private property, and to repel if a real necessity arises the foreign aggressor. We must employ force simply as the servant of liberty, and under the strongest conditions that liberty would impose upon it; we must refuse utterly and in everything to employ it so as to deprive the inno-

cent and unaggressive citizen of his own will and self-guidance.

2. We must place limits upon every form of compulsory taxation, until we are strong enough to destroy it finally and completely; and to transform it into a system of voluntary giving. Under that voluntary system alone can a nation live in peace and friendship and work together happily and profitably for common ends. In voluntary taxation we shall find the one true form of lifelong education which will teach us to act together, creating innumerable kindly ties between us all which will call out all the truest and most generous qualities of our best citizens, doubling and trebling their energies, as they find themselves working for their own beliefs and ideas, and no longer used as the mere tools and creatures of others; which will slowly bring under the influence of the better citizens the selfish and the indifferent, teaching them too to share in public movements, and common efforts; which will multiply those differences of method, those experiments made from new points of view—experiments, upon which all progress depends, and replacing the great clumsy universal systems which treat good and bad alike, which are mere developments of the official mind, and escape entirely from the control of those in whose interest they are supposed to exist; which will call into life again the proud feeling of self-help and independence which belong to this nation of ours, and which the politician has done so much to weaken and destroy.

The great choice lies before you. No nation stands still. It must move in one direction or the other. Either the state must grow in power, imposing new burdens and compulsions, and the nation sink lower and lower into a helpless quarreling crowd, or the individual must gain his own rightful freedom, become master of himself, creature of none, confident in himself and in his own qualities, confident in his power to plan and to do, and determined to end this Old World, profitless and worn-out system of restrictions and compulsions, which is not good or healthy even for the children. Once we realize the waste and the folly of striving against each other, once we feel in our hearts that the worst use to which we can turn human energies is gaining victories over each other, then we shall at last begin in true earnest to turn the wilderness into a garden, and to plant all the best and fairest of the flowers where now only the nettles and the briars grow.

We wish it to be understood that we who sign this paper are in agreement with its general spirit, reserving our own judgment on special points.

ESSAY TEN

THE PRINCIPLES OF VOLUNTARYISM
AND FREE LIFE

A series of excerpts from Herbert's writings, this essay was edited by E. E. Krott and first published, as a pamphlet, in 1897 by the Free Press Association in Burlington, Vermont.

What We Voluntaryists Believe

The Self-Owner Is Owner of His Own Mind and Body and His Own Property

We voluntaryists believe that no true progress can be made until we frankly recognize the great truth that every individual, who lives within the sphere of his own rights, as a self-owner, and has not himself first aggressed upon others by employing force or fraud in his dealings with them [and thus deprived himself of his own rights of self-ownership by aggressing upon these same rights of others], is the only one true owner of his own faculties, and his own property. We claim that the individual is not only the one true owner of his faculties, but also of his property, because property is directly or indirectly the product of faculties, is inseparable from faculties, and therefore must rest on the same moral basis, and fall under the same moral law, as faculties. Personal ownership of our own selves and of our own faculties, necessarily includes personal ownership of property. As property is created by faculties, it would be idle, it would be a mere illusion, to speak of an individual as owner of his own faculties, and at same time to withhold from him the fullest and most perfect rights over his property, if such property has been rightfully acquired (by "rightfully" we mean acquired without force or fraud), or inherited from those who have rightfully acquired it.

No Peaceful Nonaggressive Citizen Can Be Submitted to the Control of Others, Apart from His Own Consent

We hold that the one and only one true basis of society is the frank recognition of these rights of self-ownership; that is to say, of the rights of control and direction by the individual, as he himself chooses, over his own mind, his own body, and his own property, always provided, that he respects the same universal rights in others. We hold that so long as he lives within the sphere of his own rights, so long as he respects these rights in others, not aggressing by force or fraud upon the person or property of his neighbors, he cannot be made subject, apart from his own consent, to the control and direction of others, and he cannot be rightfully *compelled* under any public pretext, by the force of others, to perform any services, to pay any contributions, or to act or not to act in any manner contrary to his own desires or to his own sense of right. He is by moral right a free man, self-owning and self-directing; and has done nothing which justifies others, for any convenience of their own, in taking from him any part, small or great, of his self-ownership.

The Moral Rights of a Delegated Body, Such as a Government, Can Never Be Greater than the Moral Rights of the Individuals Who Delegated to It Its Power. Force Can Only Be Used (Whether by an Individual or by a Government Makes No Difference) for Defensive Purposes—Never for Aggressive Purposes

Nature is on the side of self-ownership, self-guidance. We see that each man and each woman is individually endowed by nature with a separate, complete, and perfect machinery for self-guidance—the mind to guide, the body to act under its guidance; and we hold, as a great natural fact as well as a great moral truth—probably from a human point of view the greatest of all facts and the greatest of all truths—that each man owns his own body and mind, and thus cannot rightfully own the body and mind of another man. We hold that what one man cannot morally do, a million of men cannot morally do, and government, representing many millions of men, cannot do. Governments are only machines, created by the individuals of a nation for their own convenience; they are only delegated bodies, delegated by the individuals, and therefore they cannot possibly have larger moral rights of using force, or, indeed, larger moral rights of any kind, than the individuals who delegated them. We may reasonably believe that an individual, as a self-owner, is morally justified in defending the rights he possesses in himself and in his own property—by force, if necessary, against force (and fraud),* but he cannot be justified in using force for any other purpose whatsoever. He cannot morally use force to further his own interests, to further his own opinions, to further any cause, however excellent in itself, for in all these cases he would be stepping outside his own rights of self-ownership, and taking away from others some part of their rights of self-ownership. All such actions would imply that he was the owner of the bodies and minds of others, and this he cannot be, for all ownership of others is forever precluded by each person's right of self-ownership. It is impossible at one and the same time for men to be self-owners and owners of others. Self-ownership leaves no place for some men to own others or to be owned by them. If we are self-owners (and it is absurd, it is doing violence to reason,† to suppose that we are not), neither an individual, nor a majority, nor a government can have rights of ownership in other men.

It is plain, then, that there is no moral function in the whole world for force to perform except to maintain the

---

* The ordinary coarse forms of fraud are the moral equivalents of force. By force the consent of the self-owner is virtually set aside; by fraud it is evaded. Consent as regards his own actions and the free disposition of his own property is the distinguishing mark of the self-owner. Take consent away from any person as regards these matters, and he ceases to be a self-owner.

† Pure critical reason obliges us to believe in self-ownership. Men either own themselves or they do not. If they do, nothing remains to be said. If they do not, then they cannot possibly own and control each other, so long as they do not first of all own their own selves. It would be like using a lever, where no point of support existed.

rights of self-ownership; for whenever it is employed on any other service, it must be employed in taking away or lessening the rights of self-ownership, and thus destroying the moral basis on which all true society rests. It is plain that force does not belong to a civilized world, that it is a mere remnant of barbarism, and (except as a defense against force) that we must allow it to find no place in our organization of society.

Again whom, then, you will ask, may force be used? Simply against users of force (and fraud) as the murderer, the thief, the common swindler, and the aggressive foreign enemy. And what are we to say if a government should use force for other purposes than the protection of self-ownership? We can only say that those who use force, whoever they are, by that very act justify the use of force against themselves. In a free country, where reason and discussion are not strangled by the authorities, and where in the end we may be sure that these moral forces will destroy force, it is in almost every case our duty to trust to reason and discussion and not to use force; but it is necesary that the moral position of all concerned should be clearly understood; and that position is: that no individual, no majority, no government, holds any true commission to use force so as to take away the rights of self-ownership from any "unaggressive" citizen; and that all those, who do so use force, justify the use of force against themselves. Haters of force, just because of their hatred of force, may not, probably will not, avail themselves in a moderately free country of this right to reply to force by force; but it is best that every majority and every government should clearly understand that when they use force (except for purposes of restraining force) they make force the law of the world, and that then force is open to everybody, since it cannot remain the moral privilege of some persons and not of others. (Note: This statement affords no defense for the dynamiting anarchist; for he uses the privileges of peace to carry on his warfare. Society rightly judges all secret treacherous force to be infinitely worse than open force.)

Voluntaryists Believe in Government, Strictly Limited as Regards Its Authority; and See in It, So Limited, a True Organ of Society

Last, while we hold that government, the delegated body, the machine created by the individuals for their own convenience, and clothed with such moral authority as the individuals are competent to confer upon it, cannot possibly be anything more than this delegated body, this machine, this creature of our own making, this servant of our daily wants, while we utterly repudiate the pagan doctrine of those power worshipers, who see in the state a sort of god, a something bigger and holier than the individuals who nevertheless create and carve and change this god of their own handiwork according to their own changing ideas, a something possessed of unbounded authority, derived nobody knows whence, and holding a roving and limitless commission to subject and crush any one set of men, if less in number, at the dictation of another set of men, if more in number—at the same time we hold that there are real duties and functions for government to perform. We hold that it is a social duty for all of us, acting freely and without compulsion, to join in organizing, and, as far as possible, perfecting government for several purposes. First of all, the common force machine, for protecting self-ownership, for resisting and restraining all acts of force directed against the life, person, and property of any citizen. We hold that for many grave reasons the individual should not attempt to exercise his own inherent rights of restraining force by force—since to do so would be to make him act as his own judge and executioner; and we hold that he chooses wisely and well in delegating these rights to a body constituted, as a government should be, in the most public, formal, careful, and deliberate manner. We believe the anarchist ideal of no fixed and regularly organized machinery for repression of crime to be founded on a mistake; and we are governmentalists, in the sense that we believe that the common instrument for the repression of ordinary aggressive crime should be formally constituted by the nation, employing in this matter of force the majority method.

Once again, in distinguishing between the illegitimate and the legitimate forms of government, we wish to point out that the forces of government can only be rightly directed against one class of persons; that is against those who are "aggressives" upon others; never against the "nonaggressives." We ought not to direct our attacks— as the anarchists do—*against all government*, against government in itself, as the national force machine, against government strictly limited to its legitimate duties in defense of self-ownership and individual rights, but only against the overgrown, the exaggerated, the insolent, unreasonable and indefensible forms of government, which are found everywhere today, and under which, those who govern, usurp powers of all kinds, that do not and cannot belong to them, laboring under the ludicrous mistake that they are owners of the nation, owners of the bodies and minds of those very individuals, who called them into existence.

Government as the Agent of the Nation in International Matters

Second, we would employ government as the mouthpiece of the nation (under carefully guarded conditions) in its relation with other nations. While we would steadily refuse to allow the government to forget its true position of being an instrument and a servant, while we would refuse to allow it to place itself in any way above the individuals of the nation, while we would withhold from it its present most dangerous powers of declaring war, or of making alliances and treaties, while we would require in these great matters individuals to come forward and declare individually their approval and support of, and their personal responsibility for, great national steps of so serious a character, while we would insist that no person should be compelled to support any war, or to perform any service, or pay any tax, either for national defense or for carrying on war, against his own will, while we would insist that the rightful supremacy of the individual as regards his own actions, should never be taken from him on any false plea of national interest or safety, yet we hold that, just as it is a patriotic duty to support the government in the suppression of ordinary crime, so also it is a patriotic duty to support the government in all measures, that seem just and reasonable to the individual, for ensuring the independence and safety of the country. We believe in patriotism—not compulsory, but voluntary patriotism. We believe that patriotism will be carried to far higher, nobler and purer levels by free men, than by those who have fallen to the level of being as the sheep of the political drover, or as simple state material, with which governments may deal and traffic at will. We believe that only as men cease to be looked upon by their governments as convenient material for taxation and fighting purposes; only as each unit in a nation gains his full and perfect right to act as a free man, and comes into full possession of his own conscience and his own sense of right, will patriotism cease to burn with its present gross and clouded flame, and become a real and true force on the side of peace and happiness.

Government as the Useful Friend, Advising and Instructing, Not Compelling

Third, we believe that government might play the part of useful friend to the people, and perform many valuable services on their behalf, provided that it renounced all use of compulsion, and never attempted to impose either compulsory services or compulsory contributions upon unaggressive citizens. Freely competing with all voluntary bodies, it might become the most valuable center, during many future years, of knowledge and help and direction in such matters as education and sanitation. It is most urgent that the great work of sanitation in all its important developments should rest on voluntary methods, should be deofficialized—that is, should be divorced from compulsion; though at the same time, it should be remembered that, if necessary, men may be rightfully restrained from polluting all earth, water, or air, that does not belong to them; or from disseminating germs of disease in public places, since all such acts are acts of aggression on the person or property of others. So, also, the government might play the part of useful friend in matters of labor and trade. It might offer to all who required it, skilled advice in such matters as the safety and healthfulness of buildings, the cultivation of land, or the management of animals: it might undertake many useful experiments of various kinds, so long as it always acted on the one condition, that it would help as a friend, and never seek to play the part of the compelling and regulating authority, or the owner of bodies and minds, of the little god supreme above rights. All force (not employed in restraining force) disturbs peaceful effort, and prevents progress. We want none of it. Our true ideal is a *nation at peace within itself*, developing every form of industrial energy and friendly cooperation, making many experiments in social life, with every citizen acting in the line of his own convictions, spending his energies and his resources in such causes as seem to him the truest and best, and with no citizen engaged in the old miserable and profitless trade of placing fetters on the hands of other citizens or of being empowered to use others against their own beliefs and desires, just because the political party, to which the A's and the B's belong, had gained its victory at the polls, and the party to which the C's and the D's belong, had suffered defeat. The rights of men are too sacred to be voted away in any contests of our political parties. Let us then once more repeat our voluntaryist principle: the rights of liberty always in the first place; the authority of government always in the second place. When once a government had accepted this limitation, and held its authority subject to the rights of the individual, it would be, we believe, loyally and generously supported by the freely given services of free men, who would no longer be called upon either to lay conscience and will at its feet, or forced to struggle with their fellowmen for the possession of that evil thing—*power*—over each other. Where the conscience, the will, the self-direction of every citizen were frankly respected, there the foolish, wasteful and mischievous rivalries of our political parties would disappear, for power would cease to be the highest prize of life, inviting all men to snatch it by any and every weapon from the hands of each other. Where governments simply protected life and property for all without difference, international jealousies, hatreds, and wars, would die out, for Americans, Germans, or Frenchmen in Great Britain, and the British in America, Germany, or France, would fare alike. Each would be protected; none would receive privileges and favors in the one country more than in the other; but all men everywhere would be left free to exercise their faculties so as to work out their own development in their own fashion. The great causes of strife and hatred would pass away. Perfect free trade and friendly cooperation would satisfy all wants, and the world at last would begin to fulfill its destiny—as the free and peaceful meeting place of all opinions, all desires and all energies.

Miracles of State Socialism

State socialism is the refusal to others and the abandonment for oneself of all true human rights. Under it a man would have no rights over his own property, over his own labor, over his own amusements, over his own home and family—*in a word, either over himself, or all that naturally and reasonably belonged to him*, but he would have as his compensation (if there were 10,000,000 electors in his country) the one-tenth millionth share in the ownership of all his fellow-men (including himself) and of all that naturally and reasonably belonged to them and not to him. It is the flinging away of natural and reasonable rights in exchange for unnatural and unreasonable rights; it is the giving up of what a man ought not to give up, and the taking of what he ought not to take. State socialism is the last shortcut, which men have invented, to Magicland. The nation is to get there without any labor, effort, or sacrifice on its own part, without any improvement in character, or development of moral qualities. Magicland is to be won tomorrow, or today if you like, by the easy method of dropping papers in a ballot box. The winning of it will cost every elector only the trouble of marking a cross on half a sheet of paper—he is not expected or desired to do anything more for himself. He may then go home quite satisfied. All the rest will be done for him by the new patent machinery of the state, while he eats, sleeps, and is directed by the officials as to all the details of his life. Happy electors! Wonder-working ballot box! Omnipotent machinery! Supernatural results!

Under state socialism the minimum of work would be done, for the energies of one-half of the nation would be always spent in compelling the other half to do what they did not want to do. This political pull devil, pull balam, would be the principal national occupation. We should talk much, work little, and probably eat still less. Under state socialism we shall have three choices of profession. We may be either a state hand, or a state official, or a state spy and informer. The last two professions will be very much crowded; but there will probably be room for us all, since the state will be much like a German colony, principally made up of its officials.

State socialism exists as an instructive mirror for the politician in which he may study his own future developments. It shows him the superstitions and defects of his political system in their most exaggerated form; it caricatures the blunders that men make in trying to govern each other on the principle of unlimited force. Our common everyday superstition of supposing that we can represent 25,000 persons on all the great subjects of life, by one marvelous person in some congress or parliament, of supposing that it is reasonable to give all the rights to three persons, because they are three, and no rights of any kind to two persons, because they are two; of supposing that numbers create moral rights; our common and everyday mistake of constructing huge machines, that nobody understands or controls, and that govern men as much as they are governed by them; of handing the nation over in a lump sum to the officials; of turning the officials into sacred persons, and turning the public into dead material, without will, conscience and intelligence of its own; of giving every individual, say, the one-ten millionth voice in the affairs of all his neighbors, and no practical authority over his own affairs; of thus allowing men who don't own themselves to own the selves of others; of destroying differences and consecrating uniformity; of massing the good, the bad, and the indifferent all together under one system, and therefore making regulations that apply to the criminal and half-criminal, apply also to the good citizen, and thus reducing the best and ablest citizens to systems fitted to the least intelligent and the least civilized citizens, as a cavalry charge is regulated by the pace of the slowest horse; of multiplying regulations till they become as the grains of the sand of the sea, and require libraries to contain them, and a professional class to expound them; of supplying the nation during every day of the year with the utmost possible material of every kind for quarreling over, of destroying those natural rewards of ability and industry, and those natural penalties of faults which belong to free life, and replacing them with every sort of artificial contrivance which can suggest itself to the perverted political imagination; of trying to dodge the great natural law of progress by making the able and industrious carry on their backs, as their compulsory burden, the less able and the less industrious; of making the workers of all kinds subject to the talkers— all these superstitions and mistakes, and many more, are the common property of the politician and the socialist, between whom there is only a difference of degree. The socialist is only the politician kept a little longer in the oven and hard-baked; the politician is only the immatured socialist.

Anarchy Does Not Understand Itself

Although we voluntaryists see with pleasure that there exists a sane, peaceful and reasonable section of anarchists—quite distinct from the reckless and criminal sections, who traffic in violence—yet we are constrained to express our belief that all anarchy, or "no government," is founded on a fatal mistake.

Anarchy, in the form in which it is often expounded, seems to us not to understand itself. It is not in reality anarchy or "no government." When it destroys the central and regularly constituted government, and proposes to leave every group to make its own arrangements for the repression of ordinary crime, it merely decentralizes government to the furthest point, splintering it up into minute fragments of all sizes and shapes. As long as there is ordinary crime, as long as there are aggressions by one man upon the life and property of another man, and as long as the mass of men are resolved to defend life and property, there cannot be anarchy or no government. By the necessity of things, we are obliged to choose between regularly constituted government, generally accepted by all citizens for the protection of the individual, and irregularly constituted government, irregularly accepted, and taking its shape just according to the pattern of each group. Neither in the one case nor in the other case is government got rid of. The more true anarchist, the man who actually gets rid of government, is Tolstoy, who preaches as Christ did, that we should bear all injuries without returning them. In that way, it is true, government can be got rid of—but then how many of us are prepared to follow Tolstoy? There still remains, as anarchists might urge, another method of dealing with ordinary crimes. Under the theory of "no government," the defense of person and property, and the punishment of crime might be left absolutely to the individual; and this method, like Tolstoy's method, would be quite consistent with the true anarchistic theory. I have heard an able anarchist defend it on the ground that men would exercise force with more scrupulousness, when obliged to act in their own persons, than when acting through a judge and policeman. But here again how many of us on the one hand are prepared to judge and to act for ourselves as regards our own wrongs; or on the other hand to consent to the self-made appointment of those—who believe themselves to be injured by us—as our judges and executioners? To most of us such a system could be described only by the word—pandemonium.

The Land Nationalizer

The land nationalizer has a touch of the old pagan worshiper about him. He turns the land into a sort of god, into something greater than men. A man can't own land, he says, exalting the mere thing, the dead material, into the first place; and degrading the man, for whom all world material exists, into the second place. It is a strange inversion of parts.

The ordinary politician is not as consistent as the land nationalizer; the land nationalizer is not as consistent as the state socialist. The politician steals with two or three fingers, and thinks it would be wrong to steal with the whole hand; the land nationalizer steals with one hand, and thinks it would be wrong to steal with both hands; the state socialist steals with both hands, and boldly glorifies the whole business. If you steal pence, why not steal pounds, we ask the politician? If you steal the land, we ask the land nationalizer, why not steal all that grows upon and comes from the land—all wool, cotton, grain, fruit and animals? In the name of reason, let us either leave stealing altogether alone, or else preach the whole gospel of stealing, pure and undefiled! The land nationalizer would take from men one of their greatest and deepest sources of happiness. He says to them: "You shall never possess your own home. You shall never possess as your own one single square yard of soil. You shall plant nothing on the face of the earth, which shall be truly yours; you shall plant no tree, and in planting it know that the fruit it bears shall belong to you and those who come after you, so long as such tree has life in it; you shall be only as a nomad race, encamped for a season, as long as it pleases those who govern, to leave you in your hired houses." Why? On what grounds does the land nationalizer venture to cut off this great source of human enjoyment from the human race? Simply, because he has not yet cleared his mental vision; simply, because he does not see, first, that if the land of the country really belongs to the whole nation, it cannot belong to that mere part of it, called a majority, and that no majority, therefore, can be competent to deal with it; and second, that if John Smith cannot morally own land, then ten million John Smiths cannot morally own land. The land nationalizer has not yet discovered that a government or state can only possess exactly the same moral rights of possessing and enjoying as the individuals who create it. Land nationalizers also forget that happiness of life largely depends upon security of conditions. They forget that under land nationalism we shall all be merely as tenants at will. At present, if we do not wish to own land, we can make such agreements for a term of months or years, or for life, as we may arrange with our landlord, and we have the protection of the courts as regards these agreements; but with government as our landlord, we should only occupy at the pleasure of those who constitute the government. No agreements bind governments. What one administration creates today, another administration a few years hence will undo and repeal. Under land nationalization it would be the constant amusement of governments to reorganize the existing system of land tenure. No question would open up such pretty opportunities for the quarrels of our politicians, or for their courageous experiments with what does not belong to them.

The Aim of the Voluntaryist

What is the work of the voluntaryist? It is to destroy the love of power; to destroy alike in himself and in his fellow-men the desire to *force* opinions or interests—whatever they may be—upon others; to be content to be a *self-ruler*, not a ruler of others; to strengthen belief in the moral weapons of reason, discussion and example; to bear patiently many evils rather than to weaken at any point the principle of self-ownership and self-direction; and to live in the faith that there is no evil which cannot be overcome by courage and resolution, no moral failure that cannot be remedied, except the one evil, the one moral failure, of abandoning self-ownership and self-direction. To abandon self-ownership is to become corrupt and servile in spirit, and for the servile and corrupt there are no great things possible. You cannot carve in rotten wood; you cannot lead to greatness those who have renounced the essence of their own manhood or womanhood.

Let the voluntaryist boldly preach the doctrine of self-ownership everywhere. Let him seek to persuade the socialist that he has no right to offer comfort and advantage at the price of the sacrifice of personal liberty; that it is quite vain to try to destroy one kind of bondage by building up another in its place; let him persuade the capitalist that all wealth, founded on any kind of state favor or privilege and opposed to free trade, is wealth taken by force from others, and rests on wrong and unjust foundations; let him persuade the members of all churches that it is a travesty and a mockery of their own creed—rightly and simply understood—to attack any kind of moral evil with state punishments; that all such persecutions are in direct conflict with the principles of the Sermon on the Mount, and that Christians, above all men, are bound to fight with the weapons of reason, discussion and persuasion; let him seek to persuade all men, whether

rich or poor, employers or employed, men of this country
or other countries, that the organization of any kind of
material force against each other is a barren and pitiful
waste of life—that a victory gained over unwilling bodies
and minds is a defeat, and not a victory, that in peace,
friendly cooperation, unrestricted experiment, constant
difference, almost unlimited toleration as regards the
actions of others, free trade in every direction, the increased mobility, life experience and self-protection of
the individual, the removal of all compulsory burdens and
services, the abandonment of the evil power of mortgaging the faculties of future generations by the present
generation, the abandonment of great political inducements for men to struggle with each other, which inducements to war must exist so long as each man desires the
possession of power for himself and dreads to see it in
the hands of his neighbor, and lastly in the perfect
security of person and property, so that the conditions
of successful effort may be recognized as constant and
persisting—that in these things are the true watchwords
of progress, to which it is our duty under every temptation to be faithful. Let us sum up what voluntaryism is—
in a few words:

Voluntaryism is the reconciler of differences.

It is the system of liberty, peace, and friendliness.

Under voluntaryism the state employs force only to
repel force—to protect the person and the property of
the individual against force and fraud; under voluntaryism the state would defend the rights of liberty, never
aggress upon them.

It takes part with no sect; it belongs to no faction.

It persecutes nobody, and, except in the defense of self-ownership, restricts nobody, regulates nobody.

It refuses to force the opinions or interests of any one part of the people upon another part.

It refuses to fight for any moral view with the immoral weapons of force.

It compels no services, confiscates no property, takes no compulsory payments.

It refuses to be the instrument of any part in any country that places the power of the state above the rights of the individual.

It is opposed to all privileges, monopolies, and restrictions, and seeks to leave men free to shape their own lives in a free world.

It protests against all forms of salvation by force.

It believes that vast sums are annually wasted in constructing the great force machines of the state and in governing by force; it believes that if human faculties were universally set free, if men were emancipated from the burdens of taxation and official interference, and if they once deliberately resolved not to struggle for power over each other, a new world of peace, friendliness, and prosperity would take the place of the world as it is today, defaced by jealousies and strife and hatred, and saddened by much unnecessary suffering.

Principles of the Voluntary State

1.   To recognize all points and under all circumstances the self-ownership of men and women, and their full right to direct their faculties and employ their own prop-

erty (within the one limit of nonaggression by force or fraud upon others) as they choose.

2.   To recognize that the state should compel no services and exact no payments by force, but should depend entirely upon voluntary services and voluntary payments.

    a. That it should be free to conduct many useful undertakings, in connection with education, sanitary matters, poor relief, insurance, post office business, trade, inspection of buildings, machinery, etc., and many other matters, but that it should do so in competition with all voluntary agencies, without employment of force, in dependence on voluntary payments, and acting with the consent of those concerned, simply is their friend and their adviser;

    b. That it should use force only to restrain the force of the murderer, of the thief and of violent persons, and certain coarse forms of fraud—thus guaranteeing the self-ownership of the individual by protecting him in person and property;

    c. That it should take no property of any kind from any citizen by force; nor regulate any part of his life; nor interfere with any exercise of faculties by force (within the nonaggressive limit); nor seek to obtain any moral purpose by force.

3.   To get rid of all public debt, central or local, by selling and mortgaging public property and by organizing a great system of voluntary contribution—certain days in the year being specially observed as holidays for the raising of voluntary revenue, local and central.

4.   To extend the voluntary defenses of the country

and to place them on a much broader basis and more permanent foundation than that on which they now stand; to depend in war as in peace solely on voluntary contributions; and to renounce absolutely the flagrant wrong of compelling those who are opposed to war to give any support to it.

5. Without abandoning in panic any duty toward those connected with us or depending upon us in other countries, to press forward the peaceful and friendly settlement of all unsettled external questions; to narrow responsibilities; to resolutely give up an aggressive and grasping policy; and to seek to establish international friendly agreements as regards all questions in dispute.

6. By thus removing all burdens, all restrictions and interferences with personal activities, by cutting down officialism, by getting rid of the mischievous interference of the politician with private property, and his constant bribing of the people, only too often for the sake of his own advancement, by destroying the reckless rivalry of political parties for place and power, and by steadily creating free trade in everything, to allow the free development not only of the almost infinite capacities and intellectual resources possessed by every intelligent nation, but also of the friendliness and natural desire of all classes to work together for common ends. By these methods to give to the world an example of the happiness and prosperity that can be won by all nations alike, where the natural right of every person to direct his own faculties and to deal with his own property according to his own desires, and not at the dictation of others, is uni-

versally respected, and all undertakings and all services
are founded upon persuasion of each other, not upon
force.

Some Reasons Why Voluntaryists Object to Compulsory Taxation in All Its Forms

1.   Because it rests on certain intellectual contradictions and absurdities. It requires that wealth should be
created by individual energy and enterprise, and then
spent collectively; that is, spent under a system which
reduces the individual almost to insignificance. It tends
to place the owner and the nonowner on a false equality
—the nonowner, if he choose to use his power, becoming
the virtual master of the property of the owner. For every
service conferred it imposes a burden—direct or indirect—and yet gives the individual no choice as to whether
he will accept the service and the burden, or decline both.

2.   Because it is essentially opposed to a state of true
liberty. It is impossible to look upon a man as free, so
long as others have unlimited command over his property.
It is impossible to separate the rights of action from the
rights of acquiring and possessing. A man acts through
and by means of the various substances of the world, and
if he is not free to acquire and own these substances as an
individual, neither is he free to act as an individual.

3.   Because it builds up the belief that one man and his
property may be used by another man against his own
convictions and his own interests. It therefore divides us
into those who are only tools and those who are the users
of tools; and perpetuates a modern form—though more

subtle and concealed than the old forms—of slave owning.

4. Because it builds up and strengthens a number of revolting superstitions. It teaches men that they belong, body and mind, to the uncounted, unknown, voting crowd called the state; for if their property belongs to the state, then we must presume that their physical and mental faculties, through which they earned their property, also belong to the state. In the same way it teaches the cowardly and contemptible doctrine that in presence of any supposed public danger or on behalf of any supposed public good, there is no longer any appeal to the conscience and self-responsibility of the individual, but that all persons are made subject to the decisions—often rash, heedless, and taken in panic—of those who exercise political power over them.

5. Because in strengthening these superstitions it degrades the view of human existence. It destroys the general perception that the judgment and the will are the highest parts of human nature, and therefore sacred beyond all other things; and it leads men to look on each other as mere material to be dealt with wholesale and in accordance with the expediency of the moment.

6. Because free countries have affirmed many years ago that a compulsory church rate is immoral and oppressive, for the sake of the burden laid upon individual consciences; and in affirming this truth they have unconsciously affirmed the wider truth, that *every tax or rate, forcibly taken from an unwilling person, is immoral and oppressive.* The human conscience knows no distinction between church rates and other compulsory rates and

taxes. The sin lies in the disregarding of each other's convictions, and is not affected by the subject matter of the tax.

7. Because it makes absolutely certain in the end a hateful war between classes. It accustoms the mass of voters to the belief that all their wants may be satisfied out of the *common compulsory fund*; it makes the fight to obtain possession of this common compulsory fund of supreme importance; and thus the nation is split up into two struggling factions—those who strive to take, and those who strive to keep.

8. Because it gives to the politician a very undue and undeserved importance. It places in his hands, often as the reward of mere successful speechmaking, the hard-won resources of large classes of his countrymen; and confers upon him a position which could only be won ordinarily through a much more laborious process and in return for qualities of a much higher order. In this way it may be a satisfactory system for the politician, endowing him with many pleasant things in return for his facile profession of certain opinions; but it is not so good for those who are made the instruments of providing, willingly or unwillingly, these pleasant things.

9. Because it favors the rank growth of a very evil form of bribery. Out of the common compulsory fund that is raised by means of taxes, the politician promises what will please his supporters; and by means of burdens laid upon the nation buys his own way into the legislative body and into office.

10. Because it tends to produce a habit of misty, confused thought and unreal generosity—generosity at

the expense of others—in our leading men, corrupting all clear sense of justice, and making them traffickers in phrases and servile to their own party interests; in other words, because in this imperfect world, no class of men, rich or poor, is to be found with sufficient honesty or impartiality to be entrusted with the compulsory taking and spending of the money of others.

11.   Because its gives every legislature—bodies which are elected under the influence of passion and strife, and by means of not very scrupulously managed party organizations—far too great power over the movements of the human mind. It gives them power to force certain forms of thought upon the nation; to crush other forms out—at least temporarily; and makes of them little gods, who dispose—but without the knowledge, judgment, or impartiality of gods—of the gravest questions of human existence.

12.   Because it makes universal suffrage an entirely unworkable arrangement. Man for man, the whole people should be on a footing of perfect equality as regards certain great national questions (e.g., questions of civil and criminal code, peace and war, monarchy or republicanism, etc.), but as regards property compulsorily taken. In all matters relating to property, it is clear sense and just sense that the opinions and desires of those to whom such property belongs, should count for far more than the opinions and desires of those to whom it does not belong. Compulsory taking of property and universal suffrage cannot reasonably be united under one system. Each makes the other ridiculous when forced to keep company. We may fairly ask—How can the nonowner preserve a

sense of justice or of self-respect, while he votes away the property of the owner?

13. Because it inevitably leads to the curse of bureaucratic government. The departments of administration, ever extending and absorbing more public money, become independent of all real control, become a separate solid nation within the nation, create—often for the benefit of parents with unmarketable sons—innumerable places and immense vested interests, and turn out second-rate work, just because such work is exposed to no competition, and is relieved from the danger of the bankruptcy court—all official mistakes being covered over by larger and larger takings from the public.

14. Because—notwithstanding the high character of many permanent officials—it increases the danger of harsh, arbitrary, and occasionally cruel things being done by these uncontrolled and irresponsible public departments, that work very much in the darkness. As their operations grow, and the authority of their agents becomes greater, the resistance of the public to their interference necessarily becomes less, both because the public cannot watch with carefulness the large area which falls under official regulation, and because the sense of public helplessness rapidly increases in the presence of these powerfully organized bodies, possessed, in far greater degree than the public can ever be, of the technical knowledge which is connected with their own class of work and their own methods. Moreover, in almost all cases, the departments are able to count upon the silent support of the government, which is in office and which has to work through them.

15.   Because in its practical consequences it is endangering the prosperity and even the existence of old and young countries. The rich and the promising countries of South America have been already nearly wrecked by their mad financial management; at this moment, it is doubtful if the United States can adopt a free trade policy, however strongly desired by a large part of the people, on account of the extravagant expenditure to which the country has been committed, and which, once incurred, necessitates a tariff; New Zealand has for many years been struggling to repair the frightful mistakes into which she was led by allowing a few men the power of compulsory dealing with the property of others; some of the Australasian colonies are suffering acutely from past extravagance, and fortunately for themselves have experienced a difficulty in borrowing; India is in a condition that should cause the gravest anxiety as regards her future; in Europe, Spain, Portugal and Greece are apparently nearly outside the possibilities of financial salvation; France has large chronic yearly deficits; Germany, Austria, and Italy—the last country in an almost ruinous condition—stagger along under burdens which they cannot bear, and which will, if persisted in, drive them over the abyss; and Russia lives in a state of constant financial difficulty, which is only partially concealed by official statements that do not err on the side of candor. Here and there are to be found some examples of saner management; but even in Great Britain, where the national debt is diminishing, municipal debt and expenditure are increasing with alarming rapidity, in Mr. Albert Pell's words, "with very little to show for it," and are now threatening the industrial prosperity

of the provincial cities. In other countries, the municipal governments of Paris, Vienna, Florence, Rome and Madrid, repeat in each instance the story of excessive expenditure, excessive burdens, and, in some instances, of grave corruption; in the United States the "boodleism" of New York has become a by-word in most parts of the world, and Boston and other cities have been removed from the hands of their municipal authorities, and placed under commissioners.

16. Because it gives great and undue facility for engaging a whole nation in war. If it were necessary to raise the sum required from those who individually agreed in the necessity of war, we should have the strongest guarantee for the preservation of peace. Once given the power of compulsorily taking the property of others, then a minister "with a light heart," a general on a black horse, a jingo press, or the shouting crowd of a capital, may turn the scale in favor of war. If neither the French nor the German governments had the power to take such property as they liked from the two nations, it would seem almost certain they would before now have arrived at a peaceful solution of their differences. Compulsory taxation means everywhere the persistent probability of a war made by the ambitions or passions of politicians.

17. Because it is unfitted—as a system—to supply the new wants of an active and expanding civilization. Where in a simple type of community there exist only a few constant wants, it is conceivable that a compulsory system—however unwise and indefensible in itself— might for a time produce no serious inconveniences. In a progressive condition, where new wants discover them-

selves from day to day, these inconveniences take an acute form. When a certain point of taxation is reached, the hurtfulness of taxes and the friction caused in collecting them advance almost in geometrical ratio, until at last a tax may be increased without producing any greater return of revenue—indeed sometimes producing a smaller return. When, therefore, taxation has once been made the principal instrument of supplying the wants of a people, a stage must presently be reached where each new want can only be satisfied with much greater difficulty and at much greater cost than in the case of preceding wants. In this way civilization—when made dependent on compulsory payments—arrests itself.

18.   Because it cannot be arranged on any system that has not far-reaching hurtful effects. It passes "the wit of man" to render the compulsory taking of property harmless. Each system of taxation has its own peculiar group of evils. To take but one example: Income taxes necessitate inquisition and odious interferences; they create a system of government spies; lead to action being taken very improperly and upon questionable guesses by officials whose one view is likely to be to increase their takings; under every imaginable system must be unequal in their incidence; cannot from their nature be decided in cases of dispute either in an open court or in a secret court without much annoyance to the taxpayer; strike all visible property more severely than the less visible forms, lead to much evasion and untruthfulness: become complicated to the last degree owing to the innumerable methods of earning income in modern life; involve metaphysical questions which recall the dialectics of the middle ages; tend to drive capital into risky employments outside the

country; whenever much raised, are likely to cause the corruption of officials on whom the returns depend; are a standing menace, [owing to the ease—a mere stroke of the pen—with which they can be increased] to traders and owners of property; are infinitely hurtful to the small men, but tend to be unremunerative, as Leroy Beaulieu has so well shown, except when they are applied to the mass of small properties, since the larger properties, when singled out for attack, even if they do not disappear, are comparatively unfruitful as a field for taxation (thus defeating by a natural check the unwisdom and injustice of trying to make any special class supply the common compulsory fund); destroy the advantage of free trade, even in a country which allows imports to enter freely, since they raise the price of articles produced in an almost excessive degree, owing to the fact that each class of producers necessarily adds his own rate of profit to the tax that he himself pays, and to the tax paid by all those who have preceded him as manufacturers of the same article in the earlier stages of its manufacture—with the consequence that each product of the market that passes through the hands of several producers and distributors, pays the tax several times over before it becomes a finished article, as well as in each case the special rate of profit added to the tax by each producer and each distributor; are therefore unfair to traders who themselves pay income tax and may have to compete with traders in other countries not burdened with income tax (though, it should be said, probably burdened in other ways); and commit the capital crime of making property less desirable, and of weakening the public desire to save and invest.

Death duties—a peculiarly mean form of property tax —assessed taxes, custom duties, stamp duties, all have their own special far-reaching consequences of mischief. One reason stands out preëminent; industrial or commercial life is free life, where men adapt themselves in their own way to changing circumstances, and are called on to display infinite tact and mental resource in their efforts to surmount difficulties and to do away with or reduce the various sources of outlay which surround production; but state compulsory payments form a solid unyielding obstacle, which cannot be got rid of or lessened except by fraud, and therefore defy all such exercise of ingenuity or invention or improvement of method. They are as irreconcilable with the free movements of the human mind and the many varied adaptations which make up the delicate process of industrial life, as a rigid iron bar would be, if thrust from the outside and without any other connection, into a complicated machinery made up of joints and flexible parts.

19. Because it introduces hopeless confusion and uncertainty—where all should be most clear, certain, and stable—into the conditions under which property is to be acquired and owned. It tends to weaken the free open market, as the great center of acquisition and distribution of property, the center through which all industrial efforts are set in motion, and through which all industrial efforts are rewarded, and to set up in its place the changing harum-scarum fancies of every set of politicians who make their way to office.

20. Because all taxes, even those placed upon the rich, injure those who are poor. They disturb the course of

production and trade; they make traders timid, and so contract industrial enterprise and depress wages; they make considerable payments in ready money necessary, and thus favor a few large houses as against the small traders, and thus again facilitate "corners" and monopolies; they disturb natural values, depreciating the property which is specially taxed; when heavy, they discourage a useful service, which the rich perform unconsciously, of encouraging those inventions which must at first pass through an expensive stage before they can be widely produced in cheap forms; they spoil markets, which in great measure depend for their cheapness and excellence upon their extent; but above all, they misdirect the efforts of the working part of the people. Grasping greedily at the common compulsory fund, out of which every sort of thing is provided, the people lose their faith in free enterprise and their natural inclination to form voluntary societies of their own in order to provide for all the growing wants of life; and instead of setting themselves to build up with their own hands a new civilization—the real work which cries aloud to be done—they waste priceless time and energy in struggling for miserable handfuls out of the devil's quarreling fund—as it has been well called—thus playing the politician's game to his heart's content.

21. Because it injures the working class in another deadly manner, bribing them to give up all real management of their affairs and to accept a purely fictitious management in its place. No better example exists than education. The simplest form of school, really managed and paid for by the working classes, would be worth far

more to them and to their children, than the present tawdry and pretentious official systems, in which everybody
interferes, and over which no individual parent has the
least real control. If they desire endowments—of which,
however, be it said, they generally spoil education—the
workmen should claim their share of the old charitable
endowments, which have been absorbed by all sorts of
institutions, and kick tax, rate, central department, and
all compulsory management and all compulsory attendance into the dust hole.

22.   Because one form of our highest education in life
is the practical education which results from our wants
and our voluntary efforts to satisfy these wants; and
because as long as we satisfy these wants by the use of
official compulsory machinery we can never learn to work
in friendly voluntary fashion with each other, and to help
each other, out of a true public spirit. Thus, the richer
classes are being constantly cut off by the effects of compulsion from learning to work with those less well off
than themselves for public ends, and in this way their
lives become less useful to others, and less happy for
themselves.

23.   Because when the common fund is placed before
the poor man—living a hard and struggling life—as his
great hope of salvation, is it reasonable to expect him to
forbear from making full use of the tempting resources
thus placed under his hand? If taxation or taking from
others is in itself a good, true method, why not employ
it to its very furthest extent?

24.   Because, from the very fact of being compulsory,
it is accompanied by great practical inconveniences, in-

separable from it. We hear much of the official checks and counterchecks, the expensive, dilatory though unsuccessful safeguards, with which the spending of public money is surrounded; and yet these irritating arrangements are necessary and cannot be dispensed with. The system under which the money of all individuals is compulsorily taken and spent in the name of the nation by a few persons is in itself so unnatural, so topsy-turvy, so opposed to common sense (since the natural safeguard which consists in a man looking after his own interest, doing what he thinks is best with his own property, and refusing to contribute to undertakings which he thinks are expensively, insufficiently, or corruptly managed, is swept away) that no imaginable reform can make any public service satisfactory, as long as it is kept on a compulsory basis. To set aside at the outset and treat as of no consequence the free agency of the individual is to commit an error of so vital a nature that everything falling under the influence of such an error is predestined to go wrong.

25. Because it is an enormous distraction as regards the work of the best workers. Where money is compulsorily taken for all sorts of objects, the most capable men must either frequently detach themselves from their own work in order to form a judgment upon any undertaking which the politicians choose to bring forward, or they must simply allow themselves to be robbed of money, which they neither consent nor desire to give, because it is a smaller loss to be robbed of money, than it is to be robbed of time.

26. Because it tends to turn us all, whether members

of legislatures, journalists, or electors, into persons who think superficially and act in a hurry on very imperfect knowledge. The enormous number of undertakings which pass under the hands of legislative bodies, and the enormous number of questions which are submitted to their decision, oblige all those who are concerned with political life to possess innumerable smatterings of piecemeal knowledge of various sorts, to form their judgments in the imperfect light of such smatterings, and to make the best show that is possible with such hastily gathered knowledge. Every member of a legislature ought to be a trained scientist in all branches of human knowledge, in order to perform the duties that everyday are thrown upon him. It has been said by some defenders of competitive examinations that their merit consists in developing the faculties that are specially required for the rapidly changing struggles of afterlife. As regards political life the plea is perfectly just; and the brilliant use of limited intellectual furniture, joined to an intrepid judgment on all subjects on the spur of the moment, is likely to be equally useful to the politician and the successful prize student. But neither the politician nor the prize student represent the best elements in the nation.

27.   Because it is essentially socialistic in principle, and offers the easiest and surest means of advance to state socialism. So long as we admit that the property of individuals lies at the mercy of the largest number of votes, we are intellectually and morally committed to state socialism, and it is only certain accidents, liable to disappear at any crisis,which stand between us and the practical realization of state socialism. To put the same

truth in the simplest terms—if what is called the state may forcibly take one dollar or one shilling out of what a man owns, it may take what it likes up to the last dollar or last shilling. Once admit the right of the state to take, and the state becomes the real owner of all property.

28.   Because this question of compulsory taking offers a decisive battleground between state socialists and those opposed to state socialism. It raises the question of the state existing for the individual, or the individual existing for the state, at once in the clearest and most comprehensive manner. Moreover, it places the combatants on more equal terms. At present, state socialists have the advantage of attacking at any point, and often win, because their solid column is rapidly thrown upon some skillfully selected spot in the widely dispersed line of defense. To a contest persistently fought on such terms there must be only one ending. The fortress that cannot attack is destined to fall; and the defense of liberty by staying behind parapets and bastions is hopeless. Henceforward, we act on the offensive. We admit of no lost or decided causes where liberty is concerned. We care nothing for the many small victories which socialists have won in the last few years. We now invade the territory of the enemy, and attack the point which is the key to his position, confident, that when once men begin to refuse to the state its evil power of taking property by force, socialism will drop into its place amongst the shadows of the past. Socialism lives and thrives upon the principle of compulsory taking.

29.   Last, because compulsory taxation is the great typical enemy of all voluntary action. We see in it the

very citadel of compulsion, the chief instrument which
which every encroachment is carried out, the chief bribe
by which men are induced to submit to these encroach-
ments, and an institution which by its very existence
preaches to men every day and every hour that they are
not really sovereign over themselves, their faculties, and
their property, *but are subject to the will of others—
placed at the mercy of these others* to be used or not used,
according to their caprices, their superstitions, or their
selfishness. We see in it one of the last remaining but one
of the most stubbornly defended strongholds of the dominion of men over men. To us, voluntary action stands
for the *good genius* of the human race, as compulsory
action, stands for its *evil genius*. We contrast what the
free individual has done, with what the compulsory
organization, called government, has done and is doing;
we see on the one side all that the human mind has
achieved in industry, in commerce, in art, in science, in
literature: we count enterprise after enterprise, invention
after invention; we see that not only the food, the clothing, the houses, the comforts and refinements which we
possess, but that our mental selves, the very thoughts that
we think, the very beings that we are, are the outcome of
the individual forces that surround us—the outcome of
the perpetual action and reaction of the spoken word, the
written page, the social intercourse, the outcome of mind
acting freely upon mind. How small, how beggarly in
comparison, is the sum to be placed to the account of the
compulsory association that is directed by the politicians!

   We affirm, then, that voluntaryism in everything is
the true law of progress and happines, and that compul-

sion, or the brute force of law, should be simply retained to hold in check brute force, to protect the individual from the murderer, the thief, and the swindler, to protect him in person and property from injurious acts, done to him in disregard of his consent. Except for such universal and simple purposes of protection, we deny that the brute force of law can ever form a true or moral basis for social relations. We affirm that the brute force of law can never be used to set aside a man's consent as regards his own actions without condemning that man permanently to a lower existence. We affirm that only as men learn to be self-directing, to take their lives and actions into their own charge, to practice and perfect the instrument of voluntary combination for all the growing wants of life, to fight their battles with the weapons of discussion and reason, rejecting all intimidation and coercion of each other, to undertake public duties and services for each other gladly, as free individuals, not driven into any path, however good it may be, by penalties and persecutions—is it possible to look forward to happier and friendlier forms of society. We affirm that there is no such hope to be found at the end of the dreary vista of organized compulsion; of new compulsions resting upon old compulsions, and again buttressed by still newer compulsions; of endless regulations, becoming year after year more minute, and penetrating more deeply into social life and home life—each action of the habit, being more and more jealously scrutinized, for fear that if freedom should be allowed to exist at any point, like a ray of light entering the gloom of a dungeon, it might prove the source from which danger at other points should arise to the huge, unstable, badly cemented fabric of universal regulation. We affirm that all such systems of compulsion are as mere wanderings in the desert, and can lead nowhere. In the breast of every person, however dimly he may recognize it, there is a moral feeling telling him that he has a right to freedom of action and freedom of thought, that he is meant to be self-guiding, and that no organization outside him, on any plea—whether the plea of his own good or of the good of others—can take these rights from him. It is because of the existence of this feeling, which, if often perverted and obscured, yet is deep as human nature itself, and is spread over every region of the world, that we who believe in liberty and hate compulsion, hold the conviction that the victory, whatever yet may be the battles to fight, must at length belong to us. You cannot build upon compulsion—human nature is in eternal revolt against it; every building you rest upon it will prove a building of strife and confusion; every seeming victory will turn against you, and in the end come to naught.

Labor Advised to Reject All Help from Coercion and Restriction

As regards the labor question, recognizing to the full the right of any and all laborers peacefully to withhold their labor, if so they choose, at every hour of every day of every year, and even—should they so elect—to starve into submission—if they can—any number of their fellow-men by such withholding of their labor, free life yet urges them to seek their ends through peace instead of war, and to do away with the terrible waste and other evils that result from employing their savings as a war fund. Believing that it is most hurtful to the true interests of labor, as well as morally unjust, to attempt to prevent any fellow laborer from taking the place which another laborer has thought right to resign; believing that each man has the right to give or withhold his own labor, as he chooses, but not in any way to interfere with the bargain which some other man may make about himself, it urges upon all workmen: (1) Where they are discontented with their conditions of employment not to strike in a body (which means almost necessarily the compulsion of some of their own number, means acting upon the instincts of a crowd instead of acting as reasonable individuals, means the danger of acquiescing—when once a struggle is entered upon—in some form of violence and intimidation), but to assist in removing those, who individually wish to be removed, to other factories and workshops, thus peacefully draining away, where the terms of employment are unsatisfactory, the best and most adventurous hands, while as a matter of right and justice they offer no impediment of any kind to the taking on of new hands by the employer; (2) To trust in such cases far more than at present to friendly negotiation, and to the increasing power of publicity and free discussion for the improvement of the conditions under which they give their labor; (3) To make their unions instruments for amassing large corporate property, to turn them from fighting machines into organizations for constructive purposes, such as the establishing of courses of education during periods when trade is depressed, the investing of their savings fund in solid bricks and mortar, in homes, which might become the property of the individual members, in lodging houses, halls, reading and recreation rooms, farms in the country, which would be held collectively, in shares of existing productive enterprises, and, as opportunity arose, in trade enterprises conducted by themselves; (4) To cultivate far more friendly and intimate relations with employers; to place employers under no vexatious rules or restrictions, especially restrictions invented by a central body; to make their conduct of business as easy as possible; to get rid of factory laws, and in their place to cooperate with employers to promote far better sanitary conditions and other conditions affecting the comfort of those who labor than those existing at present; to encourage every system under which they would become partners in the concerns in which they work; and instead of placing themselves under any universal discipline of limited hours, to favor differences as regards time and manner of work at different factories or mines, so that each class of workers—the youngest and strongest, the oldest and least strong—may gradually find that which suits them best; (5) To abandon every attempt to enforce one fixed rate of payment throughout a trade, as necessarily driving out of employment old, young, and second-rate workers, and as certain to prolong the existence of great war organizations and great war funds on the part both of employers and workmen—each side wasting more and more of its resources in the effort to be stronger than its rival, and thus imitating on a small scale the disastrous example of Germany and France; and in the same way to abandon every attempt to restrict the number of those who enter their own trade, or to turn their trade into a monopoly.

Prices Raised by Restriction Mean a Tax
Imposed by One Worker upon Another

Every trade restriction is war declared upon other trades. All attempts of one class of workers to restrict their own special industry are treason against their fellow workers, because every restricted trade implies the effort to get an artificial or heightened price for the product of such trade, while the workers in it enjoy the product of other unrestricted trades at free trade (or unrestricted) prices. They are, therefore, guilty in the great exchange of the world of taking more and giving less, and so far as they temporarily benefit themselves—and it can only be temporarily—they do it by placing a tax upon all their fellow workers in the unrestricted trades. Nor is the universal restriction of all trades less hurtful than the partial restriction of some trades. Where all professions and trades are restricted, everybody alike—worker or non-worker—is injured, because: (1) everybody has to pay the higher price that results indirectly as well as directly from such restriction; (2) all production is rendered sickly by losing the vitalizing effects which accompany free trade—the constant introduction of new methods, the constant inflow of capital brains and energy; (3) each set of restrictions in turn fails and is then succeeded by a new set of restrictions, created to make the first set more effective, and thus a state of hopeless entanglement presently results; and (4) the workers and their children cannot readily pass to the trades for which they have an aptitude or liking, and a great mass, owing to such impeded movement, is slowly formed of unemployed, incapable and indigent, who under free trade would be healthily absorbed. Such restriction, like restriction in every other matter, prevents the true solution of labor questions. The true solution can only come, as in international affairs, through friendly disarmament of opposed forces; through making the individual the pivot of all action; through creating that freedom of action, which on the one hand allows capital to work in the easiest manner, to adapt itself to new circumstances, to develop new branches of production, and, just because it is unharassed and secure, to take the lowest profit; and on the other hand allows labor not only to improve its own position constructively through its own associations—its energies being no longer misdirected and its savings no longer wasted in useless warfare—but to obtain the highest wage possible, because such highest wage depends upon the following factors: (a) peaceful, continuous production with increased amount of products for distribution; (b) improved methods, economizing labor and material; (c) the constant inflow of new capital, and the competition of capital against capital to obtain laborers—this competition being at its keenest, and the employer's profit being at the lowest, where capital enjoys perfect security. High wages and security for capital go together. Whenever an employer feels insecure he recoups himself by a higher rate of profit. At the same time it should be remembered that under a state of free trade and free movement there cannot be successful combination amongst employers to maintain profit at the expense of wages; since a high rate of profit must lead to the formation of cooperative and joint-stock companies and to the increased bidding for labor with raised wages.

The Fruits of Liberty and the Fruits of Compulsion

The *Free Life* asks of every human being to distrust coercion as a bad instrument, morally and materially for achieving progress and supplying wants. It asks them to recognize the great truth that progress abhors the dull spiritless uniformity which follows upon every form of coercion. It asks them to have faith in the all-creating power of the intellectual and moral forces, and to believe that no true living development of these forces can take place until men set themselves to reason and persuade instead of coercing, until each man asks no more for himself than to go to his own way, while he in turn concedes the same perfect liberty to his neighbor, and until every variety of thought, experiment, and system are allowed to compete freely with each other. It bids those who are of Anglo-Saxon blood to remember and cherish the special genius that belongs to their race—the personal initiative, the spirit of adventure, the steadiness in danger, the power to stand alone and resist adverse opinion. It bids them not to exchange these things for the nerveless abject life of an administered crowd. It bids them not to grasp at passing material advantages at the price of injuring themselves mentally and morally. It bids them reject all huge universal systems, not only as discouraging freshness and vigor of thought, but as necessarily fatal to the best classes of citizens, because they place these best classes under conditions framed to meet the requirements of the lowest class of citizens, and, therefore, pedantically sacrifice all the soundest and worthiest part of the people, on whom progress depends, for the sake of the least worthy—who indeed are very slightly, probably not at all, improved by the restrictions upon them. *Free Life* then calls upon the people to end the bitter strife, and the false state of progress, which must continue to exist, as long as men struggle to rule over each other. It calls upon them to get rid of the compulsory state, and replace it by the voluntary state. It holds that it is only under the voluntary state that in any true sense men can befriend each other, or work for the public good; for under the compulsory state all such services are tainted by the compulsion of those who compel, and the submission of those who submit.

The Work That Is Waiting to Be Done

It is no selfish spirit that *Free Life* preaches voluntaryism. It wishes no individual to wrap himself up in his own special interests, and to dismiss all sense of the public good; it wishes no part of a nation to retreat from any true duties which fall upon it, either within or without the borders its own country. But it denies that any good or lasting work can be built upon the compulsion of others, be they poor or rich; it denies that either by those who compel, or upon these who are compelled, can the peaceful and happy society of the future be founded. It invites all men to think out the special problems of liberty and friendly cooperation: to join in considering—while first and foremost we give to the individual these full rights over himself, his faculties and his property, without which all efforts are vain—how far we can usefully carry on a common life; how best and with the greatest respect for minorities we can manage common property; how we can work together in the perfecting of education, in the spreading of sanitary knowledge, in improving the conditions of labor, in attacking poverty, in purifying and beautifying the life of our towns, in organizing voluntary defense, in helping distant communities that are related to us or partly dependent on us—how we can do all these things, without at any point touching with the least of our fingers the hateful instrument of an aggressive and unjustifiable compulsion. With all state compulsion, that exceeds the defense of individual rights, *Free Life* makes and will make no terms. To the voluntary state it bids men offer their best gifts of body and mind; to the compulsory state it can bid men oppose their steady but and uncompromising resistance.

Index

COLOPHON

The Palatino typeface used in this volume is the work of Hermann Zapf, the noted European type designer and master calligrapher. Palatino is basically an "old style" letterform, yet it is strongly endowed with Zapf's distinctive exquisiteness. With concern not solely for the individual letter but also for the working visual relationship in a page of text, Zapf's edged pen has given this type a brisk, natural motion.

This book is printed on paper that is acid-free and meets the requirements of the American National Standard for Permanence of Paper for Printed Library Materials, Z39.84, 1984.∞

Book design by Design Center, Inc., Indianapolis
Typography by Weimer Typesetting Co., Inc., Indianapolis
Printed by Worzalla Publishing Co., Inc., Stevens Point, Wisconsin